THE UNCHURCHED

The Unchurched

Who They Are and Why They Stay Away

J. RUSSELL HALE

HARPER & ROW, PUBLISHERS

SAN FRANCISCO

1817

Cambridge	London
Hagerstown	Mexico City
Philadelphia	São Paulo
New York	Sydney

FIRST EDITION

Designed by Jim Mennick

Library of Congress Cataloging in Publication Data

Hale, James Russell.
  THE UNCHURCHED.

  Some of materials included are from the author's "Who are the unchurched?" published in 1977 by Glenmary Research Center, Washington, D. C.
  Includes index.
  1. Non church-affiliated people. 2. Irreligion and sociology. I. Title.
BL2747.H33 1980   306'.6   79–2993
ISBN 0–06–063560–6

---

80 81 82 83 84 10 9 8 7 6 5 4 3 2 1

to Marjorie, my wife

Contents

Preface

Beginning in 1977, during and since the writing of my monograph, *Who Are the Unchurched? An Exploratory Study* (Washington, D.C.: Glenmary Research Center, 1977), I have had the rare privilege of interpreting my findings to a large number of persons in denominational, ecumenical, and faculty assemblies and workshops. The Washington, D.C., Theological Consortium afforded me the opportunity to teach Protestant and Catholic students in a spring semester seminar in 1978 titled "The Theory and Practice of Evangelization." I am indebted to the participants in these discussions for their sharp questions and penetrating critiques. This book includes not only the substance, expansion, and reordering of portions of the original monograph but also some new reflections and data that these friendly critics have prompted and requested.

Not the least of the new insights is a fresh appreciation of what has happened to me, who I am, and where I stand. Thomas O'Dea's judgment that behind the analysis of any social situation, social phenomenon, or institution is "an individual experience, a particular perspective, a personal vision" is one that social scientists, in particular, need to own.[1] No investment of will or dedication to scientific detachment enables a human being to step out of his or her skin or world. The scholar is a part of the world he or she studies and, in the process of his or her studies, alters that world and is altered by it. The cues for the part I have played as a researcher come as much from my own experiential script as from the signals offstage.[2]

At the start of my interviews among the unchurched, in 1976, I was consciously aware only of pursuing a concern prompted by research interests. By the time the field phase was completed, I had become sensitive to something else: I was not an antiseptically unaffected observer. I only vaguely perceived the import of this admission at this time.

Gradually, I came to see that what was explicit in the words of the unchurched might also be implicit among the churched on the fringes of membership. I was little prepared, however, for what I would find as I tracked this logically to the center. It became increasingly apparent to me that even among the most highly committed—both among the lay "pillars" of the churches and their ministers—helplessness and apathy, hopelessness and boredom, doubt and unbelief are common existential realities.[3]

I also had to face the possibility that there may have been something of me out there. It began when a perceptive observer asked, "Why did you *really* undertake this study? After all, no researcher chooses an arena of research without some subjective reasons." Was I finding in the unchurched a certain honesty about their doubts and alienation that in myself I had cleverly, albeit unconsciously, concealed but that cried out for authentic self-revelation?

The painful discovery came one spring day in 1978 at St. Joseph's Seminary in Yonkers, New York. I had been engaged in public conversations with priests and religious of the Archdiocese of New York. At the close of one of the sessions, a young priest approached me privately. "I must ask you one question, please," he said with an enigmatic impatience. "Where are *you?*" He drew a circle on a chalkboard. "This is the church," he explained, interpreting his simple diagram, "how far from the center are you?" Spontaneously, without my usual reserve, I found myself putting a dot just inside the circle's circumference. "At the boundary," I said, "hanging on for dear life." The priest responded, with relief, "Thank God. Only we who know that about ourselves can and will take seriously what those outsiders perceive us to be." I wondered, if like Søren Kierkegaard, I too had discovered within myself and among many Christians only "habit, torpor, and the lack of spirituality."

Once I recognized the turbulence and fluctuations of my own faith —the seesaw between unquestioning belief and disbelief—and the fragility of my own relationship with the institutional church, the painfulness of my confession became liberating. With Paul Tillich, I could say my faith includes "a courage which accepts risks," even doubt about itself. If the community of the faithful can permit this among its leaders, can it permit it among its ordinary members? If so, can it also accept it among those who have left the fold?

A faculty colleague recently asked whether my study might be more revelatory of me than those about whom I write. That is the risk any author faces. I am ready to admit that, if this book reveals who I am, so be it. Thus, I make no pretense of value-free objectivity and raise with my colleagues the theoretical question whether, in fact, such neutrality toward one's data can ever be achieved. Yet I am conscious of the dangers of distortion and contamination in a method of exploration that is admittedly "disciplined subjectivity," as Margaret Mead once described all ethnological investigation. The risk is inherent in the enterprise, particularly for any reader who may attempt to move from the findings of this study to the task of evangelization. The evangelist, even more than the researcher, always communicates something of him- or herself. Communication is a matter of participation. Unless one can hear and feel the anguish, sometimes the bitterness and hostility, of those who are alienated from the churches—as indeed the echoes of one's own latent frustrations and failures—one will fail in one's best efforts to proclaim the good news.

For whom, then, is this book written? It is expected that there will be, as with the readers of the original monograph, a general audience of both the churched and unchurched for whom the descriptive material and reflections will be of interest. Denominational leaders at various levels of church bureaucracies should find this material—not available in studies elsewhere—useful, at least derivatively, for fashioning outreach programs among the unchurched. Local parish ministers and laity, large numbers of whom have already used the exploratory work in evangelization study and training sessions, will find this expanded version of increased value.

Undergraduate and graduate students in the psychology and sociology of religion, in American religious history, in theology and ethics, in research methods, and in the social sciences generally constitute a special group to whom this present book is addressed; their teachers will find here qualitative data that will help fill in the lacunae of explicit quantitative research in the field. As I have suggested in Chapter 11, this research should suggest to other researchers some clues for needed study of a neglected phenomenon in our better understanding of religion in America.

NOTES

1. Thomas F. O'Dea, "The Crisis of the Contemporary Religious Consciousness," *Daedalus* 96 (Winter 1967):116–17.

2. "There is a sense in which, in their eagerness to achieve 'scientific detachment,' "
   writes sociologist Tom Burns of the University of Edinburgh, "social scientists have
   cut themselves off from their main resource—the ability of human beings to memorize and report their own experiences." Tom Burns, "The Comparative Study of
   Organizations," in Victor H. Vroom, ed., *Methods of Organizational Analysis* (Pittsburgh: University of Pittsburgh Press, 1967), p. 155.
3. Comparable findings have been reported by John S. Savage, in his *The Apathetic and
   Bored Church Member: Psychological and Theological Implications* (Pittsford, N.Y.:
   LEAD Consultants, 1976), especially Chap. 4.

Acknowledgments

Indebtedness to others in a work such as this can never be completely expressed. Certain people, however, must be explicitly recognized. Chief among them is Bernard Quinn, director of the Glenmary Research Center, Washington, D.C., who first conceived of the possibility of an exploratory study of the unchurched in America; David Byers, who edited my original monograph; and Roy M. Carlisle, my present editor at Harper & Row. Alvin Illig, executive director of the National Conference of Catholic Bishops Committee on Evangelization, and Richard Bartley, coordinator for Evangelical Outreach of the Lutheran Church in America, have been especially instrumental in facilitating my meeting with numerous clergy and church leaders. The list of parish clergy and laity who helped me locate the unchurched in their communities is too extensive to include here. They know who they are and will, I trust, accept this belated expression of gratitude. They, along with countless public servants, community leaders, media professionals, and others, helped me find important demographic, historical, and ecological data, shared with me their "insiders'" perceptions of their own communities, and offered many unexpected hospitalities.

I am both thankful and chagrined by the international publicity given my first monograph on the unchurched by the religion editor of *Time*, by George Cornell of the Associated Press, and by media people in press, radio, television, and denominational circles, at national and local levels. This coverage of the story of the unchurched was both an embarrassment and a boon. The embarrassment was somewhat relieved by a subsequent rich correspondence and conversation with hundreds of persons—clergy, laity, scholars, and students—I would otherwise not have known. Their interest has prompted the writing of this extended report. The boon is that between 1977 and the present there is evidence of continuing research on the phenomenon of the unchurched, partially spawned by my work, some of which has already found its way into print.[1]

Not the least among the contributors is my wife, Marjorie, who suffered through the transcribing of the taped interviews and through the usual turmoil that manuscript deadlines impose, and to whom this volume is dedicated. Mary Miller, my secretary, has prepared this manuscript for publication; she is any writer's dream. What virtues and insights this book contains are largely due to my informants in six U.S. counties. Any errors of interpretation are not theirs, but mine.

J. RUSSELL HALE

Gettysburg, Pennsylvania
October 1979

NOTE

1. Two publications are especially noteworthy: *Survey of the Unchurched American* (Princeton, N. J.: Gallup Organization, 1978), conducted for the Religious Coalition to Study Backgrounds, Values, and Interests of Unchurched Americans; and David A. Roozen of the Hartford Seminary Foundation. *The Churched and the Unchurched in America: A Comparative Profile* (Washington, D.C.: Glenmary Research Center, 1978). Other research will be identified in the following chapters.

Part One

OVERVIEW

IN A notable series of lectures almost thirty years ago, Bertha Paulssen, a Leipzig-trained psychologist-sociologist, addressed the topic "Faith and Conversion in the Light of Contemporary Psychology and Theology" before throngs of theological students, ministers, and laypeople at Union Theological Seminary, New York. It was the time of the beginning of the postwar dialogue between psychology and religion, and her opening words spoke to what was deeply troubling many—the right relationship between the burgeoning religious interest in psychotherapy and Christian allegiance. "Man's superconfidence in science is being shaken today," she said. "We are beginning to see that the idolization of scientific objectivity makes us incapable of dealing with the most difficult problems of our day, namely, those problems of man versus man, nation versus nation, and our craving for a security which goes beyond nature. That science which is deterministic has little or nothing to say about the nature and destiny of man. A new epistemology is needed."

One of the Paulssen lectures anticipated my interest in the meaning of the phenomenon of the unchurched:

In the life of the church in dealing with members of the congregation and with the masses of the unchurched population, every minister and church worker today is incessantly struggling with the problem: How can I help these people find faith? How can I guide them on the road to a really Christian basis for living? Though there are still some ministers who believe that by preaching alone they can save souls, most of them add at least an effort of personal evangelism.

There are in our congregations and outside communities millions of people who are in despair, fear, anxiety, and terror who seek a way out of their dilemma. They ask, "Why?" and "What does it mean?" Neither technology nor elaborate culture can solve their problems. God is dead for them.

The procedure to help people like these requires skill and understanding. There is no 1-2-3 course in evangelism that will teach this. But the first step may be to learn how to listen to them.[1]

This is a book about what happens when one listens. But, first, whether the reader is one whose interest is in the objective study of religion or one within the church looking out, an overview of the contemporary religious scene in which the enigma of the unchurched is enacted is essential. Chapter 1 deals with some aspects of the religious history of the United States, the conceptual problems in dealing with the unchurched phenomenon, and an introduction to the method I used in exploring it. Chapter 2 is an initial glimpse of the existential dimensions of unchurchedness as it is revealed in three poignant stories told by the unchurched themselves. Chapter 3 summarizes what is known about the extent and distribution of the unchurched in the United States.

Neither this section nor the chapters that follow will solve the problem of epistemology that Bertha Paulssen raised nor provide the "quick fix" that religionists may covet. Both will be dealt with in Part Four, but more research and reflection will be required before full comprehension or action can be expected.

NOTE

1. Lecture series, Fall 1951, Union Theological Seminary, New York, N.Y.; unpublished, quoted from notes and partial manuscript in my possession. See also Henry P. Van Dusen, "Pioneer in Dialog," *Bulletin* (Lutheran Theological Seminary, Gettysburg, Pennsylvania) 45 (November 1965): pp. 7–8.

1. The Enigma of the Unchurched

"A traveler in 1700 making his way from Boston to the Carolinas would encounter Congregationalists of varying intensity, Baptists of several varieties, Presbyterians, Quakers, and several other forms of Puritan radicalism; Dutch, German, and French Reformed; Swedish, Finnish, and German Lutherans; Mennonites and radical pietists, Anglicans, Roman Catholics; here and there a Jewish congregation, a few Rosicrucians; and, of course, *a vast number of the unchurched*—some of them powerfully alienated from any form of institutional religion."

SYDNEY E. AHLSTROM[1]

Almost three centuries later, the traveler of 1979 making his or her way from Maine to Florida, from New York to Los Angeles, or from Minneapolis to Dallas, encounters more than 200 varieties of American religion, of varying shape, size, color, and intensity. He or she meets their adherents in churches and synagogues, here and there in mosques and temples, a few in communes and informal "house churches." Virtually every surviving orthodoxy, heresy, and schism in Christian history would be present. A "civil" or "culture religion"—sometimes outside, sometimes inside the religious institutions—would be found everywhere. And, of course, the traveler would encounter *a vast number of the unchurched,* some 80 million of them, many by choice dropouts or solitary pilgrims, intentionally alienated from traditional forms of institutionalized religion.

This book is about the unchurched. It is told mostly in their own words. The words tell stories. The stories describe the pictures the unchurched have drawn in their heads.[2] The pictures are real. As a construction of the reality perceived by the unchurched themselves, they represent meanings that must be understood on their own terms, from the vantage point of those who believe in them, even though in others they may strike a different response. The pictures that are drawn also have consequences—for the unchurched themselves, for the churches, and for the society as a whole. It is inconceivable that the system of meanings these variegated pictures represent, when drawn by almost 40 percent of the population, has no effect on the culture. It is important that we know what these pictures look like.

The past has also been shaped, in part, by the kind of pictures people have constructed about their world. One is impressed that alongside this nation's religious saga—"one of the grandest epics in the history of mankind," as Sydney Ahlstrom has characterized it[3]—there has been, at every stage of its unfolding, a sizable body of the population for whom the search for meaning and purpose has not led to membership in established religious groups. Often, the search has caused massive thousands to defect after previous belonging.

Contrary to popular celebrationist notions of a golden religious age, the seventeenth- and eighteenth-century American landscape was not dominated by church spires. There were more wayside inns and taverns than churches in colonial America. In 1790, there were probably fewer than 3,000 churches in the young republic. Church density was about one church for every 300 square miles (the area of New York City today).[4] Fewer than one in ten Americans were formally affiliated with any religious institution. The postrevolutionary decades were hardly the heyday of American Christianity. "The churches," Ahlstrom writes, "reached a lower ebb of vitality . . . than at any time in the nation's religious history. . . . The difficulties were the product of distraction, attack, and apathy, and the greatest of these was apathy."[5]

When Alexis de Tocqueville, the celebrated European observer of things democratic in early nineteenth-century America, commented that "there is no country in the world where the Christian religion retains a greater influence over the souls of men than in America,"[6] he was viewing a predominantly unchurched nation. Only one in six Americans were then church members, even after two Great Awakenings had run their course. It took another century before the churches would record for the first time a majority of the population with church affiliation.

One can read this data in several ways. The obvious is to reject the notion that the number of formal religious adherents is necessarily related to religious vitality or influence. The intrinsic quality of faith among church members and the ability of both laity and clergy to make their faith credible in discourse and behavior has never been a function of numerical dominance. Carriers of religious meanings, further, are not always members of religious institutions. Yet, it may be questioned whether, in the past, present, or emerging future, any faith long endures in its authentic form without sustained social support from its major institutional expressions. When such public belief systems and structures falter, lose their internal self-identity and their external plausibility, their influence in the society wanes. Generally, neither the lone charismatic prophet nor a minority of "cognitive deviants" wages successful battles, over the long run, against the profound challenges of a secularized society. Neither will churches crowded with people whose religion demands little or nothing of them survive as distinctively Christian churches.

Another way of reading the long-term data is to conclude, with Douglas W. Johnson, executive director of the Institute for Church Development, that from colonial times to the present there has been "an increasingly positive disposition in the United States toward the church."[7] Or, as historian Edwin Scott Gaustad has observed after reflection on recent religious trends, there has been a rising "broad basis of friendly interest in, and perhaps sympathy with, the tasks to which America's churches and synagogues have set themselves."[8] On the basis of church membership statistics and other religious indicators, the post-World War II surge of piety in America may have been more real than some of its detractors have argued. Notwithstanding the declines in church membership and attendance between 1961 and 1974,[9] Johnson would join with others in predicting a new stage of growth for the churches, more consistent with historical trends than the somewhat aberrant cycle of the recent past. A period of stabilization for mainline denominations, recouping the losses of the 1960s and early 1970s, it is claimed, is already apparent. And the conservative churches are still growing. In addition, the current religious marketplace now offers Eastern, mystical, and pseudo-religious faiths in hundreds of new movements, with devotees counted in the millions.[10] Lyle Schaller, church planner and staff person at the Yokefellow Institute, is confident that "we're in the beginning stages of another religious boom, different from the one of the 1950s that people look back to, but in proportions and numbers somewhat comparable."[11] George Gallup, Jr., agrees: "Evidence is mounting that the United States may be in an early stage of a profound religious revival."[12]

The same data suggest a third possible interpretation. The United States in its 200-year history has been, except for some 25 years, a nation with more people outside the churches than inside. For well over a century and a half, only a minority of the American people has committed itself, in terms of affiliation, to those institutions from which the "great influence of religion on the souls of men" might have been expected to derive. What the future holds is unclear. Linear projections from the past into the future, assuming no intervening circumstances, are notoriously misleading. It may be, too, that the meaning of belonging has changed from former times to the present and that the members today, although relatively large in numbers, exhibit a secularized version of faith without the distinctive commitments of earlier generations.

Different observers—scholars, journalists, and ecclesiastics—read the signs of the times differently.[13] When the Vatican, for example, created a Secretariat for Non-Believers and called a major international symposium on "The Culture of Unbelief," in Rome, March 22–27, 1969, it did so with the recognition that "insufficient knowledge of what is happening to religion and belief in our times . . . tend[s] to preclude the hope of acquiring a broad consensus on the problem or of specifying clear projections of developments in the coming decades."[14] If there is any consensus, it is that trends in the churches are clearly related to trends in the society at large—the transfer of functions from religious to secular agencies, religious diversity, erosion of authority among traditional institutions, demographic and ecological changes, the loss of local community bonds, and the responses of religious institutions to these trends. More than a decade ago, Rodney Stark and Charles Glock, sociologists of religion at the University of California, Berkeley, labeled the contemporary American scene "Post-Christian" and anticipated no long-term future for the church "as we know it." Their scenario was a "policy of drift, with a rhetoric of hope, and a reality of business as usual."[15] At about the same time, Peter Berger in his companion volumes, *The Sacred Canopy* and *Rumor of Angels,* saw (and argued for) a "remnant church" of "cognitive deviants" as the probable authentic church of the future.[16]

Dean Kelley, in his provocative and controversial study of liberal and conservative Protestantism, sees the future with those churches that offer meaningful responses to the ultimate questions of life and demand strictness in both doctrine and personal ethical behavior.[17] Wade Clark Roof, professor of sociology at the University of Massachusetts at Amherst, theorizes that the crisis of commitment is largely cultural—not theological, as Kelley has argued. It reflects the bifurcation of the total culture into traditional religious conceptions, on the one hand, and scientific and humanistic views, on the other.[18] Dean Hoge of the Catholic University of America observes an attendant "collapse of the middle," the inability of mainline Protestantism to put these competing views together.[19] Roof's projected future is not markedly different from that of Stark and Glock, Berger, or Kelley—"The church [that is, liberal Protestantism] may experience even further decline in the years ahead, but they should persist indefinitely as cognitive-minority institutions."[20]

My interest in the unchurched was first aroused almost ten years ago at the time of the Vatican symposium on "The Culture of Unbelief." Scholars from within and without the Roman Catholic Church participated, notably both theologians and social scientists from Europe and America. It was an historic occasion and pioneering venture. The dialogue was honest, critical, and productive. Pope Paul VI, who addressed the participants, called the moment "dramatic and symbolic." "We thank [you] for this visit," he said, "which takes on for us the character of a highly significant encounter. This is not the usual meeting of friendly persons; it is rather the encounter of diverse cultures and differing thoughts."[21] No consensus was ever reached on the meaning of the problem, but this did not prevent Charles Glock from making a proposal for worldwide empirical investigations, of various types, on the conceptualization and measurement of unbelief.[22] Bryan Wilson, sociologist from Oxford, less enamored than Glock with the potentials of survey research, proposed "an analysis of social institutions, of organizations and communities, and of patterns of social relationships within them in order to discover to what extent these communities, organizations and structures are informed by supernatural conceptions of the world and are characterized by the behavioral correlates of such beliefs."[23] In elaborating his proposal, Wilson revealed a bias, shared by many sociologists and others, that contemporary religious institutions, which legitimate belief, have "become increasingly vestigial and persist at the fringes of society."[24] Peter Berger, chairperson of the symposium probably summarized the discussions and debates accurately with his conclusion that "a sociology of contemporary religion must of necessity broaden its scope to deal with the social dynamics of contemporary nonreligious culture."[25]

About the same time as the publication of the proceedings of the

symposium at Rome, I came across a brief monograph by Colin Campbell, *Toward a Sociology of Irreligion,* which broke the apparent taboo
preventing the serious study of the social phenomenon of the rejection
of religion.[26] A decade earlier, in Germany, Gerhard Szezesny published, *The Future of Unbelief.* Szezesny argued that "unbelief is no
longer the prerogative of an especially enlightened minority, [but] the
fate of a contemporary type of Western man who may actually be in the
majority." He named himself openly as a prophet of a post-Christian
ideology.[27]

This suggested to me that in the 1950s the preoccupation of American sociologists of religion with the institutionalized forms of religion or
with the supposed religious preferences of Americans might have
screened out needed investigation of that residual category we might
label "unbeliever," "non-Christian," "no preference," or "unchurched." If Szezesny was right, could one study irreligion in its own
right, thereby effectively viewing religion as the residual?

Of course, "the irreligious" (persons without religious beliefs) and
"unbelievers" (agnostics or atheists) are not the same as the "unchurched" (not church members). The former—the irreligious and the
unbelievers—may indeed still be members of the Christian church,
especially in parts of Europe where for various reasons large majorities
of the churched are functionally without orthodox beliefs. The latter—
the unchurched, or those not on the rolls of any Christian congregation
—may indeed be crypto-believers, secretly believing without belonging.
This is especially the case in the United States, where the privatizing
of faith is endemic. In either case, might it be that the avowed non-
Christian professes his or her unbelief with a vehemence that increases
in direct proportion to an inchoate faith? Or, conversely, that contemporary men and women within the churches profess themselves to be
Christians with a vehemence that increases in direct proportion to their
loss of faith? Put more simply, as Paul W. Pruyser of the Menninger
Foundation suggests, some people may secretly envy the beliefs of others, beliefs they say they hate, just as some secretly despise their own
beliefs, to which they verbally testify.[28] If Pruyser is right, then the
boundaries between belief and unbelief may be nonexistent but, rather,
may cohere in the ambivalent character of every person.

A linguistic and conceptual interlude is essential here. We must ask
again, as did the symposium participants at Rome, what is meant by
some of the terms we have been using. Harvard theologian Harvey Cox
has written that "nonbelief or unbelief is really a Christian theological

category—it is not the name by which our fellow human beings know themselves."[29] There is, according to Rocco Caporale, director of research and professor at Pitzer College, Claremont, California, "an appalling lack of empirical data on unbelief and supreme ignorance of what really obtains in the world of the proverbial man on the street."[30] There is an undeveloped state of conceptualization on the topic and a lack of consensus on how to study it.[31] Christian theologians may have less trouble with the term *unbelief* than the social scientists if unbelief is simply the intellectual rejections of whatever a particular theologian deems comprehended by his or her own brand of orthodoxy. Some among them will be satisfied with the time-honored distinction probably first introduced from German pietism in the eighteenth century when the world's population was perceived as either "saved" or "unsaved." Such simplification would hardly be meaningful or acceptable, however, by any other today than the coterie of theologians or followers of an extremely narrow Protestant evangelicalism.

The term *irreligious* is similarly inexact. It suggests the other end of a supposed religious-irreligious spectrum without clarity about what *religious* means. Perhaps the most sophisticated analysis of religious commitment, is that developed by Charles Glock and his associates. Glock's well-known taxonomy delineates five dimensions of religiosity: knowledge, belief, experience, practice, and consequences. Operationalized, this taxonomy has spawned numerous empirical studies of the religiously committed.[32] More recently, he has proposed "four types of belief" by crossing the objectivist-subjectivist option with a supernaturalist-naturalist option.[33] Logically such systems allow for only one definition of "irreligious" or "unbelief," namely the failure to exhibit any manifestation of any of the types of religious commitment or failure to score as a believer in any one of Glock's four belief categories. The "irreligious" would thus be those whose behavior has none of the characteristics of the religiously committed. The "unbeliever" would be constituted by a failure to acknowledge or experience the sacred or to feel subject to its authority. Yet Glock admits that it is probably not possible to remove all ambiguity or to obtain definitional agreement from everyone. While full consensus may not be essential for inquiry, lack of it makes the task formidable. It also raises the question whether research in the absence of conceptual clarity reduces, in this case, a theological category to the Procrustean bed of available methodological instrumentation.

Other terms have been substituted in the research literature—"the alienated," "apostates," "nihilists," "religious dropouts," "the uncommitted," to cite a few—and in the more polemical literature—"heathen," "infidel," or "barbarian." As Pruyser observes, all such words are, psychologically and socially, "hot words"—terms of judgment, denigration, and disapprobation.[34] Each has imperialistic overtones. Each takes a particular set of beliefs or religious institution as normative, all others being beyond the pale. It is hard to use any in a merely descriptive vein. Two of the least pejorative, properly understood, are "alienated" and "apostate." Alienation is a major unit idea in the classic sociological tradition, referring to such characteristics as powerlessness, meaninglessness, cultural or self-estrangement, and normlessness. Religious alienation therefore implies separation from those belief systems and religious institutions that purvey specific meanings, values, and behaviors. Because alienation is a prominent cultural theme in the contemporary world, perhaps especially among youth, to label oneself as *alienated*, as opposed to *conformist*, is often a proud, respectable self-designation. The term *apostasy* connotes "an abandonment of a set of principles or faith" (Webster's Dictionary) and involves a disaffiliation from those religious communities that hold such principles or faith to be true.[35] Again, however, the definition is, on the surface, descriptively neutral, although it is doubtful that the disaffiliated think or speak of themselves as "apostates." It is only others who label them so.

Rather than perpetuate these conceptual ambiguities or introduce new terms further to muddy the definitional waters, I have made the pragmatic decision in this study to investigate the way the unchurched picture their world of reality. In so doing, I was aware that I would be talking with persons who might be either self-designated "religious" or "irreligious" persons. Were I to have chosen a sample from among the affiliated, I might have discovered the same. The problem of boundaries between the churched and unchurched remains an artifact of the way people themselves express their religious preference or membership and the way local churches and denominations implement the rubrics of belonging. These problems are serious but, I believe, more easily surmountable than the linguistic problem. Simplified, the designation "unchurched" results from a head count of those persons on the rolls of "inclusive members" of local congregations; those not so listed are the "unchurched." (I shall return to this later.) While most of those outside formal church affiliation do not speak of themselves as "unchurched," they seemed not, in my experience with them at the time of the interviews nor in later writing about them, to have taken offense.

The immediate, precipitating precursor of this study was the publication of *Churches and Church Membership in the United States* in 1974.[36] A similar study had been done in 1956.[37] That was the time of the alleged "revival of religion" in America. It had largely produced myopia on the part of the churches. For the denominational leaders, the decade was an era of euphoria. For the man or woman in the pew, the churches "had never had it so good!" Many sociologists and other scholars seemingly discovered a phenomenon worth studying. It is not accidental that the decade produced a spate of textbooks on the sociology of religion, indication that even in the halls of academe the "objective study of religion" was again respectable. It was the same decade that prompted the organization of the Religious Research Association and the Society for the Scientific Study of Religion. It was the period in which Martin Marty, then a fledgling doctoral graduate and parish pastor, made his debut as an author in his *The New Shape of American Religion.* [38] No one, however—sociologist or ecclesiastic—had paid more than cursory attention to the residual, the vast millions who still remained outside the churches of America.

The situation was different by 1974. Mainline churches in America were experiencing a loss of innocence and buoyancy; they were troubled. Especially Roman Catholics, for whom the winds of change following Vatican II had produced noticeable erosion in recruitment for religious vocations, the closing or underutilization of houses of studies and convents, as well as new freedom on the part of the laity openly to express views counter to those of the established church, and to begin to act more like Protestants in abstention from regular participation in the Eucharist. Mainline Protestant groups, still suffering from vast attrition of churches and members in the central cities in their inability to adapt to changing neighborhoods, were documenting record losses of members everywhere. Only the more conservative Christian churches, especially of the pentecostal and neocharismatic varieties, seemed to be flourishing. Outside the churches, a new religious consciousness was rampant among the graduates of the counterculture of the 1960s.

The first statistical analysis of the extent and distribution of the unchurched in America was the work of the statistical research division of the Glenmary Research Center in Washington, D.C.. In 1974, *Religious Population of the United States: 1971* came off the press.[39] Supplemented by colorful, dramatic religious cartography, it documented the existence of almost 80 million unchurched Americans. The maps identified, according to counties, where certain "religious families" were dominant, and more strikingly, the location of the unchurched in America keyed in color according to the relative ratio of unchurched to county population. Still, who these unchurched were, and why they were unchurched, remained unanswered.

This report seeks to illuminate the enigma of the unchurched by examining the experiences and attitudes of 165 persons in six heavily unchurched counties in the United States. I lived among them, cumulatively, for six months in 1976. With their permission, I taped our conversations, some as short as five minutes, others extending over four hours. These people were willing to discuss with me, a complete stranger, some of their most deeply felt hurts, hostilities, and convictions. They welcomed me into their homes—with hospitality, with openness, and with interest in my project. I never misrepresented what it was I was seeking from them, but I apologize to them now for withholding the information that I was an ordained clergyman unless they asked. It was early apparent to me that they were "baring their souls" in a fashion seldom matched in their conversations with other ministers they had known in the past or with whom they were presently acquainted in their own communities.

This is not a study in quantitative sociology. Andrew Greeley once remarked that, although he was skeptical of any study without numbers and hard facts, the writings of Robert Coles took him *"inside* the culture." I had to ask myself, "What's better, to look at a computer printout on the unchurched or to be able to live inside them and their culture?" It was an attempt to achieve the latter that fashioned my methodology. In a sense, it has been a fishing expedition, the casting of a large net in an effort to catch as many fish of different varieties as possible. Because the net has been cast profligately, no one can be certain that all possible kinds of fish have been caught. It is also likely that the kinds of fish caught result from the waters into which the net was cast in the first place.

The hard facts in this case are the anecdotes of the unchurched themselves. I had to ask myself as I began the task of listening to people, "How carefully do I count?" and "Do I count carefully at all?" Was my purpose the discovery of frequencies or numerical values attached to particular types of responses the unchurched made concerning their unchurchedness? I thought not, for several reasons. It would have been pretentious to have presumed that nonrepresentative samples could produce meaningful objective results. Quantification of responses, even had the sample met the usual tests of reliability, would have required a method of analysis the material did not warrant. Further, since this exploratory study sought the development of categories *from* the material rather than the imposition of categories *on* the material, the usual strict canons of objectivity seemed inappropriate. Finally, the costs of scientific sampling, manipulation of statistics, and content analysis had to be reckoned against the probable returns.

Taxonomy, or classification, of the unchurched is the primary objective of this research. Such is the elementary or beginning point of investigation in any science or in any virgin inquiry into a new field. It is an old and honored tradition in qualitative sociological studies. The classification of the unchurched presented here is preliminary, lacking in discreteness; that is, the categories are not necessarily mutually exclusive or exhaustive. They are derived from an analysis of some 2,000 pages of transcribed interviews. Only rarely does a single individual fit neatly into a single classification. The categories represent recurrent themes with labels that are my own heuristic inventions. Given my own preference for qualitative rather than quantitative reporting, I have avoided listing frequencies of occurrence.

At the outset of the field research, my question was "Can a sample as small as 165, with no pretense of scientific randomness, provide generalizations about all unchurched Americans? The answer is clearly no. Neither the choice of the six counties nor the selection of respondents was statistically representative. The counties were selected because each contained a much higher percent of unchurched in the population than was the norm across the nation. If, from the perspective of the churches, unchurchedness is deviant, I wanted to observe that deviance in its most pathological form. Further, the selection of informants was not a scientific microsample. My conversations were with persons referred to me, for the most part, by a broad spectrum of the clergy in the communities I visited. The initial list, however, was always larger than the sample I sought, which gave me the opportunity to exercise informal controls, thus avoiding oversampling or undersampling persons according to age, sex, education, income, race, and other obvious characteristics of the population of a particular county. It was necessary to supplement the clergy referrals in order to find certain types either not known to or not suggested by the ministers: ethnic minorities, the poor, and other marginal people that community data suggested to me were present.

Theoretically, the approach was eclectic. The reader will find traces of phenomenology, which claims that social reality is best understood and analyzed from the perspective of those people who experience it.[41] The use of unstructured interviews in the field owes some debt to the ethnographers who eschew armchair anthropology. I spent as much time in each location getting a feel for the community, experiencing its lifestyle, walking its streets and driving its roads, talking with its leaders, and participating in what was going on as I did in conversations with the unchurched themselves. It was important for me to know, as best I could in four weeks' stay, the context of living through which oral communication was filtered. In Part Two, "Odyssey into the Land of the Unchurched," it will also be obvious that I did my homework, perusing census documents, histories, local folklore, maps and charts, telephone directories, planning reports, agency analyses, local and county government records, and all else that helped shed light on the kind of place each county was.

Most importantly for me, both in the conduct of the research and in this writing I have found it essential to be honest with myself. I was not an antiseptically unaffected observer. Things happened to me that made my life exciting or austere. I cannot be the same again after the immersion. In one county, I found myself not wanting to leave; in another, I never got over the culture shock and had trouble forcing myself to stay. Some of my informants could have become friends. Most of them were beautiful people, "happy pagans" if you like, but nonetheless genuinely engaging, magnetically authentic persons. Despite the temptations and invitations, I never succumbed to the chance to share my own faith. I practiced active listening and sought to enter into the experience of the other, but I am not deceived that who I was or who I was perceived to be did not affect what was said. The first person singular is preserved at those places in the text where the reader deserves to know and take account of my own subjective feelings.

I have chosen not to be coy about the identification of the communities I studied. The names are real. I am convinced that no pseudonym has ever hidden the place of an investigation for long, however honored this tradition is in social research. I take the risk of naming places and the characteristics of those places with no ingenious scrambling of details. Journalistic reports and newspaper editorials that followed *Time* magazine's coverage of my preliminary findings, especially in Sarasota and Orange counties, proved that the risks were real. This means, of course, that I also take responsibility for possible errors of fact or judgment. No county in America is homogeneous, and its social construction of reality is never one-dimensional. I can only hope that residents of these counties will recognize my descriptions as plausible reductions of a complex array of details into central themes, a dominant mentality, or a pervading ethos.

The names of the unchurched people, however, have been fictionalized. Although they gave me permission for the publication of their words—in every case quoted exactly as they were spoken, with every attempt to preserve the context—I have not used their real names. Occasionally, I have used a substitute Christian name; in other cases, I have simply indicated the person's occupation, age, or other characteristic that helps provide a context for the words spoken. I have invented some names and altered other possibly identifying characteristics. Not particularly envious of the fate of Arthur J. Vidich and Joseph Bensman, whose figures were hung in effigy after the publication of their ethnographic study of Springdale, New York,[42] I have—where it seemed judicious for further protection of the informant—"relocated" a person in a community far separated from the place in which I actually found him or her. I have given the real names of community leaders who shared, without confidentiality, knowledge of their communities.

I trust that the reader can accept the material for what it is worth. Although the findings may have no "proven" applicability to a larger universe than the persons represented, numerous oral reports of this material have uniformly elicited expressions such as "That's my experience," or "I've met these people before," or "It's believable to me." Hundreds of letters I have received since October 1977, testify that the stories I first heard from my informants in six counties are echoed throughout the land. Again and again, the alienated have written, "It's interesting that a person like *you* is making a study of *us,*" or "I am one of your groups you label —————," or "Right on! I'm one of them; let me tell you my story." Some experienced ministers have even commented cynically, "So what else is new?" If this study does no more than document the obvious, I would still want to claim that a modest contribution has been made in an area of investigation not previously explored in any systematic fashion. If the words of my informants are not new, the question must be asked why it is that the things said and the experiences revealed have been so largely ignored for so long by the churches. If the response to these verbal signals has been one of self-justification or rationalization, one can only conclude that the church's previous listening has been faulty.

After completing six months of travel and logging more than 30,000 miles by air, car, foot, and boat, I returned home with the tantalizing consciousness that I might have found the same material in my own backyard. That may be so. But I could not have known this in advance, nor would my access to it have been the same. There was value in entering communities that I had never visited before, where the towns and people were complete strangers to me and I to them. I would like to go back.[43] My feeling is that they would have me back. There is still more to be heard, at greater depth, than has yet been heard.

NOTES

1. Sydney E. Ahlstrom, *A Religious History of the American People* (New Haven, Conn.: Yale University Press, 1977), p. 4. Italics mine.
2. This imagery was first suggested by Lippmann in his classic essay, "The World Outside and the Pictures in Our Heads," in Walter Lippmann, *Public Opinion* (New York: Macmillan, 1922), pp. 3–32; 79–100. See further discussion of this concept in Chapter 2.
3. Ahlstrom, *A Religious History*, pp. 3–4.
4. Calculations here and below are based on secondary analysis of early U.S. Census data, discussed and charted by Edwin Scott Gaustad, *Historical Atlas of Religion in America* (New York: Harper & Row, 1976), rev. ed. See also the discussions by Martin Marty and Douglas Johnson in Jackson Carroll, Douglas W. Johnson, and Martin E. Marty, *Religion in America: 1950 to the Present* (New York: Harper & Row, 1979), pp. 51–90.
5. Ahlstrom, *A Religious History*, p. 365.
6. Alexis de Tocqueville, *Democracy in America* (New York: Vintage, 1945), vol. 1, 12th ed., p. 314.
7. Carroll, Johnson, and Marty, *Religion in America*, p. 94.
8. Gaustad, *Historical Atlas*, p. 170.
9. For documentation, see *Yearbook of American Churches* (New York: National Council of the Churches of Christ in the U.S.A., 1960–1975).
10. The best analyses of the "new religious consciousness" are in the pioneering ethnographic studies from the Berkeley Project, published in Charles Y. Glock and Robert Bellah (eds.), *The New Religious Consciousness* (Berkeley: University of California Press, 1976); in Robert Wuthnow's examination of broader cultural patterns, *The Consciousness Reformation* (Berkeley: University of California Press, 1976); and in Wuthnow's more recent *Experimentation in American Religion: The New Mysticisms*

and Their Implications for the Churches (Berkeley: University of California Press, 1978). For a brief popular summary of Wuthnow's conclusions, see Wuthnow and Glock, "The Shifting Focus of Faith: A Survey Report," in *Psychology Today*, 1974, *8*(1), 131–36, and Wuthnow, "A Religious Marketplace," in *Journal of Current Social Issues*, Spring 1977, *14*(2), 38–42.

11. From an interview with Schaller by Richard L. Critz, "The Future of the Church in America," *Your Church Magazine*, September–October 1977.

12. George Gallup, Jr., "Afterword: A Coming Religious Revival?" in Carroll, Johnson, and Marty, *Religion in America*, p. 111.

13. For two different journalistic perceptions of the so-called "evangelical revival" see the cover story, "Back to That Old-Time Religion," in *Time*, 26 December 1977, pp. 52–58, and Garry Wills, "What Religious Revival?" in *Psychology Today*, April 1978, pp. 74–81. More substantive treatments include Charles Y. Glock, ed., *Religion in Sociological Perspective: Essays in the Empirical Study of Religion* (Belmont, Calif.: Wadsworth, 1973); N. J. Demerath, III, "Trends and Anti-Trends in Religious Change," in Eleanor B. Sheldon and Wilbert E. Moore, eds., *Indicators of Social Change: Concepts and Measurements* (New York: Sage, 1968); Andrew M. Greeley, *The Denominational Society: A Sociological Approach to Religion in America* (Glenview, Ill.: Scott, Foresman, 1972); and Andrew M. Greeley, *Unsecular Man: The Persistence of Religion* (New York: Shocken, 1972).

14. Rocco Caporale, in his "Introduction" to the studies and proceedings from the First International Symposium on Belief, Rocco Caporale and Antonio Grumelli, eds., *The Culture of Unbelief* (Berkeley: University of California Press, 1971).

15. Rodney Stark and Charles Y. Glock, *American Piety: The Nature of Religious Commitment* (Berkeley: University of California Press, 1968), Chap. 11.

16. Peter L. Berger, *The Sacred Canopy: Elements of a Sociological Theory of Religion* (Garden City, N.Y.: Doubleday, 1969); and Peter L. Berger, *A Rumor of Angels: Modern Society and the Rediscovery of the Supernatural* (Garden City, N.Y.: Doubleday, 1970).

17. Dean M. Kelley, *Why Conservative Churches Are Growing: A Study in Sociology of Religion* (New York: Harper & Row, 1977), new paperback edition. For two responsible critiques of the Kelley thesis see Thomas R. McFaul, " 'Strictness' and Church Membership," *Christian Century*, March 13, 1974, pp. 281–84; and Reginald Bibby, "Why Conservative Churches Really Are Growing," *Journal for the Scientific Study of Religion* 17, no. 2 (June 1978): 129–37

18. Wade Clark Roof, *Community and Commitment: Religious Plausibility in a Liberal Protestant Church* (New York: Elsevier, 1978), p. 7.

19. Dean R. Hoge, *Division in the Protestant House* (Philadelphia: Westminster, 1976), pp. 40–46.

20. Roof, *Community and Commitment*, p. 215.

21. Quoted in "Address by Paul VI," Caporale and Grumelli, *The Culture of Unbelief*, pp. 302–3.

22. Charles Y. Glock, "The Study of Unbelief: Perspectives on Research," in Caporale and Grumelli, *The Culture of Unbelief*, pp. 53–75.

23. Bryan Wilson, "Response to Glock," in Caporale and Grumelli, *The Culture of Unbelief*, p. 126.

24. *Ibid.*, p. 127.
25. Peter L. Berger, "Foreword," in Caporale and Grumelli, *The Culture of Unbelief*, p. viii.
26. Colin Campbell, *Toward a Sociology of Irreligion* (London: Macmillan, 1971).
27. Gerhard Szezesny, *The Future of Unbelief*, trans. Edward B. Garside (New York: Brasiller, 1961). See especially Chaps. 1 and 14.
28. Paul W. Pruyser, *Between Belief and Unbelief* (New York: Harper & Row, 1974), especially Chapter 10.
29. Harvey Cox, "The Viewpoint of a Secular Theologian," in Caporale and Grumelli, *The Culture of Unbelief*, p. 92.
30. Rocco Caporale, "Introduction," in Caporale and Grumelli, *The Culture of Unbelief*, p. 3.
31. For one attempt, see Martin E. Marty, *Varieties of Unbelief* (New York: Doubleday, 1964).
32. Stark and Glock, *American Piety*, pp. 11–16.
33. Glock, in Caporale and Grumelli, *The Culture of Unbelief*, pp. 56–57.
34. Pruyser, *Between Belief and Unbelief*, pp. 246–48.
35. David Caplovitz and Fred Sherrow, *The Religious Drop-Outs: Apostasy Among College Graduates* (London: Sage, 1977) is probably the most thorough social scientific investigation to date on "apostasy." The thesis is that "Apostasy indicates not only a loss of religious faith, but rejection of a particular ascriptive community as a basis for self-identification" (p. 31). See also the replication of the Caplovitz study, with modified conclusions: Bruce Hunsberger, "A Reexamination of the Antecedents of Apostasy," unpublished mimeographed paper, Wilfred Laurier University, Ontario, Canada, October 1978.
36. Douglas W. Johnson, Paul R. Picard, and Bernard Quinn, *Churches and Church Membership in the United States: An Enumeration by Region, State and County, 1971* (Washington, D.C.: Glenmary Research Center, 1974).
37. Bureau of Research and Survey, *Churches and Church Membership in the United States* (New York: National Council of Churches of Christ in the U.S.A., 1956).
38. Martin E. Marty, *The New Shape of American Religion* (New York: Harper & Row, 1959).
39. *Religious Population of the United States: 1971* (Washington, D.C.: Glenmary Research Center, 1974). A mimeographed report "correcting" Johnson, Picard, and Quinn, *Churches and Church Membership*, for unreported members. The statistics show the number and percent of Catholic church members, other Christian church members, and the unchurched people in each state and county within the United States.
40. John Runda, "A Preliminary Research Proposal to Identify and Classify the Unchurched in Six Rural Counties," prepared for the Glenmary Research Center, 1971. Also, by the same author, *An Annotated Bibliography on the Unchurched in Rural America* (Washington, D.C.: Glenmary Research Center, 1971).
41. See, for example, Maurice Natonson, ed., *Phenomenology and the Social Sciences* (Evanston, Ill.: Northwestern University Press, 1973). I have taken the position, with Peter Berger and Thomas Luckmann, *Social Construction of Reality* (New York: Doubleday, 1966), that reality is never simply given; it is constructed. Its apprehension

is always an active process involving subject and object. Reality becomes manifest when people unfold its meaning for them. Such meaning, whether true or false, constitutes a person's "definition of the situation," and has objective consequences in the actor's behavior. While ethnomethodology is not employed consciously in this study, several scholars have pointed to a compatibility that I do not reject.

42. *Small Town in Mass Society* (Princeton, N.J.: Princeton University Press, 1968), Chap. 14.

43. I have, in a sense, returned by proxy. One researcher, Edward A. Rauff, of the Lutheran Council in the USA, has gone back. Rauff reentered each of the six counties I had studied two years earlier. His interest centered on the question, raised by some of my ecclesiastical critics who have sought evangelistic prescriptions, "What makes a person who has been unchurched for five years or more decide to join again?" Interestingly, he has discovered a few who were in my unchurched sample in 1976 and who have now returned to the church. See Edward A. Rauff, *Why People Join the Church, An Exploratory Study* (Washington, D.C.: Glenmary Research Center, 1980).

2. Mary Lou, Emily, and Carlos

> "We are tendencies, or rather symptoms," Emerson once said. "We touch and go, and sip the foam of many lives. . . . Other men are lenses through which we read our own lives."[1]

In this Emersonian sense of representative biographical types[2]—not in a statistical sense—let us begin our entrance into the minds and culture of the unchurched. Three sketches provide an initial glimpse at the sort of pictures the unchurched draw of their experiences and their world. In Part Three, I shall classify the types of unchurchedness they represent, their range and variety with excerpts drawn from 165 such stories and pictures. Here, each of the three autobiographies contains its own pathos and hostility, its own intrinsic plea for understanding, its singular inner contradictions and ambiguities, its unfinished search for meaning and purpose. They are the real stories of real people (fictionalized at crucial points only to protect their identities). They are retold here in the language and with the passion in which they were first heard; only the sequence has been altered slightly, in some instances, in order to reconstruct the order of events in the stories told. For Mary Lou, Emily, and Carlos, their constructions of reality had real consequences.

Let me start with a talented young jewelry designer, Mary Lou, whom I encountered in a casual excursion to the local artist colony near Laguna Beach, California. "Artistic Accents" was the last craft exhibit I visited one evening in March 1976, as I strolled in and out of the quaint little shops overlooking the Pacific beach. I had admired a pendant of contemporary design. Mary Lou inquired where I was from, who I was, what I was doing in Orange County. I told her the purpose of my survey. She asked to be interviewed, and we made an appointment for the following noon. The conversation began at her shop, continued over lunch in a nearby restaurant, and concluded on the street as we returned to her place of business where several of her college-age friends waited, at her initiative, for interviews with "that religious sociologist from the East."

I was brought up Roman Catholic in San Francisco. As a child, I felt very close to the church, very, very close to its teachings. It made me *feel*, I had a rich spiritual experience. It was beautiful and poetic. The teachings were beautiful—the catechism, the nuns, the feelings of holiness. When I think of God, I think of everything beautiful, everything kind, everything magical, everything holy, everything wonderful. The teachings of the church were that to me.

I went to religion classes in the parochial school. To me, I looked forward to them. It was like fairytales. It made me feel very close to God. I've always had this very close feeling to God anyway. I felt a union.

When I was a little older, nine or ten, I think, I went to first communion. It was a total, complete, fulfilling experience. To me, it was more than just a religion—it was a communication with God in a beautiful way. I loved the way they put it. First communion is an exciting time, a spiritual preparation. It makes you feel good. I felt very close to God. I wanted to be good, and I wanted to be a part of what he wanted me to do here on this earth. It is like a magical thing and a story thing. It was my own little world. I don't remember whether my family was involved. I really don't think so.

Afterward, there was confirmation. Instead of communication with God, confirmation gets into your responsibility with the church. Somehow I was a very different child. I stayed strong about my opinions and my feelings.

Then, I had an experience with a nun. I was eleven then. They had at times tended to be too harsh. It's almost that they take the religion too seriously. They almost forget God. They make too many rules and forget the spiritualism. I used to go to school where these elderly nuns took the little children off the streets, you know, little tiny ones. We would have different little things for them, little parties, and things to do.

One day, there was a little boy—this is something that I now understand, I forgive her, but at the time it was very upsetting to me—a little tiny boy I liked so much. He was so much in need of attention. We had little packages and put them in a big basket—we would play games. And if they were good, we would open all the little packages for them. And there was a boy, just a child, just a child, much younger than I. He got into the packages and started opening the presents. And the nun—she was a little frustrated old nun—got very angry and slapped him. That upset me very badly. So—I kicked her. I said, "You are an agent of God, and you should have more understanding." She got very angry then. I said, "I don't want to work with you again." I left and went home. She came back—I was somewhat of a little rebel anyway—and told my mother that

I was a bad girl and I belonged in a juvenile home and that sort of thing, you know. And I said to her, "You just don't have any understanding for people, and you shouldn't be a nun." That made it worse. I almost got beaten out of my mind. My mother, of course, sided with the nun—they were supposed to be godlike or whatever. And I got punished over this, and I resented the church because I felt—I should have understood that no one is perfect—it left a bad taste in my mouth, bad feelings.

There was a series of other incidents, too. I'm saying that most religious groups and their priests and parishioners—they try to take the place of God. I'm still searching, none of us have the answer. No religion or person can tell me what my communication with God is. It is between God and me. I think we have to have some kind of leadership, but I'm saying that I just don't think that any one person can have the right to make themselves take the place of God. Remember, they said we would have a lot of false prophets, false preachers, and false churches. It is up to us in our understanding and our communication that we be able to feel which is right and which is wrong. I know when something is right and when it is wrong.

I remember when I was excommunicated from the church. I got divorced. I got divorced, and I thought that was the most hypocritical thing in my life. Here they had raised me Catholic! All of a sudden I cannot receive the host unless I live in sin with someone and come in and confess it every week and be forgiven, be a hypocrite. I threw my husband out the door—physically—and I would do it again and again and again and again. Even Christ threw the gamblers out—does that mean that all of a sudden he was a bad person? My husband was very offending. He was breaking the regulations of the marriage. He was a liar. Although I cared for him, I couldn't make him see any other way than the way he was, and I wasn't going to continue living with him under those circumstances. When I divorced, I realized that every church sets their rules and one thing I wasn't going to be was a hypocrite. Well, I am a hypocrite at times, but, you know, I tell God.

I stopped going to mass. Well, maybe once in a while. But particularly since I was little I used to have a phobia about mass. My mother had to push me out the door to go on Sundays, it was like being forced into a sacrifice. When I was in church, I felt like I would suffocate. My stomach hurt, my knees hurt, my back hurt. Everything about religion and about God was beautiful, but the actual mass on Sunday was a torture. It was the same thing over and over every Sunday. I guess you could say I just don't like that much crowd anyway. I was led to believe that you have to go to church on Sunday—you have to get together with this group of people. But I feel wherever I am there is God. I know that there is a great need for the unity of people getting together, and back in the Catholic Church, but I wish that things would be more understanding and different so that all those people would gather back together with a different understanding.

There is only one God, and the church is not God. The priests are not God.

The Pope is not God. We are just instruments. The most important part is to show love—to extend this love. There isn't any set rule except the rules you set within yourself. As a divorced person, I don't care whether the church accepts me or not. You have to make rules. Certain rules have to be there. Most people have to be led, they have to be told, they have to be punished. But they also have to be forgiving, because God is forgiving. The church is hurting people when it should be loving. I think they should try to teach people better understanding and about life and about God and, you know, purity and reaching. I mean, they are changing the rules, but accepting me is not what I'm after. Because I accept myself, and I am higher than the church. I am a child of God.

Sometimes I think that I might want to go back to the church, but I don't think I ever will. I'd like to be able to be a part of helping, understanding, giving someone my time, to help other beings. If that is what my church became a part of, I would be a part of that. Because it is what God wants me to do. But as long as it is going to be in rules and punishment and "I'll slap your hand if you do this," or "You are out of the church"—no, I will never be a part of that. I feel that whatever I do God is in control. I'm just doing his bidding. He has shown me many ways—the unbelievable miracles like I could tell you—he has shown me many times, many ways that it is right and I am doing his bidding and I leave it up to him. I think eventually in the end, just like they say, we are going to be a part of God or we are going to stop existing.

I have to tell you something else. Not too long ago I heard they were going to start a new church, a Catholic mission, you know. I wanted to give them something—like a gold cross to hang over the altar. I called up the priest, and I told him about my idea. What do you think he said? "Well, young lady, are you Catholic?" I said, "Sort of." He said, "Then you come on over for confession, and we'll see about your crazy idea." You know what? They won't even let my gold cross be near my beautiful Jesus.

The second autobiographical sketch was contained in a letter I received following a *Time* magazine item, "Looking from the Inside Out," which summarized my typology of the unchurched. The writer was Emily, a mature adult now living in the deep South. In a letter to me, she wrote, "I am glad that you cared enough for the unchurched to investigate us." Although she appended a postscript that read, "I trust that you will destroy this letter immediately," she later granted permission for me to reprint it, after removal of several identifying features. Her poignant and articulate story follows.

As an unchurched person, I can speak for many like myself in some respects, but only for myself in others. The use of the pronouns *we, us,* and *I* will distinguish my usages.

We are the working poor, and we are legion. Our churches were the usual

Protestant lunatic fringe, Church of Christ, Baptist varieties, and Pentecostal varieties. Instant salvation was the promise; immediate torment was the delivery.

God was a huge, larger-than-life-sized man who demanded poverty, ignorance, and endless, ready-made, unnecessary suffering, especially of women. Belief in the literal, verbatim magic of every word in the Bible was mandatory; attempting to understand even one precept was forbidden. We not only were commanded to obey precepts we did not understand, but also to teach them to others, spreading our afflictions.

This God we had delighted in the smell of the burning flesh of sinners who smoked, drank a drop of liquor, or missed attending church for any reason. The list of condemned practices was very, very long; it included reading anything except the literature published by one's particular church.

These churches, their God, and their peculiar practices are very much alive, and they continue, as always, to manage their people by pulling their emotional strings, by silencing reason—which is "evil"—and playing upon man's deepest fears and highest hopes.

Most of us who left simply consigned ourselves to lives of misery on earth and an eternity of hell after death. We felt like God's hate for us was too great to appease. That God seemed to hate everything, even the light of the sun. In spite of all the bibliolatry these churches taught and teach, if a person chanced on a sublime and beautiful passage such as "Doubtless thou art our father even though Abraham be ignorant of us" or "All shall be taught, from the greatest to the least," that person was immediately, strongly reprimanded. Such beauty does not and did not enter into such a monstrous, ugly god's "plan of salvation."

The Christ they presented to us was not a savior; he was a weak, mindless nonentity who demanded our submission to evil in every form. It was a horrible caricature, and I used to think how terribly the Christ was crucified every Sunday morning and evening and every Wednesday evening.

Like all of my sisters and brothers who I felt were God's stepchildren, I left the churches in painful confusion, deeply hurt, not knowing my right hand from my left.

Before I turned my back on the church's God, I had an extremely frank talk with him.

One of my young children was almost dead because I had turned the other cheek too many times, because I had "obeyed in all meekness and submission, calling him (my husband) *lord*" (Paul's commandment). My children and I were hungry and we were destitute; we were also 2,000 miles from the nearest relative or friend.

I told this church God that while I was somehow certain that he was right and I was wrong, nevertheless I had followed him into a mire and must leave him long enough to get myself and my young children out of the desperate condition he had willed on us. I told this God, moreover, that whatever his Jesus said, it could not include child sacrifice—we saw, and see, a lot of that in these churches. I promised this ugly God that once I pulled us to high ground I would repent of leaving the church for which his Christ died, and when the worst troubles were over I would return. With Paul's handcuffs fastened on my wrists and Jesus' commands starving my children to near-death, I had to take my leave of them long enough to help us myself. I pointed out to this God that a bird defends her young and her nest, a dog her pups, but human mothers are forbidden to do this, according to the New Testament.

With the speed of light, our desperation soon became inspiration, our sickness turned into health, and our long, terrible confusion and pain receded into calm confidence.

I kept my promise to the church God, and I returned, but very briefly. Very, very briefly. After that, I began a search that lasted for twenty-five years; through Salvation Army used-book stores and public libraries; through wild woods and mountains; across rivers; through towns and cities. Finally, the Infinite God, the Most High and Holy, the One of whom Isaiah spoke—that One showed me a gleam of genuine light. It is no larger than a grain of sand, but it is light— beautiful, eternal, everlasting, wonderful. No church will ever get the opportunity to snuff out this gleam.

My only regret is that I cannot communicate this bit of light to my sisters and brothers out here in this "pagan, sinful world on its way to everlasting damnation"—for missing a church feed, maybe.

Again, however, my regret is foolish. No mortal hand ever closed on a sunbeam and then attempted to hand that sunbeam to another mortal. In time to come, my brothers and sisters will receive their bit of light; no doubt many already have, although it might not be dressed in religious garb. Shall not "all be taught (saith the Lord)"? Who knows, however, if any shall be taught in church?

Thank you for listening. If you have a bit of light, I bid you goodspeed. If you do not, keep searching.

Yours truly,
Emily

A third sketch comes from an interview with Carlos, a middle-aged former farm worker, then the "token Chicano," as he put it, in an antipoverty agency, now a factory worker in a food-processing plant near Salem, Oregon. He had been referred to me by a younger Mexican-American, a political science student at Oregon State University at Corvallis. We met in the living room of his modest home, facing a mantlepiece holding pictures of his wife, family, children, and grandchildren. He began with reminiscences about his childhood in Mexico, then gradually unfolded his love-hate relationship with the church of his adolescence and later years.

My parents came from Mexico, and I was born in Texas. But I was taken back right when I was about eighteen months old because of the recession at that time. So I grew up in Mexico until I was 18 years old.

Most of the people in Mexico, say 50 percent of the people in the community in which I was raised, went to church or mass every Sunday. Back there, it seems like as far as I can remember I was going to church every Sunday. My mother was real active. I was baptized when I was a baby and took my first communion when I was seven or eight. While I was home with my mother, I attended church most every Sunday—it was a rarity that I missed it.

But after, when I was nine, ten, or eleven, I went my way. Then, there was nobody to send me, or pressure me so I stopped going altogether. I had already begun working by this time. I traveled quite a bit. It was a kind of stop-and-go situation. When I came to the United States, I believe I spent about a month in Texas, and then I went to Chicago. I spent about nine months in Chicago, went back to Texas for a year, back to Chicago for another seven or eight months, then back to Texas again.

I've been here, in this town, about ten years. There have been times when I have been very, very active in my church. Actually, it started way back in 1956. I was living in a community in Texas then. There was no church there, so the priest used to come to that community and began celebrating mass in public buildings—like theaters, the courthouse, the American Legion hall, you know, wherever he could rent space to hold mass. Accidentally, I was invited by a friend of mine, and I became involved with this group. It was mostly Chicano.

It was suggested that we could build a church if we wanted to. So everybody agreed, and I went along with the crowd. I was involved in raising funds. We organized people with talent who knew how to sing or to act, people who knew how to play the guitar or to dance. Once we set up a wrestling match. So we made quite a lot of money in a very short time. By 1958 we had a church.

Then, in 1960 the Cursillo Movement[3] moved into Texas, a sort of revival in the church. I was kind of lucky. It was very compact religious instructions for three intensive days. I was friendly with the priests. There were times when I suddenly found myself low. So I kept close with the team—eleven laymen and one priest plus. There was singing, open feelings, and activities. Before this, I can remember the priests very separate—on the pulpit to say the sermon. I had contact in sort of a fatherly situation. I doubt many people have that opportunity.

Then, the Cursillo came up here. It come; it die. There was a misunderstanding. A lot of Chicano families became very interested, very excited. They can see the change in their lives. Everybody was very happy. Then, there was another group who refused to go. They thought Cursillo was another denomination. It was because, well, it was natural, you know, whenever something new comes along some people are making a step forward to seek this experience. Some refuse to make this step. This is what happens here. They begin to talk against us and making statements that we believe this, that we do that—they became sort of our enemies, some priests, a few seminary students, and the people itself. We advise each other not to get mad with them, to try to understand, not to get into arguments. Sooner or later they might go through the experience and change. But it happens, and at that time we don't have no help, no help in Spanish. We have to go to Pasco, Washington, to have a Mexican priest. The excitement of the Cursillo kind of dies. Things are kind of cool now.

Then, there was the times when we have these seminarians here. They came with the intention of helping the community. They didn't have the wisdom to try to unite the community, but rather they divided. They went with the non-Cursillos, and they listened to them. They asked questions like, "Is it true that we need to go to the Cursillo for our salvation?" They say, "No, you don't have to." They stopped there. You never know where you are going to find the tool to find salvation—maybe in one sermon, maybe in one retreat, maybe in talking to a priest. You never know—maybe in the Cursillo. And the people misinterpret. They come back to us and say, "You are a bunch of liars." It was a very hot 1970, 1971, and 1972. There has been no Cursillo since then—our last was 1973.

Now, I begin to feel emptiness. It seems like a routine. Something is missing; something is missing! Cursillo really opened my eyes. I don't feel fulfillment any more. The service itself is so routine. Maybe God wants something else to be taking place instead of just going through the process of saying different things in the same manner Sunday after Sunday—the first reading, the second reading, the Gospel, and communion, a few more words, and that is it.

Maybe the time will come when things will be different. Some day, somehow, something will happen. Maybe something happen to myself, and I might see the light. I'm sorry that I am not capable mentally or spiritually to participate. Some day something happen.

A Chicano priest would understand how we feel, how we live, and how to approach the message. They kind of identify with us—the Mexican priest, the Chicano priest from Texas, a Spanish priest from Spain, recently a priest from Columbia—they have the feeling of our community and culture. They really hear us and touch the bottom of consciousness. Anglo priests are very kind, very knowledgeable, very intelligent persons, but a world apart from reaching us consciously. They are very cool.

I have twelve kids. Back in 1972, we all went back to Mexico. My mother and father still live in Mexico. I could sense and feel the change. But we don't have that much opportunity to go back. Most of the Chicanos are too poor.

These kids are going to lose that part of their culture. They want to become real Anglos—not want to, but they are conditioned that way by the system.

I used to work for the Opportunity Center here back in the 1960s, then I quit and went three years to —————— college. Then, they give me an administrative position with the state. But I soon realize I was all window-dressing. I was just an excuse for the organization to tell Washington they have an exmigrant worker on the staff. I am not a token. The director said, "We need you." I say, "I don't be your token. So goodbye," and I quit.

I went back to the fields. Then, I got the job in the cannery. I stay there for the winter—it is close to the house. It is steady work. But I'm not going back to the fields this year. My son, he don't want to go. My girl, she is working over here so she is going to make as much as if I take her with me. What's the use? So I stay here. Even if I am a part of an Anglo community, it is going to change. My kids, they don't know very much any more about a Chicano priest. I'm just going to hang around.

These representative biographical types mirror the spiritual ethos of our time. They provide lenses for discerning some common perceptions of the churches seen through the eyes of the unchurched.

Mary Lou still carries the sentimentalism of her early childhood when religion was "like a magical thing, a story thing"—everything beautiful, kind, holy, and wonderful—"like fairytales." That swiftly fades with her divorce and excommunication. There is a wistful longing to go back; she even tries to return vicariously through the proferred gift of her own crafted cross to a new mission. But her innocence is lost. She must make her pilgrimage alone. "I don't care whether the church accepts me or not. . . . Because I accept myself, and I am higher than the church."

Emily's life story is one of exposure to the Protestant "lunatic fringe," an exposure, which she explained to me in a subsequent letter, is still the only church option available to her today in her small, Southern, rural community. Both intellectually and experientally, the gospel she had heard had been perverted into bad news—a common testimony of many of the unchurched I encountered. Having finally after twenty-five years experienced "that One [who] showed me a gleam of genuine light," she still travels alone. Twice, she reiterates, "No church will ever get the opportunity to snuff out this gleam" and "Who knows if any shall be taught in church?" Like Mary Lou, Emily has retreated further and further into a private, personal realm, her faith "exiled to that last frontier" where the person becomes the "sole judge of his own truth."[5] Mary Lou and Emily are representative of those who have lost by imposed or voluntary exile the very religious communion they seek. They live in a lonely, private world, bereft of the shelter, instruction, hope, voice, and connections of any meaningful religious community. It is doubtful that they will ever return, and they become vulnerable in their insecurity to the latest claims of newly discovered truths, their gurus and evangelists.

Carlos is the classic marginal man who belongs nowhere—a "token" in the Anglo world and unable to return "home" to a world he has long since abandoned. He "just hangs around" in a Chicano community that has lost its roots. His personality seems compatible with the warmth of the Cursillo and its excitement, which make "everybody happy." His life has been marked by more "lows" than "highs," but now even the amphetamine effect of the Cursillo has subsided: "It come, it die." He resignedly tries to cope with his emptiness and lack of fulfillment. His life has become "cool" like the priests and like the "system" that conditions his life and that of his growing children. He has only one mechanism left for adjustment, a stoic "What's the use? I stay here."

There is, of course, always a problem in viewing the world of the actor through the actor's own eyes.[6] How does one know whether an informant has engaged in a colossal deception? How much of one's recalled autobiography is selective? Why are the painful traumas often remembered longer than the ordinary successful life passages? Are there, moreover, hidden depths of meaning that are buried beneath the repertoire of language and the vocabulary of accounts? And, to what extent did my respondents tell me what they thought I wanted to hear? Answers to these questions are neither new nor simple; they have been dealt with by the ethnographers, the psychologists, the historians, survey researchers, and the public opinion pollsters.[7] The questions may be unanswerable given our still primitive knowledge of the human psyche.

What we do know is that people have pictures in their heads of the world outside that, given an empathic listener, they unveil in story form. Their stories often determine, as myths have for the preliterate, their acted reality. Some of the pictures are ludicrous pictures of the world as others know it. Sometimes the tellers of the stories deceive themselves, consciously or unconsciously. Yet, ludicrous or self-deceptive, these stories still constitute the beliefs and perceptions on which they act.

Walter Lippmann has provided apt illustrations of this. He once recalled an island, far off from the mainland, where a few Englishmen, Frenchmen, and Germans were living in 1914. There were no cable communications, and the British mail steamer docked at the quay only once every 60 days. When the ship pulled in, the captain told them that for over six weeks their English and French compatriots had been waging war against the Germans over the sanctity of international treaties. "For six strange weeks," Lippmann observed, the islanders "had acted as if they were friends, when in fact they were enemies."[8]

For centuries, both Christians and scientists drew their topographies of the world as a flat parallelogram. Their maps were not in the least absurd. Only in our superior hindsight can we argue that the world as they needed to know it and the world as they did know it were two different things. Similarly, men wage battles or give political speeches believing in their pictures of their enemies. Our Puritan forebears diagnosed evil and burned the witches they believed spread the deadly pestilence of Satan. Thousands of soldiers died on the battlefields of Europe in World War I in the final five days before news of the real armistice reached the front. A sexist culture was spawned, in part at least, on the lack of knowledge, before the early nineteenth century, that the female egg played an essential part in conception.

These representations of reality are not lies. They are common, recurrent, inevitable "social fictions"—often limited and distorted by the perceivers—by which the human scene is painted and by which the pictures work themselves out on the scene of action. As Lippmann has concluded, "The way in which the world is imagined determines at any particular moment what men will do. . . . It determines their effort, their feelings, their hopes."[9] This reportage puts high confidence in the ability of local actors to give meaningful descriptions of the events of their lives, descriptions that color their self-understanding and their view of the world in which they live.

Such pictures and stories may also be interpreted in terms of the functions they perform. The functional clues derive from the sort of stories they are. Many of them are "accounts"—explanatory statements of the reasons for and causes of their behavior.[10] A common form of this is "scapegoating"; that is, "My behavior is a response to the behavior of others." This is a frequent function of the stories of the unchurched. Mary Lou explains her adult bahavior as a result of the dissonance she discovered, first, between the ideal and lived behavior of a "frustrated old nun" who slapped a defenseless little boy, and, again, in the imposed status of excommunicate as a result of her divorce and remarriage. Emily embarks on her long pilgrimage, perhaps like Martin Luther centuries before, in a search for the gracious God denied her in the preaching of those who consigned her to a life of misery and an eternity of hell. Carlos' response is more ambiguous. He appears, as far as his recorded story goes, not explicitly aware of his immigrant marginality and social alienation (at least not in these terms). Clearly, however, he recognizes that he lives in a "cool" world with its "cool" religion. His own "cool" behavior he attributes to the behavior of others. Even his faint hope that "something may happen" pushes the responsibility largely to the initiative of others.

Some "accounts" take the form of "atrocity stories."[11] In unconscious ways, the stories function to preserve one's own integrity against the assaults or norms thought to be inflicted by others. So, the practical nurse or aide has a full repertoire of atrocities she alleges have been committed by registered nurses. The registered nurse has similar stories of the stupidities or incompetence of physicians and surgeons. Lawyers demean the wisdom, integrity, and fairness of judges in whose courts they have lost cases. Tales are legion of the "crookedness" of used-car salesmen, of misplaced parts in an engine by bumbling auto mechanics, of dentists who pull the wrong teeth, of historians who "don't know the facts," of quarterbacks who call the wrong plays, of janitors who "really know" what their tenants are like. People who relate the atrocities—real or imagined, or, as is often the case, routinized in their telling within cultures, subcultures, and groups—may feel that they thus gain power over others, especially the others the society tends to legitimize or honor. They take umbrage at another's advantage, advancement, or status. The atrocity stories of the unchurched may be vehicles of self-justification, proofs of the appropriateness of their own behavior in the face of the hypocrisy of the churched.

One might be tempted to ask people like Mary Lou, Emily, and Carlos, "Who is really talking through your stories?" Or, "Whose mouthpiece is this voice?" It may be that the stories I heard were words spoken by ventriloquists, to use a colorful metaphor invented by Helmut Thielicke in his study of nihilism.[12] These stories may be the foamy crest on an ocean of oral tradition, the extent and communication of which has never, to my knowledge, been investigated. Emily's explicit distinction between *we, us,* and *I* is a rarity in most of the anecdotes of the unchurched. In fact, redundancy abounds everywhere. Similar stories are reiterated by persons who have never met and live a continent apart. One is forced to conclude either that the incidents from which the stories derive (like the priest who gets drunk at the Eucharist) recur, or that people think they do because "It's just common knowledge" (for example, "everyone, of course, knows . . .") that has become internalized *as if* it were one's own experience.

This is not to charge that the challenges against the churches, their beliefs, and their leaders, are void of personal conviction. Whether the words are those of a ventriloquist or not, I heard them from the mouths of live human beings, not dummies. And it is no more possible to detach the words from the storytellers than to detach art from the artist, music from the composer, or memoirs from the autobiographer. To dismiss the stories is to question the integrity of their authors.

Pictures in the head, then, are his or her reality for the person who so pictures the self and the world. Mary Lou's angry nun is a real person who has affected her life. Emily's God "who seemed to hate everything, even the light of the sun" was the real God of the churches she fled. Carlos' perception of the Sunday mass as routine ritual "Sunday after Sunday . . . a few more words and that is it" has made him "not capable mentally or spiritually to participate" any more. As the internal pictures become shared stories, the potential for distortion and self-justification, as in vintage "atrocity tales," is a common human occurrence. It is a sustaining fiction that helps preserve the self. It thrives wherever people are dependent on one another's company.

NOTES

1. Ralph Waldo Emerson, *Representative Men: Seven Lectures* (Philadelphia: Altemus, 1892), pp. 11, 25.
2. I am indebted to Thomas F. O'Dea, *Alienation, Atheism and the Religious Crisis* (New York: Sheed and Ward, 1969), pp. 15–41, for this "ideal typical" approach to what O'Dea terms "the crisis of the religious consciousness."
3. "Looking from the Inside Out," *Time*, 3 October 1977, p. 85.
4. The Cursillo Movement, central to Carlos' story, began in Majorca, Spain, in the late 1940s, and spread to other countries in 1953. The best single apologetic work by movement leaders is *The Fundamental Ideas of the Cursillo Movement* (Dallas, Texas: National Ultreya, 1974).
5. Robert Wuthnow, "A Religious Marketplace," *Journal of Current Social Issues* 14, 2 (Spring 1977): 38–42.
6. Philosophers point to the "solipsistic fallacy," the tendency to view the self as the only

existent thing. Phenomenologists and ethnomethodologists have been particularly vulnerable to this charge. See, for example, the discussion by Helmut R. Wagner, "The Influence of German Phenomenology on American Sociology," in Myrtle Korenbaum, ed., *Annals of the Phenomenological Society* 1, 1 (1976): 1–29. For a critical assessment of the potential trap of solipsism, see Robert S. Perinbanayagan, "The Definition of the Situation: An Analysis of the Ethnomethodological and Dramaturgical View," *Sociological Quarterly* 25 (Autumn 1974): 521–41.

7. See, for example, Roy Turner, ed., *Ethnomethodology: Selected Readings* (Baltimore: Penguin Books, 1974), for a series of "working papers," with self-conscious discussions of "theorizing as practical reasoning" in the social sciences.

8. Walter Lippmann, "The World Outside and the Pictures in Our Heads," in his *Public Opinion* (New York: Macmillan, 1922), p. 3. Several of my illustrations here and following are from this classic essay.

9. *Ibid.*, pp. 25–26.

10. See Marvin B. Scott and Stanford M. Lyman, "Accounts," *American Sociological Review* 33, no. 1 (February 1968): 46–62.

11. For an interesting analysis of "accounts" as "atrocity stories," see Robert Dingwall, " 'Atrocity Stories' and Professional Relationships," in *Sociology of Work and Occupations* 4, no. 4 (November 1977): 371–96.

12. Helmut Thielicke, *Nihilism: Its Origin and Nature with a Christian Answer*, trans. John W. Doberstein (New York: Harper & Row, 1961), pp. 22–23.

3. The Extent and Distribution of the Unchurched

"We are being spied upon. . . . The eyes of all men are fixed on us." Jacques Ellul, noted French social scientist and lay theologian, made this observation in his recent *The Ethics of Freedom.* "Every act on the part of the Christian is observed, evaluated, and analyzed by the non-Christian." Those outside the church are able to say of those on the inside, "Look, their lives and acts are just like our own. They do not correspond in the least to what they are saying." Ellul grants that this may be "mere excuse for their not following the Christian way. . . . Nevertheless, it is a real excuse that we ourselves provide for them."[1]

Who are these spies, who when debriefed reveal the intelligence they have gained from forays into the camps of the unchurched? Most of them are indistinguishable from most of those on the inside, except that they are on the outside. Some were once themselves insiders; that is, members with varying degrees of involvement in the churches. They report what for them the inside was like. They draw pictures in their heads that are their own real pictures, however different from the pictures the committed insiders draw. Some have spent almost a lifetime inside and have only recently joined the outsiders. Others have been outside so long that they must recall their adolescence or childhood to recover what it was like to be a member or participant in the church. Some few have never really been on the inside at all, only infrequently in their entire lives having known what the inside of a stained-glass window looks like. A handful of these have not only not themselves been inside but also are totally unacquainted with insiders. At best, they only know the inside from rumors they hear now and then from other outsiders who were once insiders. Finally, there are those who have moved in and out with reckless abandon. They have joined the ranks and quit the ranks, spending shorter or longer periods in and out. The spies, in short, report what they know for themselves or think they know. Their pictures are drawn from their own perceptions, gained from their own remembered life experiences.

On the basis of recent research, we can make some generalizations about the social location of the unchurched, when compared with the churched population in the United States.[2] Males are more likely to be unchurched than females. The unchurched tend to be younger, under thirty-five, especially among inactive Catholics. More singles than marrieds are, proportionately, unchurched. The unchurched have fewer children. Contrary to many previous studies, the thesis that parents return to the church for the religious upbringing of their children has been seriously questioned. One study,[3] for example, indicates that "age of children" differences among churched and unchurched Protestants are negligible. Among estranged Catholics, the unchurched are more likely to have children under six and less likely to have children of school age. Among those with no religious preference at all the tendency to have children of school age is least likely, compared with those who still express Protestant or Catholic preference.

Social class differences between the unchurched and the churched are not as clear as those who view the church as a haven for the socially dispossessed have held. In fact, there is a tendency among churched Protestants and Catholics to identify with the middle and upper classes. Both Protestants and Catholics tend to be more highly educated, more likely to fall into white-collar occupations, and with negligible income differences, when compared with the unchurched.[4]

The unchurched are less rooted than the churched.[5] Thirty-eight percent of them have lived in their present community for five years or less, compared with 26 percent of the churched. They also move more frequently, 30 percent of the unchurched two or more times in the past five years, compared with only 18 percent of the churched.[6] Further, the migration patterns of recent years may exacerbate the problem of the churches, for several reasons: (1) the flight from places where religious institutions have been historically strong (such as the Northeast) offers no guarantee that the mobile will take their religion with them; (2) the population movement to Sun Belt regions (Florida, Arizona, and California, for example) puts the migrant into areas where religious influences have not been historically strong; and (3) population dispersal in the 1970s into nonmetropolitan areas is creating a new lifestyle—"living in the country, working in the city"—disruptive of patterns that favor church involvement.[7]

Depending on the definitions of *urban* and *rural,* two different profiles result. If *rural* refers to "counties where a majority of the population lives in open countryside, or in towns of 10,000 or less, away from cities, suburbs, and urban fringes" (one-third of the population), collectively, the rural counties do not differ significantly from their urban counterparts in percent of the population unchurched.[8] If, however, *rural* means places under 2,500 population, as in U.S. Census rubrics, the percentage of unchurched in "urban America" is unquestionably more pronounced than in "rural places." In either case, some distinctive characteristics of rural counties, however defined, may have some relationship with unchurchedness: lower educational attainment, poverty (twice that in urban counties), poorer health care and housing, lower income, and low population density. This suggests that the force of these variables may be greater than place of residence independently. Obviously, more analytic work is needed to supplement existing qualitative and descriptive studies before the correlations are objectively known.

How Many Unchurched Are There?

Estimates of the extent of the unchurched population in the United States vary with the definition and the method of counting. There is common agreement among most researchers that to be churched implies "some kind of participation in or association with the ongoing life of a local religious institution; that is, a congregation, a parish, a synagogue, a tabernacle, a mosque, or so on. The emphasis is on 'belonging' or 'involvement' as opposed to 'believing' or 'faithfulness.' "[9]

Agreement breaks down when the "churched" or "unchurched" are counted. What kind of "belonging" is implied? How much "involvement" or "participation"—and of what kind—qualifies for the designation "churched"? Whose judgment do we trust, the reporting person or the reporting religious institution? If the latter, the religious institution, what does "membership" mean—the baptized, the adult confirmed, total adherents, church attenders, financial givers? Are the reported figures reliable?

These questions plague all researchers who would make sense out of religious statistics. Any discussion of the extent of church membership in the United States must therefore clarify the costs and benefits of using the available data. We know considerably less than we need to know, and what we do know is less precise than is often supposed, given the present chaotic status of statistical, religious data gathering.

The problem is theological as well as methodological. Some local communions, perhaps the American counterparts of the German *Volkskirche*, consider every baptized person a member unless transferred to another congregation or removed by death or excommunication. Anabaptist groups count baptized adults only, consistent with their doctrine of "believers' baptism." Pentecostalists and some other sectarian groups equate membership with participation in worship, especially revival or dedication services; tests of membership may also be imposed, such as a "born-again" experience or personal moral attributes. The so-called intentional religious communities insist on a "covenant of belonging," which may include tithing, daily Bible reading, regular worship attendance, and some form of lay involvement in the secular community. At least one American religious group, the Church of Christ, Scientist, holds that "numbering" members is inappropriate. Jews variously define themselves as religious practitioners or as a people, not necessarily religious, of a specific culture. It is unlikely that these theological hurdles will disappear in the near future. The leaders of religious institutions will understandably not easily compromise their theologies to meet the operational needs of researchers.

Researchers agree that either membership or some frequency of church attendance is a major criterion to distinguish the churched from the unchurched—a consensus that is useful only if we further limit the terms and identify the sources of data. "Membership" statistics depend on one or more of three common sources of data: (1) Religious Census reports by the U.S. Bureau of the Census, discontinued after 1957; survey samples, as, for example, the General Social Surveys of the National Data Program for the Social Sciences (National Opinion Research Center—NORC—Chicago), or public opinion polls by such organizations as Louis Harris, Ben Gaffin, George Gallup, the Kettering Foundation, and Samuel Yankelovich, to cite a few; and (3) denominational statistics, reported by local congregations, and tabulated by national interfaith agencies, sometimes adjusted to achieve uniformity of definition and to account for nonreporting local churches or denominations.

U.S. government compilations of religious data began in 1850 and continued on a regular decade basis until 1936. A special count of religious preferences was made in 1957 but has since been discontinued on the grounds that it compromises civil liberty and church-state separation. Two typical questions by which survey researchers—NORC, for example—determine "religious belonging" are "What is your religious preference—Protestant, Catholic, Jewish, some other religion, or no religion?" and "How often do you attend religious services?" Secondary analysis of the responses permits a classification, as in the recent David Roozen study,[10] of five mutually exclusive categories: the Protestant churched, the Protestant unchurched, the Catholic churched, the Catholic unchurched, and those expressing no religious preference or identification. In its 1978 survey of the unchurched American, The Gallup Organization (based in Princeton, New Jersey) used as its working definition of the unchurched "a person who has not attended church or synagogue in the last six months apart from weddings, funerals, or special holidays such as Christmas, Easter, or Yom Kippur or who is *not* a member of a church."[11] Both approaches—NORC and Gallup—assume the essential reliability of the answers respondents give. But some people who think they are members are not actually on the rolls of local churches. More people claim church attendance than actually appear in the pews. Further, although standardized questions may be useful to establish long-term trends (the same questions asked at periodic intervals), it is questionable whether the answers mean the same thing at different times. Dominant motifs in the society may affect the way individuals reply. As Gary Wills observes cynically, what the polls record is the spread of the *term*, rather than common or changing answers.[12] The meaning of a particular religious experience, membership, preference, or participation may change as certain behaviors gain or lose legitimacy in the culture.

Vidich and Bensman discovered, in their classic study of Springdale,[13] that the bustle of religious activity in many small communities creates the impression that church membership is larger than is actually the case. The religious zeal that characterizes a minority of the heavily involved may be deceiving. The general conformity to the notion that this is a religious nation creates an unconscious, self-imposed thought control that inhibits many dissidents from publicly acknowledging their defection. Many simply do not wish to bear the disgraceful stigma that results from being perceived as blockheads, eccentrics, macabre outsiders, pariahs, spoilsports, or betrayers of national ideals. How else does one interpret the consistent results of Gallup polls that almost everyone in the American society believes in God? Is it plausible to conclude that only 2 or 3 percent of the American people do not believe in God? If so, what does this mean? Does the fact that most pollsters, like Gallup, sample the "civilian" public—that is, the "noninstitutionalized," ruling out interviews with college and university populations on their own turf[14]—effectively diminish the effect of the seriously committed, hardcore secularists in the American society? So, as Tracy Early writes, "we must assume that a certain percentage of respondents tell Gallup what they think good Americans should tell him."[15]

In this study, I have placed greater reliance on officially recorded statistics of membership. *Church members are those persons listed on the rolls of Christian religious bodies. The unchurched are the residuals left over after the churched have been counted.* This simplification does not remove some problematic characteristics in the tabulations of the churched population. Neither the 1952 nor 1971 county-by-county studies of U.S. church membership, the most ambitious and sophisticated to date, claimed to account for all U.S. church members. While both include "the vast majority of Christian church members in the United States,"[16] neither accounts for more than 80 percent of Christian church members. Eastern churches, for example, numbering some 4.2 million in 1971, declined to participate. The Assemblies of God, reported to have more than doubled its .5 million membership of 1952 by 1971, were not reported. Black churches without national systems for reporting were not included, nor were many smaller, independent local congregations who have no national offices. Jews, estimated to comprise over 6 million, and Moslems, claimed by some to have 3 million adherents in the United States, constitute a major omission.

The more critical problem in counting members is definition, but there are ways of partially solving it. To avoid the theological problems, membership designation rests with the denominations themselves. Comparability of data can be relatively achieved by establishing two categories of membership: (1) communicant, confirmed or full membership, as defined by the respective denomination; and (2) total adherents, estimated where necessary by adjusting for nonreported members under thirteen years of age.

Such tallies may result, in some cases, in overcounts, exaggerations originating perhaps at the local community level, where religious leaders inflate statistics to obscure known attritions or simply guess at their numerical strength, perhaps at higher levels than controlled records would warrant. There is also evidence that churches may undercount their members in order to escape higher financial quotas set by their national headquarters for church-wide benevolences. Whether these two contradictory tendencies cancel one another out is simply unknown. Cautiously, one must make one's own judgment, which in the final analysis will rest on some subjective assumptions. The tallies can only be accepted as the most reasonably accurate at hand; that falls short, admittedly, of objective certainty.

Tabulations of the Glenmary Research Center, Washington, D.C.,[17] used in this study, have compensated for many of the known errors in Johnson, Picard, and Quinn's study. Adjustments were made for the estimated 10.4 percent of the total U.S. church members belonging to black denominations. The Eastern churches, the Church of Christ, and the Assemblies of God, which account for most of the 8.8 percent of the total church population not reported, have been included by arbitrarily increasing the church count in each county. Finally, denominations that reported state totals and not county totals were given representation by distributing members to counties according to the ratio of members to population known to exist at the state level. County data for Jews and other world religions in the United States do not exist; an artifact of this count therefore results in including members of such groups among the unchurched. Mormons, whom many Christian theologians do not classify as Christian, are tabulated in the Glenmary study as church members.

The unchurched in the United States, then, as defined in this study, comprise some 78,425,146 people—that is, persons not included in the number of total adherents (communicant, confirmed, full members plus actual or estimated child members, and adjustments for nonreporting churches) reported by or estimated to belong to local congregations in 1971. Compared with first count 1970 U.S. Census data, which recorded the total population as 203,211,926, *the unchurched percentage of the population is 38.6 percent.* These figures, rounded, make it possible to speak of approximately 80 million unchurched, or 40 percent of the population.

This estimate roughly corresponds to the 1978 Gallup survey, which counted roughly 61 million adults who do not belong to any church or religious institution, or 41 percent of the adult population, eighteen years of age and older (150,116,000, as estimated by the U.S. Department of Labor in April 1978). Projected to the total population, the Gallup figures would run higher than the Glenmary estimate, about 88 million. The Roozen study, based on NORC data, concludes that the total unchurched in America represent 32 percent of the population, but the data base, as with the Gallup poll, consisted of a national cross-sectional sample of noninstitutionalized adults, eighteen years of age and older, and absolute numbers must be adjusted accordingly. A more recent Glenmary study (1978),[18] which claims to have compensated for unreported Jews, still approximates the unchurched population in the 38–40 percent range. Some other estimates run higher. Donald McGavran of the Institute for American Church Growth, for example, estimates that "about a hundred million Americans are nominal, marginal, or slightly lapsed Christians."[19] Alvin A. Illig, of the Catholic Bishop's Committee on Evangelization, estimates up to 90 million Americans with no religious affiliation whatsoever, including about 12 million "estranged Catholics," so alienated from the church that they may be considered "churchless."[20] Given the probability of large numbers of marginal members among the 79,890,288 Protestants also, the estimated 80 million unchurched, or 40 percent of the population is likely conservative.

Where Are the Unchurched?

There is unanimous agreement among all who have studied the distribution of the unchurched in America that the South, not surprisingly, contains the largest share, proportionately, of the nation's church members. The West, by contrast, is the most heavily unchurched. This has been an historical phenomenon, not new. According to Glenmary, 65.7 percent of the southern population today belong to churches; 53.8 percent of American westerners do not belong to churches. (See Appendix.) The North Central and Northeast regions of the nation are 35.5 percent and 35.8 percent unchurched, respectively.

Within these four regions—Northeast, North Central, South, and West—are nine divisions: New England, Middle Atlantic, East North Central, West North Central, South Atlantic, East South Central, West South Central, Mountain, and Pacific. The Pacific and Mountain divisions (13 states, including Alaska and Hawaii) rank first and second in their percentage of unchurched people (Pacific, 57.8 percent; Mountain, 41.1 percent). The remaining seven divisions rank in the following order: East North Central (5 states, 37.5 percent); South Atlantic (9 states, including the District of Columbia, 37.9 percent); Middle Atlantic (3 states, 36.9 percent); New England (6 states, 32.3 percent); East South Central (4 states, 32.2 percent); West South Central (4 states, 29.8 percent); and West North Central (7 states, 28.5 percent). Conversely, the South and "middle America," as long perceived by most Americans and now documented, are clearly the dominant areas of churched Americans.

The states of Oregon and Washington have the largest proportion of unchurched persons in the nation (60.9 percent each). Only one of Oregon's thirty-six counties, for instance, registers a majority of its population as church members. Other states with a majority of their populations unchurched include California (57 percent), Hawaii (56.2 percent), Alaska (56.1 percent), Nevada (53.6 percent), West Virginia (52 percent), and Colorado (51.4 percent). Among the fifteen states ranked highest according to unchurched percentage, ten are in the Mountain-Pacific region. The rest are all east of the Mississippi—West Virginia (ranked 7), Maine (ranked 9), Indiana (ranked 12), Florida (ranked 14), and New Hampshire (ranked 15).

The distribution of the unchurched is dramatically portrayed when the statistics are plotted by counties in religious cartography. (See Figure 1.) California, the most populous state in the nation, stands out as having the single largest concentration of the unchurched, 47 of its 58 counties (81 percent) being dominantly unchurched. (Tiny Alpine County, population 484, situated atop the Sierra Nevadas just south of Lake Tahoe, has the dubious distinction of ranking first among all counties in the forty-eight contiguous U.S. states in percentage of unchurched persons; only 36 known church members are recorded there.) A similar phenomenon continues north into Oregon and Washington and east into the Great Basin state of Nevada. East of the Mississippi, the unchurched population runs the length of the Appalachians, with concentrations in northern New England (especially in Maine's more rugged interior and in the White Mountains of New Hampshire), in the Allegheny Plateau counties of New York, Pennsylvania, and West Virginia, through the Cumberlands of Kentucky and central and western Tennessee, to northwestern Alabama, where the Appalachians finally disappear into the Gulf Coastal Plain. In general, then, the unchurched are bimodally distributed, on the West

Figure 1. PERCENT OF POPULATION UNCHURCHED

By Counties of the United States: 1971

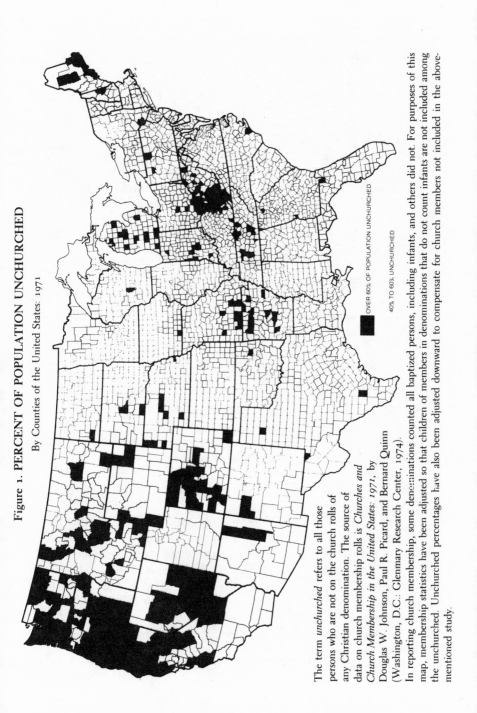

OVER 60% OF POPULATION UNCHURCHED

40% TO 60% UNCHURCHED

The term *unchurched* refers to all those persons who are not on the church rolls of any Christian denomination. The source of data on church membership rolls is *Churches and Church Membership in the United States: 1971*, by Douglas W. Johnson, Paul R. Picard, and Bernard Quinn (Washington, D.C.: Glenmary Research Center, 1974).

In reporting church membership, some denominations counted all baptized persons, including infants, and others did not. For purposes of this map, membership statistics have been adjusted so that children of members in denominations that do not count infants are not included among the unchurched. Unchurched percentages have also been adjusted downward to compensate for church members not included in the above-mentioned study.

Coast and along the eastern Appalachian strip.

Four additional minor concentrations are also evident. The Ozarks of lower Missouri and northwestern Arkansas contain forty counties, the majority of whose populations have no church affiliation. The mountainous sections of Colorado and New Mexico are also heavily unchurched, one out of five of Colorado's counties having unchurched populations over 70 percent. (Park County, population 2,185, east of the Continental Divide in central Colorado, registers fewer than one in ten of its people as a church member.) Michigan's sixty-nine Lower Peninsula counties are heavily unchurched, as are about half of Indiana's northern and central counties. Finally, Florida's five Gulf Coast counties of Charlotte, Citrus, Manatee, Pasco, and Sarasota—each with 50 percent or more unchurched—help push this state well above the national average of unchurched.

To summarize, the unchurched may be thought of as "spies," persons who have had access, either directly or indirectly, to the camps of the churched. The intelligence they have gained from observable manifestations of the life of the churches and their adherents is useful both for understanding the pictures they have drawn in their heads and what may, indeed, be the "reality" of the churched world. Profiles of who these people are are beginning to emerge from research studies and will be further elaborated in the excerpted stories in later chapters of this book.

The number of the unchurched is roughly 80 million, about 40 percent of the population, according to the best estimates presently available. Counts by denominations and by survey researchers are not markedly dissimilar. The answer to the question, "Where are the unchurched?" can be answered by reference to cartography that plots, county-by-county, the degree of unchurchedness across the nation. It suggests primarily a bimodal distribution, one concentration along the West Coast, the other running the course of the eastern Appalachian strip. Other minor concentrations are observable in the mountain states of the West, in the Ozarks, in the East North Central states, and in the southern Sun Belt. Less obvious from the cartography is the relatively universal diffusion of the unchurched throughout the American society; they are present as minorities in every county of the United States.

I shall submit ethnographic evidence in the next chapter that suggests that the pictures in the heads of the unchurched tend to "go with the territory." The "spies" have been influenced not only by their life experiences but also by the places in which those experiences have taken place.

NOTES

1. Jacques Ellul, *The Ethics of Freedom* (Grand Rapids, Mich.: Eerdmans, 1976), p. 271.
2. These observations are drawn primarily from David A. Roozen, *The Churched and the Unchurched in America: A Comparative Profile* (Washington, D.C.: Glenmary Research Center, 1978); and George Gallup, Jr., *Survey of the Unchurched American* (Princeton, N.J.: Gallup Organization, 1978).
3. Roozen, *The Churched and the Unchurched*, pp. 15–16.
4. *Ibid.*, pp. 14–15, 18–19.
5. See Gallup, *Survey of the Unchurched*, "Tables—Demographic Data."
6. *Ibid.*
7. For further discussion of the effects of mobility on religion, see Carroll, Johnson, and Marty, *Religion in America: 1950 to the Present* (San Francisco: Harper & Row, 1979), pp. 88–89, 102–103.
8. Roozen, *The Churched and the Unchurched*, p. 14; also Bernard Quinn and John Feister, *Apostolic Regions of the United States: 1971* (Washington, D.C.: Glenmary Research Center, 1978), pp. 38–41.
9. Roozen, *The Churched and the Unchurched*, p. 4.
10. Roozen, *The Churched and the Unchurched*, pp. 4–5.
11. Gallup, *Survey of the Unchurched*, pp. 2–3.
12. Gary Wills, "What Religious Revival?" in *Psychology Today*, April 1978, p. 77.
13. Arthur J. Vidich and Joseph Bensman, *Small Town in Mass Society* (Princeton, N.J.: Princeton University Press, 1968).
14. Wuthnow and Mellinger contend, for example, that in the early 1970s, over half the students on certain elite campuses claimed to be without religious beliefs and that nationally at least 20 percent of all college students denied any religious affiliation. Numerous research studies support this, among them Robert Wuthnow, *Experimentation in American Religion* (Berkeley: University of California Press, 1978), Chap. 7, who suggests that countercultural beliefs and values, often associated with campus experimentation, have diffused to larger and larger audiences; Daniel Yankelovich, *The New Morality: A Profile of American Youth in the Seventies* (New York: McGraw-Hill, 1974); and the several studies of Dean R. Hoge, beginning with his *Commitment on Campus: Changes in Religion and Values over Five Decades* (Philadelphia: Westminster Press, 1974).
15. Tracy Early, "Gallup Polls the 'Unchurched,'" in *Christianity and Crisis* 38, no. 11 (17 July 1978): 182–85. For a rejoinder, compare Peggy Shriver, "Polling the 'Unchurched'" (letter to the editor), in the subsequent issue, *Christianity and Crisis* 38 no. 12 (21 August 1978): 203.
16. Douglas Johnson, Paul R. Picard and Bernard Quinn, *Churches and Church Member-*

ship in the United States: An Enumeration by Region, State and County, 1971 (Washington, D.C.: Glenmary Research Center, 1974), p. x.

17. Statistical Research Division, *Religious Population of the United States: 1971* (Washington, D.C.: Glenmary Research Center, 1974). Computation procedures for adjustments of data are described in "Introduction."

18. Quinn and Feister, *Apostolic Regions*, pp. 38–41.

19. Donald McGavran, "Sheep Stealing and Church Growth," in *Church Growth: America*, March–April 1977. McGavran works implicitly with an older typology that includes the "marginal" and "dormant" members among those who have become alienated. See Joseph Fichter, *Social Relations in the Urban Parish* (Chicago: University of Chicago Press, 1954). The Fichter typology includes four groups: the nuclear member (the "hard-core faithful," about 3 percent of a local parish); the modal member (the "typical Christian," about two-thirds of the members); the marginal member (only minimally involved); and the dormant member (one who no longer defines him- or herself as a church member). Fichter's typology is operationally defined; McGavran's is not.

20. In an address by Illig, "The Beneficiaries of Evangelization," delivered at III National Encounter, the Cursillo Movement, De Kalb, Illinois, July 6–9, 1977; unpublished, summary available from Alvin A. Illig, 3031 Fourth Street, NE, Washington, D.C. 20017.

Part Two

ODYSSEY INTO THE LAND OF THE UNCHURCHED

"TELL ME your landscape and I will tell you who you are," was José Ortega y Gasset's way of suggesting that environment, circumstance, and ethos have a profound impact on attitudes and behavior.[1] People are conditioned not only by their genetic endowments but also by the kind of place in which they reside and the ways they have been socialized to cope with their surroundings. Relationships—to persons, kin, reference groups, the physical environment, the technological environment, values, knowledge, and so on—make the person.

But the landscapes in which people have grown up or in which they choose to locate vary both in their influence and scenery. Secularization —the seclusion of many realms of life (occupation and politics, for example) from religious influence—is universally rampant. But there are important variations from place to place, and from person to person. Similarly, the religious landscape in America provides a scenery that looks different in different places. Suggestively, Martin Marty views the maps showing the distribution of dominant religious groups in various places and concludes, "There are five nations within a nation": (1) the Latter-Day Saints empire in Utah and adjacent spill-over states; (2) the Baptist empire in the South; (3) the Lutheran complex in the Midwest; (4) the Methodist band "south of the North and north of the South"; and (5) the Catholic empire in urban areas across the country.[2] He might have added another—the Jews, almost 80 percent of whom live in eight large metropolitan centers, three million or half of the total in the environs of New York City alone.

If one has spent significant lifetime experiences in one of these "chambers" (enclaves of the like-minded) of American religion, one is affected by its pervasiveness, either positively or negatively. If, on the other hand, one belongs to the "corridor" people (the cosmopolitans who move from place to place, from group to group, from value to value), one is affected by the loss of locality bondedness and may occupy progressively several of the chambers or none at all. We will find both types among the unchurched who tell their stories, but first it is important to sketch a profile of the six counties in which the unchurched were found.

The six counties chosen for this study were Boone County, West Virginia; Marion County, Alabama; Orange County, California; Polk County, Oregon; Sarasota County, Florida; and Waldo County, Maine. Seven interrelated factors were considered in the selection.

Time Management. I assumed at the outset that the completion of 20–30 usable interviews in each county selected would take two to three weeks of intensive field work: first, to identify the potential informants, and, second, to locate them and conduct the interviews. I estimated another one to two weeks' time to make initial contacts with a representative spectrum of the clergy from whom I would draw my initial referrals, and to complete interviews with 10–15 knowledgeable local persons from whom I would gain some insights into the milieu of the county. Unscheduled time would also be essential to swim in the lagoon of the native village, as anthropologist Malinowski once described the essential methodology of the field ethnologist. Thus, the data-gathering period was bracketed to include roughly four weeks in each of the six locations. Such time management proved adequate for the task. Time constraints, however, prevented in-depth followup interviews even when the content suggested the desirability of probing for more information and feelings. The data-gathering period was the six-month period between February and July 1976.

Regional Representation. In order that the interview material might emerge from as many settings as possible, I sought regional diversification of the counties selected. I anticipated that the study of heavily unchurched regions would serve two purposes: to provide settings in which the unchurched rates were exceptionally high, and to reveal the degree and manner in which such contexts might influence the way people express their unchurchedness. This dictated the first broad cut of possible counties: representation from the concentrations of the unchurched in the Pacific portion of the West and in the Appalachian strip in the East.

Some sample also was needed from several of the minor concentrations of the unchurched in America. This was more difficult. Colorado-New Mexico was eliminated in order that oversampling of the West be avoided; the Pacific states would receive priority. The Ozarks of Missouri-Arkansas lost in favor of the more heavily unchurched, relatively proximate, central Appalachian section. The Gulf Coast of Florida offered a special opportunity to survey an area with rapid, recent population growth, relative affluence, leisure orientation, and substantial numbers of retirees. Northwestern Alabama provided a setting in a dominantly sectarian portion of the South where the traditional culture, based on farming, mining, and lumbering, was changing to one based on industrialization. Michigan-Indiana was eliminated after other criteria led to the selection of my quota of six locations.

Special Features. Within each region, several factors combined to favor the specific counties chosen. Obviously, I wanted to avoid demographic and ecological duplication of characteristics in the six places, however geographically separated. On the West Coast, Orange County, California, supplied a large, highly diverse, mushrooming metropolitan setting[3] that many contend is a bellweather county of the nation. It is part of the Los Angeles-Long Beach-Anaheim consolidated metropolitan area, with over 10 million people, the second largest such area in the nation. Polk County, Oregon, located in the middle standard metropolitan statistical area of the Willamette Valley, with its suburban eastern development and its forested western frontier, was an appropriate county representing the highest unchurched states in the nation, Oregon and Washington. I found Sarasota County, Florida, a major Sun Belt winter resort and retirement center of predominantly urban characteristics,[4] an apt choice to sample the Gulf Coast. I included Boone County, West Virginia, in the center of one of central Appalachia's major coal-producing areas, also located in that state with the highest unchurched population rate east of the Mississippi. Waldo County, on the mid-coast of Maine, is also located in a high-ranking unchurched state and region. Although a resort area, tourism is not its dominant characteristic, nor does it reflect Sarasota's opulence. At the lower end of Appalachia, Marion County, Alabama, might be considered the aberrant selection in the group, located as it is in a heavily churched state but with high unchurched percentage of population.

Land Area. Physical size of county was a consideration in the selection. I wanted to minimize the danger of possible incomprehensible heterogeneity and to maximize ease of access throughout the county. The six counties range in land area from 500 to less than 800 square miles: Boone, 501 square miles; Sarasota, 587 square miles; Polk, 736 square miles; Waldo, 737 square miles; Marion, 743 square miles; and Orange, 782 square miles. Such land areas approximate half the average land area of counties in the nation.

Population: Size and Density. The population size and density in the selected counties offered demographic variety without approaching U.S. extremes.[5] Both urban and rural counties were chosen, although other studies, published after this field research was completed, show negligible differences between unchurched people in urban versus rural places. The populations range from 26,000 to 27,000 in Boone, Marion, and Waldo counties, to the moderate 163,000 of urban Sarasota, and to the giant metropolis of Orange County (over 1.5 million). The population densities range from the comparatively sparse densities of Waldo and Marion counties to 2,117 per square mile in Orange. (Both higher and lower densities, of course, may be found among the 3,143 U.S. counties.) Orange is the largest of the six in size and density of population. Waldo is the smallest. Second highest is Sarasota, second lowest, Marion. Boone and Polk are small in size and density. I deliberately avoided counties so small as to suggest gross deviance, although such counties as Alpine, California, and Park, Colorado, might be useful for future comparative studies. Los Angeles, San Francisco, Chicago, Detroit, and the large cities of the Northeast would have been unmanageable even if they had met other criteria. Orange's well-known freeways eased access to its twenty-five cities and towns. Boone, small in land area, population size, and density, was, by contrast, more difficult to cover because of the poor roads and the separation of settlements by precipitous mountain ridges.

High Unchurched Rates. All six counties have unchurched rates well above the national average of 38.6 percent. Three are over 70 percent: Boone, 76.5 percent; Waldo, 75 percent; and Polk, 72.3 percent. The remaining three are counties with the majority of their populations unchurched: Sarasota, 50.4 percent; Marion, 56.9 percent; and Orange, 57.4 percent. Other counties, of course, show higher absolute numbers of unchurched. Here, the emphasis was on relative proportions.

Note again that the selected counties are not those with the highest proportions of the unchurched in the country, although they are among that group. Nor is there any implication that their unchurchedness necessarily implies irreligiousness. Both of these errors of interpretation gained wide credence as a result of media coverage of early incorrect reporting of my survey findings.

Center in Cluster. Each county was surrounded by or adjacent to other similarly unchurched counties. When a cluster of counties met other criteria for selection, a county near the geographic center of the cluster was chosen. This was done in order to avoid selecting a fringe county that might rank high in unchurchedness because large numbers of its population were members of churches across the county line. Membership statistics include churched populations according to church location, not members' place of residence.

The following county profiles will convey to the reader some salient features of each of the six counties. It is out of such contexts that 165 people tell about themselves and paint pictures in their heads of the churches they have known or avoided. Their stories and their pictures are colored by the ethos of the distinctive environment in which each resides. There is an affinity between the themes that describe a person's reasons for opting out of a church and residential ethos. Put another way, the exegesis of the human document requires an understanding of the *Sitz im Leben,* the context or "seat" of one's living.

This odyssey, as the word implies, is a firsthand account of my wanderings in these six heavily unchurched counties of the nation. The odyssey lasted six months. I walked, drove, hiked, boated, biked, bussed, and flew from place to place within and between the locations. My abode was usually a motel or rooming house, in one location a trailer, generally in the county seat or geographic center of the county. I talked cumulatively to hundreds of very important and very ordinary people in addition to the more formal interviews with the unchurched. They included public officials and civil servants; librarians; local historians; journalists; storekeepers; funeral directors; realtors; parish clergy and ecclesiastical bureaucrats; oldtimers, newcomers, and transients; men and women in business and industry; college students and counterculture youth; planners; teachers; community organizers; and social workers, as well as the habitues of bars, beaches, shopping centers, street corners, and other places of assembly. I joined groups whenever I was invited or could find them: on the fishing piers of Florida's west coast and the marinas of the

Pacific; at a gymnastic competition at a local high school; clergy meetings in each of the six counties; cocktail parties; counterculture communes in Oregon and Maine; the circus at Venice, Florida; the superintendents' office at a planing mill in Oregon and at a mine shaft in West Virginia; masses and revivals, healings, decorations, singings, and more conventional church services, usually several times a week; university and community social and cultural events; the annual "Fireman's Carnival" at Dallas, Oregon, and the "Swallow's Festival" at San Juan Capistrano; tours of historic places everywhere—wherever people gathered to play, learn, relax, study, plan, or carry on their ordinary, everyday activities. I tried to "make like the native" without "going native" insofar as time permitted and discretion allowed.

The style is intentionally impressionistic or dramatic rather than objective, although statistical, journalistic, historical, topographical, literary, ecological and other sources of data have been consulted. Often I have used the first person singular to personalize the account. Certain experiences are parsimoniously highlighted to pinpoint dominant motifs and chief foci of the experienced milieu. Only the reader, ultimately the "native," can judge the degree to which I have caught the flavor of everyday life in each of the settings.

It is useful to couple the county profiles in three groups: Yankee and Frontier Land, Appalachia, and the Sun Belt. Waldo County, Maine, and Polk County, Oregon, belong in the first set. Boone County, West Virginia, and Marion County, Alabama, make up the second pairing. Sarasota County, Florida, and Orange County, California, comprise the third set. The pairings do not necessarily suggest demographic or ecological likenesses, although there are some similarities. Rather, some dominant themes tend to emerge more strikingly when pairs of counties are profiled in concert.

NOTES

1. Quoted by Julian Marias, *Jose Ortega y Gasset: Circumstance and Vocation* (Norman: University of Oklahoma Press, 1970), p. 362.
2. Jackson W. Carroll, Douglas W. Johnson and Martin E. Marty, *Religion in America: 1950 to the Present* (New York: Harper and Row, 1979), pp. 52–53. In another look at the same religious cartography, Marty invents four additional metaphors to describe the general surfaces and outlines of American religion: the "young, rugged mountains" (fundamentalism and evangelicalism), the "old, worn-down mountains" (main-

stream Protestantism and post-Vatican II Catholicism), "steep hills standing alone" (esoteric and exotic groups), and the "nondescript plains" (the unchurched)—in "A Map of Religious America," *Journal of Current Social Issues* 14, no. 2 (Spring 1977): 4–9. Rosemary Ruether, in the same issue, demurs: She argues that the whole notion that historical denominations still contain monolithic typologies that can be assigned to landscapes or spectrums has too many fissures within each type ("Martin Marty's Mythical Moonscape," pp. 10–13).

3. Of U.S. counties with populations 500,000 or more, Orange ranks as the fourth fastest-growing county (1970–1975) in the nation, only exceeded by Broward and Pinellas counties in Florida and Maricopa County, Arizona. U.S. Bureau of the Census, *Estimates of the Population of Counties and Metropolitan Areas,* Series P-25, no. 709 (September 1977).

4. Of U.S. counties with populations between 100,000 and 499,999, Sarasota is the third fastest-growing (1970–1975) in the nation. See U.S. Bureau of the Census, *ibid.*

5. Population data used in Chapters 4–6 are from 1970 U.S. Census, first count statistics, and 1975 estimates, unless otherwise noted. Unchurched calculations are from Research Division, *Religious Population of the United States: 1971* (Washington, D.C.: Glenmary Research Center, 1974).

4. Yankee and Frontier Land

Polk County, Oregon
County seat: Dallas
Land area: 736 square miles
Density: 53.5 per square mile
Population: 35,349 (1970), 39,400 (1975)
Population change, 1970–1975: 11.5%
Population rank: 896 among 3,143 U.S. counties (1975)
Unchurched population, Polk County: 25,550, 72.3%
Unchurched population, Oregon: 60.8% (Rank 1 among states)

Polk County has historically been a "pass through" county, with trails or roads on the way to some other place. In the 1840s and 1850s, the cry was "Oregon or Bust." The Oregon Trail, the guidebooks boast, became the scene of one of the greatest migrations in human history.

The migrations continue today. The road markers are ubiquitous, reading "To Ocean Beaches." They lure the out-of-state tourists a few miles farther west, through the Van Duzer corridor of the Coastal Range, to the strip of Pacific resorts from Lincoln City to Newport. People pass through Polk County unaware. And they mark with some consternation former governor Tom McCall's celebrated advice, "Come and visit, but don't stay." Oregon does not want to grow, many Oregonians tell you—"We've seen what has happened in California, we don't want to pay that price for progress!"

For the Polk County natives, the lure of "some other place" is everywhere apparent. They go to Salem, the state capital just east across the Willamette River, to shop, to eat out, to get services, or to work. The college student commutes to the Oregon State University campus at Corvallis in less time than his or her New York counterpart takes to travel by subway from Times Square to Columbia University. From Dallas, the county seat, the resident drives south to the industrial city of Albany in thirty or forty minutes or north to Portland and south to Eugene—two of the state's major metropolitan centers—in a little over one hour. Everyone seems to be on wheels—to get around near home by car or bike, or to get away in the station wagon, camper, or recreational vehicle for a day, weekend, or summer holiday. You see parked on the driveway or on the front lawn of a modest ranch house in Monmouth or Independence a veritable fleet of vehicles and trailers poised expectantly for their pilgrimage to the lakes, mountains, or beaches. Back in the isolated town of Valsetz, sixteen miles west from Falls City along an unpaved forest road, I found a local schoolteacher already packing his camper on the final day of the school year, preparatory to his annual exodus to the coast.

Many stay, even if as an Oregon College of Education historian at Monmouth put it, "Everybody initially comes to stay for a year." More than 70 percent of Oregon's people live in the Willamette Valley, which contains the state's three standard metropolitan statistical areas: Portland, Salem, and Eugene. Since 1950, the valley has grown at a faster rate (23.8 percent between 1960 and 1970) than any other region of Oregon. Polk County, now included in the Salem standard metropolitan statistical area, experienced a 33 percent population upsurge in the 1960s; it grew another 11.5 percent in the first half of the 1970s. This surge will likely continue over the next thirty years, planners predict,[1] as Polk County participates in the expansion of the SMSA and the state. Today, 59 percent of Polk County residents live in urban places, a marked change from 1950, when the county was 70 percent rural, or from 1960, when it was still 66 percent rural. West Salem, characterized now by suburban subdivisions, will become the most populous urban area in Polk County. This will increase the cosmopolitan orientation of the county and reinforce the historic tradition of a people "on the way to some other place." West Salem will become increasingly a bedroom community for its metropolitan neighbor, Salem, on the other side of the river, where large numbers of its wageearners already work.

Polk County as a whole, however, is viewed by neither the outsider or the insider as a "big, populous, and powerful" place, as urban Americans self-consciously view the nation. One has only to walk the streets of Dallas (population 5,072), Monmouth (2,229), and Independence (1,930), or read the pages of the county's *Itemizer Observer,* to sense the small-town character of the county and the county's desperate efforts to keep it that way. Only about 1 percent of the land is used for urban purposes; 90 percent is devoted to natural resources—farms and forests. Even the major industries of Dallas, the county seat, betray what it is that Polk County people do for a living (if they do not commute elsewhere)—tanning, planing, manufacturing paper products, and building lift trucks. Less than ten miles from the city of Salem, westward-bound travelers cannot miss the radical shift in scenery and know that they have left the metropolis for the farm. The entire eastern half of the county, invaded by densely settled urbanites, is still predominantly agricultural or idle land. Livestock, grain and seed crops, and fruit and nut trees dominate the landscape.

Farther west, as one moves toward the foothills of the Coast Range, just fifteen miles west of Salem, to the uplands where the tributaries drain into the Pacific, one finds oneself in Douglas fir and hemlock forests. Second-and third-growth timber is harvested in abundance. Hundreds of trucks loaded with logs daily roll along the highways and back roads from forest to sorting and storage areas. Falls City, in central Polk County, Willamina, in the northwest, and Valsetz, one of the few surviving company-owned towns in the West (a Boise-Cascade operation), and their adjacent farm and forest territories, occupy more than half of the county's land area though populated by less than 15 percent of the people. Thus, despite suburban developments in the east, the county will retain for years to come its dependence on forestry and agricultural resources.

The frontier mentality of the people is the dominant ethos of Polk County. "A decent amount of self-respect plus a decent regard for the self-respect of others," Will Hutchison, a western historian, writes, "was a vital part of frontier individualism. The supreme worth of the individual was spawned in the open spaces of the western frontier and followed a religion-based ethic and a Lockean liberalism," still characteristic of the Northwest.[2] Conversations with both natives and newcomers convinced me that these values are still alive in Polk County. This remains a "haven for those who want to start something new," a Dallas funeral director told me. A friend of Ken Kesey (author of *One Flew Over the Cuckoo's Nest*) related how young boys are still socialized into manhood as they join their fathers on the annual spring float trip down the river and learn to "drink, cuss, and tell dirty stories like all free he-men." Numerous Dallas folk recalled for me their town's Ripley "Believe It or

Not" citation of almost forty years ago: "More churches and more liquor sold per capita than any town in America." They seemed to be saying that nothing much has changed. I was told proudly that Oregon's governor in 1976, Bob Straub, a Polk County resident, relaxes around home in blue jeans, "like an ordinary country guy." A local politician explained the legal basis for the people's independent spirit, guaranteed by the state constitution, which affirms that "all power is inherent in the people" and which "at all times" grants the people the "right to alter, reform, or abolish the government in such manner as they may think proper." "That goes so far as to make treason legal here," he said. "We trust our office holders—from governor on down—only so long as they serve the independence of the people. We kick them out by recall and change their policies by initiative and referendum if they forget that."

Such radical independentism has an affinity with what I learned about the religious outlook of the countians. A local historian described the types of folks who had come to Polk County during the last 140 years. The largest number of first settlers were from Missouri; then Ohio, Tennessee, Virginia, Illinois, Indiana, and other states farther west. Usually, they had been somewhere else on the way—Michigan, Arkansas, Nebraska—"often failures economically," he said, in the course of their two or three generation trek to Oregon. Almost exclusively Anglo-Saxon Protestants, they brought with them a "Bible Belt fundamentalism" of the Presbyterian, Baptist, and Disciples of Christ variety. The churches have always been noted for their extreme congregationalism and rejection of hierarchical authority.

Mennonite immigrants came to Polk County as early as 1870, some directly from Russia, others from Minnesota, Kansas, Nebraska, South Dakota, and Canada. They arrived with "wagons or cars full of belongings and kids, a kitchen pot and a Bible," one oldtimer said. Proselytized by German Baptists and torn by internal fights, the original congregations have split to form at least ten separate Anabaptist groups with numerous parishes in the county. The spectrum ranges from the Mennonite Church ("guardians of the traditions of the Fathers"), the Evangelical Mennonite Brethren (a schismatic group with a conservative evangelical identity), the Mennonite Brethren ("twice-born, primitive Anabaptists") and the more liberal General Conference Mennonites, to the Baptist sects, which include the American Primitive, North American, Southern, Conservative Baptists, and the Old German Baptist Brethren.[3]

Other groups are all of twentieth-century vintage, Catholics from 1910, and Lutherans and Episcopalians so recent as to be considered "basically missions" by the locals, even though statistics show 1,000 or more each in the Catholic and Lutheran churches, second only to Mennonites in percentage of total church adherents. Mormons in Polk County, very recent immigrants or converts, are considered to be a "fast-growing [group] here, with perhaps a thousand members," I was told by county clergy. The varieties of Pentecostalists are quite recent. Scientology, using the name the Delphian Foundation, has been firmly ensconced for the last few years in a palatial abandoned Catholic monastary at Sheridan; it has a small coterie of followers in Polk County.

One county pastor gave me this personal analysis of the religious scene:

> There are a lot of people here who have never been socialized. The social stratification is sharp. You don't put hillbillies, intellectuals, the poor, and the rich together. They don't fit, don't know how to get along. It's reflected in our churches and communities—contentious, fighting, "I'll do my thing so get out of my way!" Our northwest values give rise to this sort of individualism, and it results in lack of community in all our institutions. The churches tend to define their doctrines so narrowly that the bulk of both the oldtimers and newcomers are automatically screened out. Each group says, "We are the true believers," but doctrinal antagonisms are really just camouflage for intense personal and social differences. Newcomers, when they come here, "test the waters" in our churches. Many of them say they find the same old fundamentalist baggage here they left behind. They quickly cut the ties and are not at all interested in reestablishing their roots.

The Polk County archivist talked to me about the dispersion of the churches: "You drop a pebble in the waters at Dallas, and you get a ripple effect as the rings move to the county's edge." The churches at the edge, he noted, get smaller and smaller, the parishes so tiny that they can only afford visiting part-time pastors or untrained lay leaders.

The vast majority of Polk countians do not belong to any Christian congregation. The total number of recorded church members in 1971, according to Johnson, Picard, and Quinn, was only 6,900, about 20 percent of Polk's 35,349 people.[4] This small minority of church folks belong largely to fractionalized, independent, and individualistic sects, divided into as many as thirty different denominational, "free," or autonomous groups. After adjustment for the unreported sectarians and others from whom only state totals are available, Polk County's 72.3

percent unchurched rate makes the county the second highest unchurched county in the top-ranking unchurched state in the nation. It
is eighth highest among the counties of Washington and Oregon. Polk
is the only county in the Northwest where, in counties with a population
over 30,000, seven out of ten residents are unaffiliated. If the total
population were all members of the county's more than fifty congregations, each would have a membership of over 700. In fact, only one
parish even approaches that size.

Several conversations with Polk leaders dramatized for me the pervasiveness of the unchurched culture here. John Bollman, a Dallas funeral
director, noted that the Northwest ranks highest in the nation for
"immediate disposition of the body at death. It's not unusual here at
all," he said, "for funerals to be conducted without benefit of clergy."
The implication was that the family of the deceased frequently has no
pastor to whom to turn. Sometimes, it's a matter of "doing one's own
thing." He told the story of a young man who died recently. His body
was carried one-half mile from the house where the death had occurred
to a burial plot out on the farm. The interment was a "therapy session
for dogwood-carrying youth—a lot of openness, honesty, and love" but
no minister or traditional God-talk. Jim Travis, superintendent of the
Boise-Cascade plywood mill spoke to me about the company-subsidized,
undenominational church in Valsetz. "About 40 people attend from this
community's 450–500 people—ten or twelve families are very interested. I can almost name them all," he said. "I've been here for six years,
and during that time I've hired about 400 workers. When they come,
they ask about housing, how much rent we charge, the schools, recreation and all that, but I can't remember anyone ever asking 'Do you have
a church?' or 'What kind of church is it?' "

Joe Blaha, publisher of the *Itemizer Observer* and a sixteen years'
resident of Oregon, talked to me about the "Oregon spirit." "It's a place
where people contend for ideas and try to preserve the right of the
individual to determine his own destiny." This, he felt, is not only a
tradition-centered political, social, and economic ideal, but it carries
over today into the religious arena. "People here don't like hierarchies
—they want the right to fight among themselves, and, if they can't reach
consensus, to splinter off into new groups. . . . Oregon is like a virgin,
rather naive, innocent and trusting. She gets screwed occasionally, but
the costs are worth it." Polk County is an "open, but fragile class
structure. It changes all the time. People don't invite you in. No one

takes responsibility for the individual, the individual has to take initiative and responsibility for himself." Blaha's parting word to me was "Be kind to the ministers and churches here—tell them they are doing a good job, they really are—but they're out of their sphere of influence when they try to tell their people what to think or do, or how to behave or act. People here don't listen to that kind of thing."

The ministers in Polk County, another informant said, "have to earn their right to leadership, to learn how to touch base with the common people, with their fierce individualism." He guessed that might be one reason ministers who were ex-Marines or other military men did better than others. But, in the final analysis, "the only approach that works here is the soft sell, 'My church is here—if you need anything, call on me.' " Most never do. Not uncommonly, they protect themselves from the invitation itself. They post "No Religious Solicitation Here" signs on the lintels of their homes.

Waldo County, Maine
County seat: Belfast
Land area: 737 square miles.
Density: 36 per square mile
Population: 23,328 (1970), 26,500 (1975)
Population Change 1970–1975: 13.4%
Population Rank: 1,268 among 3,143 U.S. counties (1975)
Unchurched population, Waldo County: 17,498; 75%
Unchurched population, Maine: 49.6% (Rank 9 among states)

Waldo County lies 3,125 miles east of Oregon, a nation apart from Polk County. Maine is no longer frontier, if it ever was, unless Leif Erikson considered it that when the Vikings sailed along its coast in 1003 A.D. Its original natives were not immigrants but indigenous Americans, as the recent claims by the Penobscot and Passamaquoddy Indians for rights to two-thirds of the state, including much of Waldo County, attest. They settled in the late 1970s for much less. Its remembered history, however, is in the Yankee tradition. Its ethos is not expressed in Oregon-style "Don't fence me in" as much as in Yankee-style "I'll respect you if you respect me." Toleration is the spirit of Maine, like that of the rest of New England, toleration of those who go to church as well as those who do not. Most don't. Gorham Munson, a Penobscot historian, after reviewing Waldo's history and assessing its present, wrote of Belfast: "It gives an impression of a self-reliant town with roots in a past of sea captains that is minding its own business."[5] This was my first impression of the place and its people too. It remained so after my month's sojourn there. I arrived at Bangor, Maine, via Delta from Boston at 10:30 A.M., Sunday, May 2, 1976. Thrifty Rent-a-Car leased me an old Vega for an easy hour's drive, south along Route 1A, to the county seat, Belfast, prearranged as my headquarters for my stay on the mid-coast of Maine. I quickly left behind all signs and sounds of the "big city." Bangor's 1970 population was 33,168. I zigzagged along the two-lane highway to avoid the potholes still left from the winter freeze and the spring thaw. I soon entered Waldo County, too long before Memorial Day to find the antique and gift shops, museums, and most of the motels and restaurants open for the tourist season. It was rainy, a wet reception, so misty that I missed seeing until a week later the bicentennial attractions of the Penobscot river towns of Winterport, Frankfort, and Prospect. I got only a momentary glimpse of Penobscot Bay at the Searsport harbor.

I entered Belfast, by the "back door," as the locals told me later, along Searsport Avenue with its strip of motels—Colonial Gables, Belfast Motor Inn, the Yankee Clipper, not to mention Jed's Restaurant, the Lobster Pound, and Perry's "Original" Tropical Nut House. In the next several days, I made my usual expedition through large portions of the county's 737 square miles and twenty-five towns, through coastal communities, up the Penobscot to the river towns again, into the inland towns of Waldo's upland hills, and across the mountain areas of the center and the farm lands of the northwestern corner. I found unpretentious Unity College and before the month was over, on another stormy day, took the 24-car Governor Muskie ferry to tiny Isleboro Island, three sea-miles from Lincolnville.

After scanning Joseph Williamson's monumental three-volume *History of the City of Belfast in the State of Maine from Its First Settlement in 1770 to 1875* in a local library, I made an historical pilgrimage into this community's past, to a dozen or so of the town's fifty homes of the Federal and Greek Revival periods, stately old Hydton House (1845), the White House (1840), and Admiral Pratt House (1812) among them. Belfast had been a "city," I discovered, since 1853, but its population has never exceeded 6,000 in 120 years of record-keeping (1970 population, 5,957). Here a century ago, a contemporary historian notes, "the shore resounded with shipbuilding; there were several wharves, a congestion of sailing vessels, a few steamers, plenty of maritime activity." Now, I found the harbor comparatively quiet except for the morning tugboat whistles that called the early morning shifts to work at the poultry-packing houses and the sardine cannery.

I walked almost daily to the downtown business quarter, its brick buildings, some empty, centering at Main and High streets. I visited the Courthouse and Belfast City Hall several times in an unsuccessful search for significant county vital statistics, unearthed later by helpful county agents at the state's Cooperative Extension Service office, out of town. I poured through files of the county's weekly, *The Republican Journal* and was interviewed for two stories by its feature writer, Denise Goodman, an expatriate from Dayton, Ohio, who turns colorful phrases like "The boom in potato shipments from the Searsport docks has apparently cushioned the bust on the local clam flats." My car took me through a county that the passenger trains had deserted twenty-five years before and Interstate 95 had bypassed in the early 1960s. There were signs everywhere—dilapidated, vacant stores and factories and quarries and homes—that more people had been moving out of Waldo than in. There were almost 1,000 unoccupied housing units in the county. Waldo's population of 37,229 in 1850 had shrunk to 23,328 in 1970, was climbing again in the early 1970s but still far short of its nineteenth-century peak. Most of this had happened, I was told by everyone "in the know," in the last century, when Maine's maritime industry died. The small coastal town of Searsport had once produced one-tenth of all the deep-sea shipmasters in the American merchant marine and had built, during one century of activity, over 250 topsail schooners, square-riggers, and wooden ships of larger tonnage. Today, eight gangs of longshoremen can load 800 tons of newsprint in containerized cargo onto the diesel-powered "Petra" in a few hours. The local hyperbole was less than the truth, but it was still spoken, "Searsport was put in dock seventy-five years ago; it hasn't gone to sea since."

After its thousands fled, they left behind a largely native Yankee population—77 percent born in Maine—and one out of four living in poverty, making Waldo one of the poorest counties in the state. Twenty-six percent of the housing units lack some or all plumbing facilities, almost twice that of Maine.[6] But the casual stranger "from away" misses this. The "other America" in Maine, as Michael Harrington found throughout this nation, is neatly hidden to the point of invisibility until

one tries to navigate the almost impassible roads back in the hills. "You
have to 'cut your feet' in the pastures, follow the brooks, and leave the
roads," one guide told me, "if you want to see what's really here."
Things are somewhat better in the coastal towns where two-thirds of
Waldo's people live, but the inland highlands, hardest hit by the out-
ward migrations to Bangor, Augusta, Portland, Boston, and points south,
and by the rugged mountain winters (temperatures averaging 20° F with
70 inches of snow) are almost depleted. Only the high-stacked piles of
fireplace and stove wood alongside isolated mountain cabins remind one
of the hardy souls who stick it out when their neighbors leave.

In "Another Man's Poison," Ben Ames Williams once described the
Searsmont (fictionalized as *Fraternity Village*) of 1919. Some gracious
counterculture youth who run the Grasshopper Book Store in Belfast
helped me rediscover this classic I had almost forgotten from my own
youth. Fraternity Village was

> . . . one of those little communities so common in the New England hills—a
> cluster of white houses, a store or two, a church whose white spires rose above
> the trees. There was a mill dam just above the bridge; and the mill itself squatted
> in a litter of piled lumber, barrel heads and staves, soft edgings, slabs, and
> sawdust. . . . A clear, well-pointed, frugal, happy little village. Worth knowing.
> Its neighbor towns included Liberty, and Equality, and Union, and Freedom.
> All cut from the same pattern.[7]

The Down East Enterprises imprint edition (1969) of sixteen of Ben
Ames William's corpus of a hundred or more *Fraternity Village* stories
carries the publisher's judgment, "Fraternity, Maine, . . . is little
changed, today, from what it was more than 50 years ago when he wrote
his first story about it."

The physical features of that description continue to be accurate. The
"frugal, happy little village" and its "neighbor towns," although still
little, translate frugality today to mean bare subsistence. Infant mortality
in Waldo County is the highest in Maine, and only ten physicians are
available, twenty-five short of national minimum standards. So, it may
be asked whether the "happiness" of 50 years ago has now gone sour.
The poor, young housewife in Waldo today has difficulty with Thoreau's
nostalgia and romanticism about the Maine woods. She doesn't see "the
tops of the pines waving and reflecting the light at a distance high over
all the rest of the forest." For her, for the unemployed husband who

waits for someone to call for men to cut pulpwood, and for the aging, "the light at the distance" is often shaded by the nearer darkness. Nor do they wax eloquently any longer with Edna St. Vincent Millay's refrain, "Lord, I do fear / Thou'st made the world too beautiful this year!" What the Lord made is almost gone, and what's left is not too beautiful to a quarter of Waldo's people.

A storekeeper in one of the out-of-the-way highland towns refused an interview with me, "No, sir," he said. "I've stayed in business these forty years keeping my lips tight. I don't discuss politics, sex, or religion. I'm not going to spoil it today talking religion to you. People believe and do what they want. That's their business. Not yours. Not mine." With a crispness I learned to expect from my Waldo informants, he was telling me what my recorded interviews documented again and again—"Our ancestors came here," one woman told me, "to worship as *you* please or not to worship as *I* please." Most admitted that without the churches their communities would be "the poorer for it," but they couldn't specify what contributions the churches were making other than providing some sort of "balm and comfort" for those "who need that sort of thing." One relative newcomer in Winterport, active in a community effort to restore an old nineteenth-century meeting house, made it clear that if successful the drive would open the closed doors of that church twelve times a year as a museum for townsfolk and tourists.

Perhaps the churches of Waldo still function, like the stately houses of Belfast, as relics of the past, for the few who belong or go. The only vital church to which people thronged was the conservative charismatic Searsport Full Gospel Church. The rest, 75 percent of the total, more than 17,000 of the population, "mind their own business." The churches are there for those who want them, and most would call the churches assets to their towns, but they neither attract nor repel— church involvement is simply a peripheral activity the large majority abstain from, as others might abstain from meat or sweets. A librarian in one town (population 470), where only one of four old churches is still operating, hazarded the prediction that "if Jesus Christ were to come back today, he wouldn't draw much of a crowd." Formerly from elsewhere in New England, she said, "This is a nice quiet place to get away from it all." She doesn't hesitate to say the church is "one thing I don't miss."[8]

NOTES

1. Mid-Willamette Valley Council of Governments, "Population Growth in the Mid-Willamette Valley," *Population Report,* Annual Series, no. 7, March 1973.
2. W. H. Hutchison, "Ambiguous Legatees," *The American West,* September 1967.
3. For the distinctions among Mennonite groups, see J. Howard Kauffman and Leland Harder, *Anabaptists Four Centuries Later: A Profile of Five Mennonite and Brethren in Christ Denominations* (Scottdale, Pa.: Herald Press, 1975). Clergymen James Riede, Robert Ross, Frederick Stiles, and Theodore Fast were of invaluable assistance in introducing me to the religious scene.
4. Douglas W. Johnson, Paul R. Picard, and Bernard Quinn, *Churches and Church Membership in the United States, 1971* (Washington, D.C.: Glenmary Research Center, 1974), p. 170.
5. Gorham Munson, *Penobscot, Down East Paradise* (Camden, Maine: Down East Enterprise, 1959), pp. 374–75.
6. This and other statistics here, from Vance E. Dearborn and Steven J. Uzman, *Waldo County Statistics, from 1970 Census and Other Sources* (Orono, Maine: Department of Agricultural and Resource Economics, Cooperative Extension Service of the University of Maine, 1973). See also *1976 State O' Maine Facts* (Rockland, Maine: Courier of Maine Books, 1976).
7. Ben Ames Williams, *Fraternity Village* (Camden, Maine: Down East Enterprise, 1969), p. 1.
8. For confirmation of the major motifs of this profile in an empirical study, see Wade Clark Roof, William M. Newman, and Peter L. Halvorson, *Religion in New England: A Social Profile* (Hartford, Conn.: Hartford Seminary Foundation, 1978). The authors conclude, for example, that switching from church to church in New England is greater than elsewhere and that "religious defection is quite high for Catholics as well as Protestants" (p. 17). Also, Protestants in New England have less confidence in religious leaders than Protestants in the nation generally (p. 37).

5. Appalachian Counties

Central Appalachia consists of some sixty counties in eastern Kentucky, southwestern Virginia, northern Tennessee, and southern West Virginia. Southern Appalachia includes Mississippi, Alabama, South Carolina, North Carolina, and parts of Tennessee and Virginia. I have chosen one county from each region: Boone, in West Virginia, in the center of one of the East's major concentrations of unchurched people, and Marion, in Alabama, a heavily unchurched county in relatively churched southern Appalachia. The two counties have different topographies, industries and mentality. The majority of Marion County is unchurched, 56.9 percent, Boone County, the highest unchurched county (76.5 percent) in my survey.

Boone County, West Virginia

County seat: Madison
Land area: 501 square miles
Density: 54.7 per square mile
Population: 25,118 (1970), 27,400 (1975)
Population Change: 1970–1975: 9.1%
Population Rank: 1,237 among 3,143 U.S. counties (1975)
Unchurched population, Boone County: 19,208, 76.5%
Unchurched population, West Virginia: 51.9% (Rank 7 among states)

Boone County lies southwest of the central part of West Virginia, about twenty-five miles (an hour's drive) south of the capital of the state, Charleston. It is drained by the Coal River and its tributaries, running in a northwesterly direction through the entire county. Kanawha and Raleigh counties lie above Boone and to the east. Wyoming County is south of Boone, separated by 3,000-foot-high Guyandot Mountain. The southwestern edge borders Logan and Lincoln counties. The roads run serpentlike along creeks and rivers at the base of precipitous hills with little stretches of level land called *hollows,* or "hollers," in which many of the county's thirty or more small settlements are located.

Like the state, which has been losing population for the past 25 years, Boone County had lost more than 20 percent of its 1960 population by 1970. The population in 1970 was 25,118; its largest town, Madison, the county seat, had 2,343 people. County inhabitants overestimate the growth in population since the last census and believe the recent return of exiles has boosted the total to as much as 35,000. U.S. Bureau of Census figures do indeed show a reversal of the downward trend of the 1960s but estimate no more than 27,400 in 1975 and project no more than 32,000 by 1990.

Coal is king in Boone County, the third-ranking county in the state in coal production. In 1975, seventy-five mines were in operation, 70 percent of them underground. About thirty corporations employ almost 5,000 workers. All other means of livelihood are pale in significance compared to mining. Very little farming is done even on the ridge plateaus that were once stripped of their virgin timber; there are less than 300 farmers in the entire county today. More than one in three of the adult population has had only eight years of schooling. In 1970, 26.1 percent of the county's families had incomes below the poverty level. The vast majority of the people are American-born, West Virginia natives, long-term residents of the county, and work in Boone County. The small influx of immigrants come from nearby West Virginia counties, from the South, or from the North Central states, from which they are returning after having left for industrial jobs a decade or so ago. Anglo-Saxon names predominate, the McCoys outnumbering the Hatfields five to three.

Boone County is a harsh environment. Destruction and death and human despair are nothing new to this sparse settlement of people. Floods, coal mining, poverty, and neglect have taken a heavy toll on the land and its people. King coal has exacted a price from the land and his subjects. There has been persistent poverty in the county, even though mines have recently reopened since the massive depression of the 1960s. Spirits for many are still broken, and hopelessness abounds. People don't smile much.

Proponents of a "foxhole theory of religion" would argue that such a place is ripe soil for the Christian faith. It is, if the tent-meeting revival conversions are an index to the vitality of faith. Evangelist Eugene

McCallister was the first of the 1976 season to set up his "ole Gospel tent" in Nellis. It is not unusual to find individuals who have been "born again" six or eight times, with a baptism by immersion to seal each rebirth. Few, however, find their way regularly into the pews of the churches, even though they too tend to favor an emotional brand of religious experience with rigid prescriptions for moral behavior.

I visited Joe Turner in the company of one of his parishioners, Brother Delbert Johnson. Turner is a rough, bombastic character possessed of an overdose of self-confidence. Son of a Camp Creek moonshiner, he is minister of the "Jesus Church." "It's a free and open church of Jesus Christ," he told me. "Anybody can use it for revivals, and we let anybody testify or preach who wants to—but he'd better be on his guard. Like as not somebody's goin' to make him prove what he says by the Bible."

Joe doesn't go to his own church much, he says, except when he's in charge—that's Friday and Sunday nights when 25 to 200 folks gather for his own virtuoso performances. Attendance often depends on how many curious ones file into his ramshackle frame building up on a hill overlooking Camp Creek. The curious and Joe's fellow travelers—"They come from all around, Pennsylvania, Maryland, Kentucky, Tennessee" —are there hoping to catch the featured attractions—the handling of rattlesnakes, copperheads, or cobras, or the drinking of strychnine. It is hard to account for his appeal otherwise, for his brand of fundamentalist religion is regular fare in scores of churches in the hills and "hollers" of Boone County.

But Joe Turner, on one's first meeting with him, sets himself apart from the rest. He appeared to me the con artist without subtleties. He has mastered the art of attack—a product perhaps of the scores of times when reporters, television camera crews, and sociologists have entered his "holler" to do a story, a spectacular, or a study. I told him I had come to invite him to be my guest for a breakfast meeting with county church leaders. I gave him my card and a printed invitation. He asked me to read it to him. I thought at first that he couldn't read or that he had left his glasses in his handsome new mobile home 50 feet from the shed where he was doing some repairs with his twenty-five year-old son. But the hammer he held in his hand, his wrestler's physique, and his booming voice told me quickly that Joe is a man used to taking charge, giving orders, pontificating on the truth.

"Are you saved?" "Do you have the gift of tongues?" "Do you baptize in the name of Jesus Christ?" The questions, interspersed with memorized Bible texts strung together with no apparent logical sequence, came with a rapidity that made answering impossible. It was clear too that he did not want answers. He was establishing his authority as the resident expert on the scriptures. He wanted to size me up as friend or foe. For Joe Turner, there seemed no other possibility—even the "friend" bows before his unimpeachable, towering presence and power.

Joe Turner likes the word *power.* "Buddy, I want you to go off in the hills soon, kneel down, and ask Jesus Christ for the power—right in here, *inside* you," he said, pounding his own bulging, hard-muscled stomach. "Unless you got the power, you ain't got the truth, ain't got the Holy Ghost, can't speak in tongues. But when you do, buddy, you'll be perfect. I believe in holiness—no more weeds or booze, no more lusting after women, no more cheating and gambling. That's where I was once," as he began his own testimony, "before I was born again and baptized in the Baptist Church. But that didn't give me the *power.* Those revivalists and preachers were just putting on a show to get my dollars in their pockets. I needed the power, the *power—fire*—the *Holy Ghost,*" he shouted in rising crescendo. Then, with condescension, "And I know you ain't got it, buddy. That right, Brother Delbert?"

Brother Delbert said, "Amen, Brother Joe, Hallelujah!"

"I love you," Joe said as I left, "but you're on the road to hell if the power isn't in you. And I don't believe you got it! I'll probably never see you again, buddy. Come back when you've got the power."

Brother Delbert Johnson walked back with me to my car. On the way, Mrs. Turner said, "Hello," very pleasantly and told me that Joe sometimes talks too much. "He doesn't mean to be unkind, just that he's got so much power it's hard to shut it off. He's a good man." In the car as we returned to the Camp Creek General Store, Brother Delbert allowed as how sometimes Brother Joe "comes on a bit heavy." "Why don't you come out Sunday, Brother Hale?" he asked. "Will Joe be handling serpents then?" I inquired. "That depends," he answered, "if it's the right season. The Lord will decide."

On Sunday night, I saw Joe's power in action for three hours. I was impressed and revised my first impression that he was a con artist.[1] Behind the shoutings, electronically amplified to almost unbearable decibels, behind the fiery, bombastic, unintelligible words, behind the alternation of frenzied dancing and trancelike behavior, behind the convulsive contortions of a congregation that got caught up in the excitement, was a Joe Turner who was preaching a very practical kind of religion. "Jesus ain't somebody far off in the sky but somebody who's right here within you and me. And he'll make a difference in your life, brothers and sisters. He'll make you pay your debts. He'll make you honest. Let Jesus, Jesus, *Jesus* rule your lives." The people cried out, "That's right, Joe . . . Amen . . . Amen . . . Hallelujah . . . Jesus, Jesus, JESUS, J-E-S-U-S!"

The box of rattlesnakes was brought to the front, but Joe Turner ignored them that night.

Any stupid old drunk can handle snakes, and he might get bit. I been bit, can't remember how many times now. It paralyzes you and busts you inside out. I know. I thank God for those bites. Amen. It surely helped me to acknowledge God's power. 'Cause I'm alive today. God's promises are still true, brothers and sisters, "They shall take up serpents and they will not die." But not tonight, the spirit isn't here tonight. Let's pray for Brother White tonight. He's dyin' over there in the hospital. Go, visit him. Tell him you're praying for him. Don't tell him *your* troubles, tell him to put his troubles on the Lord. The Lord's got the power. Amen.

He reminded us that the snakes were brought in under the direction of the Spirit, but they were also carried out under the direction of the Spirit. "The Spirit tonight's telling us to pray for Brother White. . . . Let him get healed, O Lord. O-o-h, Lord, heal him."

Joe Turner's "Jesus Church" is a one-of-a-kind church in Camp Creek and in Boone County. He has little support among the clergy of the county, less from most of the church people. He is scoffed at by the unchurched, "If that's what religion is all about, it ain't for me." But it seemed to me that Joe Turner was a genuine article. He epitomizes the harshness of these West Virginia hills. He knows the miners who inhabit the hills and "hollers." He knows the dangers of the holes in the earth. He knows what "black lung" is; people told me he has it himself. If people can't find a power that helps them transcend it all, or control it, there is not much left. Most find no help in the traditional churches. They called them "dull, a bore." I visited some of them and tended to agree. The Pentecostal churches, the unchurched told me, were not much better. They weren't dull, but "the rules and regulations are so tough that you got to be perfect before they let you in." The average man or woman felt he or she "wasn't good enough" to be a church member and wasn't ready to be "that good." At least in Joe Turner's church, they throw their arms around you and kiss you, as they did me, and they told me "I love you, Brother." With the love and certainly with the "power," one might survive.

Hard data about Boone County was almost impossible to find in Boone County. I searched the offices of the county courthouse at Madison, but found little. Most of what I learned was in the library or state offices in Charleston, the state capital.[2] A newspaper man told me to look at the history books, "That's where many of the people still are, back in the last century," he said. I followed his advice and scanned an immigrant's guide from 1870.

The genuine rural West Virginian is not much addicted to precipitous motion, rarely loses his temper or self-possession, and beyond the acquisition of the necessities of life, limited by almost Spartan frugality, is disposed to leave the improvement of things around him to time and chance. This unprogressive disposition is the more striking, as his native intellect and sagacity are extraordinary and susceptible of high development under proper direction or the stimulus of personal ambition. . . . The West Virginian seldom inquires into his neighbor's business with indelicate curiosity, and no matter how strong or antagonistic his convictions, never intrudes them upon strangers in aggressive or controversial discourse.[3]

But, my informant reminded me, "Don't call them 'Yesterday's People.'[4] They don't like that even if they are." Their isolation from the rest of the nation, even from the rest of West Virginia—Morgantown, I discovered, was perceived by most as alien territory—has made Boone County residents a separate breed, a proud breed. They may not be in a position to control their own destinies, but no one dares deny them their wish to do so. The wildcat strike of coal miners (July–August, 1976), according to sources in United Mine Workers Local 1759, was precipitated by a federal court's "interference" with local working conditions. "We're sick and tired of the federal courts taking the side of the coal operators," leaflets said during the month-long walkout. The textbook controversy of a few years back had originated in adjacent Kanawha County. It quickly spilled over into Boone where the issue, a local school official told me, was "less the content of the literature children were reading in the schools than who was in charge of the children's education, the parents or the state."

There is a massive "outside interference" over which the locals have no control. All roads are owned and maintained, for example, by the state, and Boone County residents are unhappy that state revenues—

much of it supplied by taxes that come from coal operations in Boone
County—never seem to reach Boone County. Many of their back roads
remain almost impassable. They are aware, as the county sheriff told me,
that most of the land is owned by outside interests with headquarters
out-of-state. "Five business firms own 29 percent of Boone County,"
Sheriff John Protan said, "and twenty-three business firms own 86 percent of West Virginia." The giant corporations like Eastern Associated
Coal Corporation at Bald Knob and Armco Steel Corporation at Robin
Hood No. 8 Mine limit the freedom the people would like to keep for
themselves. Only one television channel in the state is owned and
managed by West Virginians.

Impotent with respect to most of the environment that surrounds
them, Boone County people strike back with all they have—pride and
a fierce resistance to all and sundry who attempt to quench that dogged
spirit. They are enthusiastic promoters of the state's slogan, "Wild and
Wonderful," and they display on their license plates the familiar "Almost Heaven." One wonders, however, whether under that proud ve-
neer there is not the lurking sense that they live out their daily lives in
hell or the fear of it. Retired miners I met, all with black lung and many
with amputated figures, hands, or arms, could still remember their youth
when 500 men were killed in West Virginia mines each year. Little
comfort that only 70 died underground each year of the past decade, or
that only 266 suffered nonfatal injuries in the mines at Barrett and Bald
Knob in 1974. It was still hell for the 4,828 miners who went into the
mines every day, some on back-to-back shifts to swell their average $300
weekly gross wages (before overtime pay). The visible mark of pride for
many was what that income bought—booze, guns, and the latest model
pickup truck. One wonders how much had changed since 1781 when
Francis Asbury, Methodist circuit recorded in his journal, "I preached
to about 300 lifeless people . . . but there were so many wicked whiskey
drinkers, who brought with them so much of the power of the devil, that
I had little satisfaction in preaching."

If impotence breeds alienation, the isolation of persons from community breeds loneliness. Boone County people can do little about that,
either. Except for four settlements—Madison, the county seat, with a
population of 2,342; Whitesville, 781; Danville, 713; and Sylvester, 245
—almost 85 percent of the people live in unincorporated places like Bob
White, Wharton, and Barrett on the Bald Knob road; like Seth, Orgas,
and Sylvester on the way to Whitesville; like Low Gap, Coalbottom,

Secoal, and Ramage on the route to Jeffrey; or like Ridgeview, Brush Creek, Nellis, and Costa on the hollow road southwest of Ashford and Rumble. Few are settlements of more than a score of homes, and the distances from place to place are doubled by the twisting roads along creeks and around mountains that one must travel to traverse the terrain. Even within the tiny communities, I was amazed to hear so frequently, "No, I'm sorry, I really don't know the folks just down the road."

Impressions like these are dangerous, for there is always "another Boone County" that these observations leave out of account. But this was what I saw and felt. As I left, I wrote these words in my notebook:

In Boone County, there are many religious mansions. They are peopled by ideological families that are not always friends and—if their passion for splitting for the least provocation is any indication—often bitter enemies. (Will I ever forget that first day I called a group of church leaders together for breakfast at the Gateway Drive Inn? I was not just the stranger who had to introduce myself to them. I had to introduce them to one another!) But they are linked by loyalty to the scriptures and the desire to keep all godless, modernist enemies from their doors.

I found no one really trying to build a unified house. Two young Franciscans, the first resident priests in the county, will not soon be embraced by the overwhelming Protestant populace and the still simmering anti-Catholic milieu of Boone County. I felt for them, for their service last Sunday in Madison seemed to me to be what the whole county needed. I heard good news from them, not the judgmental bad news I was hearing from the sectarians.

The Church of Christ ministers here, mostly untrained laity, are thriving on sectarian separatism in their dozens of little chapels at every hamlet crossroad. The Pentecostalists, whether in the Holiness or Church of God varieties, are insisting on an interior decoration of their mansions so particular as to make its habitation by others uncomfortable, if not abhorrent. The Methodists, rocking from their own massive membership losses of recent years, will be tending their own mansion.

The Baptists (I wondered what went on in the "Morningside Ba*b*tist—sic! —Church" near Brush Creek) will fight a losing battle keeping all their local churches in the convention. Even the West Virginia Mountain Project of the United Presbyterian Church seemed to be running a miniscule operation compared with publicity it received in the late 1960s when Jack Weller and his successors preached that God was a God of the poor. There are no Lutherans or Episcopalian churches here to chart a middle course.

So the many mansions will likely multiply, each claiming its own distinctive merit and each with shrinking membership.

That is a dismal prognosis. I could have been wrong. I may still be. The people's pride will likely persist, but it may drive them farther away from the churches than closer to them. Only the future will tell.

Marion County, Alabama

County seat: Hamilton
Land area: 743 square miles
Density: 36.7 per square mile
Population: 23,788 (1970), 27,300 (1975)
Population Change: 1970–1975: 14.6%
Population Rank: 1,244 among 3,143 U.S. counties (1975)
Unchurched population, Marion County: 13,526, 56.9%
Unchurched population, Alabama: 31.7% (Rank 35 among states)

Less than 600 miles south of Charleston, West Virginia, the southbound traveler arrives at Birmingham, Alabama. One hundred miles northwest from this state capital city of 300,000 is Marion County,[5] located in the lower hills of Southern Appalachia. Fully 80 percent of its 743 square miles is timberland, mostly pine-forested, but with some oak, chestnut, hickory, and gum trees. There are still some small farms —growing cotton, corn, wheat, peas, potatoes, and sorghum. Poultry, soybeans, hogs, and beef cattle provide the largest gross farm income. The county is rough and hilly. In the lower portions, the hills are relatively low and rounded. In the center and northern portions, the rolling surfaces become rough and broken and rise to 1,000 feet.

The towns are small, as one would expect in a county of 27,300 people (1975). The principal communities are Hamilton (population 3,088), the county seat located near Marion's center; Guin (2,220) and Winfield (3,292), seven miles apart on the county's major thoroughfare linking Birmingham and Memphis; Hackleburg (population 726) 14 miles northeast of Hamilton; Brilliant (726) whose environs on the east show the ravages of strip mining; and Bear Creek, a tiny settlement in the northeastern corner.

Marion County's western edge borders the state of Mississippi. Tupelo, Mississippi, a small-sized city of some 20,000 people, is an hour's drive from Hamilton; it offers shopping, medical and other conveniences not available in Marion County. The major trading orientation, however, is southeast, toward Birmingham. Sixty miles north are Sheffield and Florence, twin cities of 50,000 population at Wilson Dam, a key installation of the Tennessee Valley Authority's hydroelectric complex. Huntsville, site of the NASA Space and Flight Center, which registered a phenomenal growth of almost 100 percent in the 1960s, is more than 100 miles northeast. The other major metropolitan areas of the state—Montgomery, Anniston, Mobile, and Tuscaloosa—are all remote from day-to-day contact. The rapid industrialization of the state obviously will have major impact on such places as Marion County in the future, but that time has not yet fully come.

Situated in an area once part of the Chickasaw Indian domain, Marion County was first settled by the English, then in the early nineteenth century by migrating pioneers from Tennessee, North and South Carolina, Georgia, and Virginia. The South Carolinians brought the county its name, recalling the legendary exploits of the "Swamp Fox" of the Revolution, General Francis Marion. The settlers were of English, Welsh, Irish, and Scotch stock. Names like Abercrombe, Aldridge, Atkinson, Bailey, Burleson, Dickinson, Gann, Holcomb, Kirkpatrick, Logan, McDonald, McNutt, Owens, Sizemore, Tidwell, Watson, Wiginton, and Young still crowd the local telephone directory. Eighty-five percent of the residents today are Alabama natives.

Change has never been easy for Marion County. As far back as 1861, there were those—the "Tories of the Hills," as they have been called by local historian W. S. Thompson—who hid in the coves and hills of northwestern Alabama rather than serve in the Confederate army. Their opposition to the Secession, headquartered at Montgomery, where Jefferson Davis had taken the oath as president of the Confederacy, led them to seek secession from the Secession. They failed. Civil rights for blacks, which led to boycotts and demonstrations in the state in the 1960s, accompanied by periodic forays by Northerners into this heretofore "untroubled" terrain, were resisted. One gains the impression, however, that the transition is being made. Consistent with Alabama's "law-and-order" mentality, desegregation in the schools has been largely achieved. Socially, the blacks still "stay in their place," and local residents are hard put even to identify where they live, even though their presence on the streets of Winfield and Hamilton is common. A northern visitor is impressed by the omnipresence of police and sheriffs, even in the out-of-the-way small towns, and wonders why. The native appears sheltered from the outside world and may want it that way. The supply of metropolitan daily newspapers is slim, and one hears from the storekeeper, "No, weekly news magazines don't sell too well here. We'd rather stock the monthlies; they can stay on the shelves longer." *Playboy* and *Hustler* are available but discreetly hidden.

The new industrialization has already taken its toll. Whether the new inmigrants, representing threatening cosmopolitan values, will infuse Marion County with new leadership or retreat to their own enclaves is moot at this time. County residents clearly welcome the economic boost the industrial invasion brings, but the value conflicts are severe. The Marion County of the future will still wrestle with the strain between the traditional ethos, which says, "I still believe that the old way of centering life in the home and church is the best way,"[6] and the emerging ethos, which centers on the economic development of the county. Symbolic of the strain is the fall "Farm-City Week," sponsored by county leaders, during which 200 or more rural and urban people get together and try to understand one another and recognize their mutual dependence. But one wonders what is being celebrated when the featured event of the annual farm-city luncheon is the "Maid of Cotton Contest." Which values will prevail?

Thus, Marion County is in transition and has been for a long time. Neither cotton nor cattle is king, as they are in some other counties of the state. Textile firms such as Toll Gate Garment, Winfield Cotton Mills, and Munsingwear together employ over 1,500 workers. Federal Mogul Corporation, 3M, and Continental Conveyor and Equipment, new industrial firms in the county, employ another 1,500. Industrial production and employment dwarf the $1 million sales from timber and the timber-related jobs of about 600. Industrial expansion is increasing the population, almost 15 percent since 1970, especially in the Hamilton-Guin-Winfield area, bringing to the county management personnel and highly skilled workers from the North Central states. The mobile home industry, which flourished for a decade or more, had all but disappeared by 1975.

Despite the changes, much remains the same. The main street in Winfield, for example, reminds one of a western frontier town. There is a drugstore, barber and beauty shop, two discount stores, a Western Auto store, garages, a couple of banks, the county newspaper office, and a scattering of quick-serve food outlets. But no bars or liquor outlets; they are prohibited by local option law. Off the main street, one moves into residential areas to the north, shopping and industrial areas to the south along and across the St. Louis and San Francisco railroad tracks. Within the town is a public housing project and a U.S. Army depot, where surplus tanks and trucks are the backyard view of residents in $50,000 to $70,000 homes. Here and there in a grove of trees is a small trailer park. On the periphery are some homes of dubious stability and value, mixed with others indicating modest or great prosperity.

Poverty has always been in Marion County. In 1976, with the exodus of the once-burgeoning mobile home industry, unemployment was said to be about 10 percent. The percent of the population living in poverty (22.5 percent) was more than twice the U.S. average and above that of Alabama. Wages were low for most workers, the 47 major companies paying about 50 cents above minimum wage. The average annual income of the staff of the county schools in 1974 was under $7,000. More than 628 cases were on public assistance rolls, 587 individual recipients receiving aid for dependent children in September 1974. In the average month, 3,550 people used food stamps. There was an aggregate of almost 6,000 disadvantaged senior citizens, according to reports by the County Community Action Committee.

Marion County has numerous churches, perhaps seventy-five or eighty in all, located at every cross roads and in the hollows and draws. A few, mostly Baptist and Methodist, have memberships of several hundred each, but the bulk of them have fewer than 100 members. Many of the country Church of Christ congregations have only 20 to 30 adherents, but their influence in the county is considered substantial. Few ministers have had college and seminary training. One striking exception was the Roman Catholic parish at Winfield, served by two full-time priests, three full-time women religious, and occasional part-time visiting seminarians and brothers. This team served 137 Roman Catholics in 1976, most of them from among the newcomers in the professional and managerial class. They are widely scattered in a three-county area. There are no Episcopal, Presbyterian, United Church of Christ, or Lutheran congregations in the county, but the diaspora from such bodies is abundant.

Although Alabama is heavily churched, 63.3 percent affiliated, Marion County has 13,526 residents not on the rolls of any congregation in the county. It is the highest unchurched county (56.9 percent unchurched) in Alabama and one of two counties in the state with a majority of its people unaffiliated. The reasons are not completely clear. My unchurched informants seemed agreed on only one thing—the churches they knew held no attractions for them. The poor, the blacks, and the aging among them felt exploited or ignored, not welcome.

I tried to summarize my feelings after my first week in Marion County:

> I'm sure there's beauty somewhere around, but I find it terribly depressing. The strip miners have left their holes and piles behind when they've exhausted the profitable seams of coal. Railroads seem to chug and shift cars on sidings that run up and down hollow after hollow. A four-year-old in a Munsingwear Factory Outlet store said "Hi!" then kicked me in the shins. Immigrants from the North greet me like a long-lost brother. The natives are kind, warm, but reserved and a bit suspicious when they learn I'm a "professor from up north."
> Among the church folks, especially the clergy, I get the feeling they are waiting to find me vulnerable so they can give me their pitch and "get me saved." A small coterie who have supported my project have gone all out— personally cooperative, hospitable, concerned. Father Pat Brehenny, in whose trailer I'm staying, brings beauty to my moments of depression. If all the Glenmary priests are like this human being, a dedicated and effective priest, I'd like to meet the rest.

Three weeks later, I experienced some of the beauty I had missed at the start. The suspicions I had felt proved a mild paranoia, a function perhaps of my own initial culture shock. But the stories I heard from the unchurched were uniformly sad—tales of hurts and tragedy and wistfulness. One young man gave me a poem he had written, titled "Yesterday's Child." Fugitive from the police and refugee from the drug scene of the 1960s, he closed his doggerel with these lines:

> Maybe sometime we'll awake to a world full of love,
> And not have to shake our heads and give a man a shove.
> Yes, I hope that some day we will all soon find out
> That beyond all this bullshit there's peace without doubt.
> Yesterday's child, Oh Lord, what shall he be?
> A lost city dweller, or a man who is free.

An older man, stroke victim and bedridden, husband of one of my informants, became agitated several times during our interview and tried to speak. His voice said simply, "One. Two. One. Two. Whoosh. O shit." His wife, embarrassed, explained what it meant. This was his memory of the tornado of April 3, 1974, when in a matter of minutes the nearby town of Guin was "practically wiped off the map of Alabama." Ten million dollars' worth of damage was done by the 500-mile-per-hour winds; 300 homes were destroyed, twenty-one people killed, and hundreds seriously injured. Apparently, there had been a new scare a few weeks before I arrived when another "big, black funnel" moved in one Saturday night, as if to celebrate the second anniversary of the "great destruction." It passed over. But the dread of it was still in the air.

Where were the unchurched in Marion County? I found them on a Sunday morning eating alone in the restaurant of a Winfield motel. In Ma Tucker's bootleg haven near Glen Allen. In the shacks of the blacks, back in the hills on the depleted farms near the vandalized, formerly all-black Ada Hanna High School. In the plush homes of transplanted midwesterners above Guin and in the sylvan woods outside Hamilton. Among the housewives shopping in a country store on the side of the road to Brilliant. In the trailer courts and "project" units. Among the elderly everywhere, lost and forgotten. In the towns and out in the hills —mostly in the hills. Within walking distance of most was a church.

Marion is a county in transition. Perhaps it has always been so, from that time when, before 1818, those early settlers arrived from the hills of Tennessee and the Carolinas or from Georgia. Perhaps there are still "Tories in the Hills" of northwestern Alabama who, like their antisecessionist ancestors, hide out in modern-day caves and mountains, out of touch with the main stream of contemporary culture and its institutions. Perhaps, like newcomers and transients everywhere, they don't fit in with what they find, and can only experience community with other strangers like themselves. For them, the "decorations" and the "singings" in the old-style, family-centered churches are foreign to their pasts in another place. They can't understand the Ministerial Association, which is preoccupied with pornography, X-rated movies at the county drive-ins, and the traffic in marijuana, when other concerns seem more important to them. They feel like aliens and are certain they are perceived as such by the natives. Marginal people all.

NOTES

1. It was here that I met Eleanor Dickinson. Her book *Revival* (New York: Harper & Row, 1974) has been compared by Walter Hopps of the Smithsonian Institute with James Agee and Walker Evans's *Let Us Now Praise Famous Men* (New York: Ballantine, 1960) as a similar example of "the fully esthetic union of visual images, words and data relating to specific members of our culture." Dickinson was on a return visit to Joe Turner's church, this time with audio and video tape, camera, and her usual felt-tip marking pen and large sheets of newsprint clipped to a Masonite board. I

talked with her before the meeting, saw her move with ease among a people with obvious empathy, and watched her sketch Delbert Johnson while the congregation prayed and danced and spoke in tongues. Weeks later, I read *Revival* and looked at her photographs and figure drawings. That experience caused me to look back on my evening at the "Jesus Church" differently. I began to see what she saw and felt. I appreciated the text written by Barbara Bensinger, based on Dickinson's tapes, and listened again to my own tapes. I know now what Dickinson meant when she said, "I believe they feel me to be a kind of missionary."

2. Among the most useful publications are such items as J. C. Dillon, *West Virginia Blue Book* (Charleston, W.V.: Jarrett, 1975) and Sam Cipolette and Steve Ellis (eds.), *1976 West Virginia Economic Profile* (Charleston, W.V.: W.V. Department of Commerce, 1976). Also helpful were details on the mining situation from two different perspectives: John Ashcroft, *Directory of Mines* (Charleston, W.V.: Department of Mines, 1974); and *West Virginia Coal Facts* (Charleston, W.V.: West Virginia Coal Association, 1975). Dale Bowman, of the West Virginia Department of Commerce, located maps, census data, and the most recent population projections. Topographical information is from C. E. Krebs and D. D. Teets, *West Virginia Geological Survey: Boone County* (Wheeling, W.V.: Wheeling News Lithograph, 1915) and from current U.S. Coast and Geodetic Survey quadrangles. Sigfus Olafson, local retired engineer and amateur historian, supplied valuable "oral history."

3. J. H. Diss Debar, *West Virginia Handbook and Immigrants Guide* (Parkersburg, W.V.: n.p., 1870), pp. 33–34. A parallel estimate of the West Virginia mentality of more than fifty years ago appeared in James Morton Callahan, *History of West Virginia, Old and New* (Chicago and New York: American History Society, 1923), vol. 1, p. 21, as follows: "Mountain regions discourage the budding of genius because they are areas of isolation, confinement, remote from the great currents of men and ideas. . . . They are regions of much labor and little leisure, of poverty today and anxiety for the morrow, of toil-cramped hands and toil-dulled brains."

4. Jack Weller's *Yesterday's People: Life in Contemporary Appalachia* (Lexington: University Press of Kentucky, 1965) was his obvious reference. Weller described a people who have "slept through a revolution, having missed the industrial age." Many West Virginians, like my informant, have not noticed that this was a compliment Weller was paying the mountain people. Because of their missing the industrial age, Weller contends (pp. 159–60), "The mountaineer may well be ready and able to help us enter the new cybernetic age, in one leap from the agrarian age."

5. Sources of demographic information about Marion County are the 1970 U.S. Census reports for Alabama, especially volumes on "General Social and Economic Characteristics." Valuable data have been summarized by the Cooperative Extension Service, *Marion County Progress Report* (Auburn, Alabama: Auburn University, 1974), mimeographed. Historical information was given me by local informants.

6. Florence Sizemore, "My Fourscore Years and More in Marion and Lamar Counties," in Carl Elliott, *Annals of Northwestern Alabama* (Tuscaloosa, Ala.: SWS Printers, 1959), vol. 2.

6. The Sun Belt

People in the United States are among the most mobile people in the world. In recent years, they have been moving from place to place with increasing frequency. One wonders whether roots have completely disappeared and whether anyone any longer can name his or her home town. The migratory route for many is to the south and west. They end up in the southern tier of states called the "Sun Belt." American workers, their families, and particularly the retired, are moving to a sunnier clime when they get the chance. A middle-management executive, "on the way up," will tell you how he calculatingly accepted every transfer his company offered him over the years until he was asked to go to Alberquerque or San Diego. From then on, "I refused transfer, even if it meant the end of promotions." Or, from the affluent retired, you will hear, "For the last ten years, we've gone to Florida every winter—first for two weeks, then a month, finally for the whole winter season. After that we never went back north."

Sarasota County, Florida, is one of those counties at the end of the migration trail. Orange County, California, is another. Both have become large metropolitan centers, but with enough of the "back home" friends and relatives around to preserve a semblance of rootedness. They often tend to huddle together, like the Indiana folks who set up trailers in the same enclave between Sarasota and Bradenton, Florida, or the Minnesotans who populate the same subdivision in Huntington Beach, California. Sarasota's 1975 population had reached 162,600 and Orange's 1,655,100, and they are still growing rapidly.

Sarasota County, Florida
County seat: Sarasota
Land area: 587 square miles
Density: 277 per square mile
Population: 120,413 (1970), 162,600 (1975)
Population Change: 1970–1975: 35.0%
Population Rank: 240 among 3,143 U.S. counties (1975)
Unchurched population, Sarasota County: 60,646, 50.4%
Unchurched population, Florida: 44.5% (Rank 14)

Sarasota County exudes conspicuous wealth, bourgeois culture, and the virtual takeover of the community by senior citizens. In the state of Florida, in 1970, 14.6 percent of the population was sixty-five years of age and over, in Sarasota County, 28.6 percent.[1] Two coastal census tracts at the northern end of Sarasota City have populations in which nearly one-half of the people are sixty-five or older. The same phenomenon is developing in the southern portion of the county. There are two ways of calculating Sarasota's population, I discovered in this land of sunshine: the census enumerations that form the data base line and the "functional population" between January and March "for whom service must be planned and provided."[2] The county's 1970 population was 120,413; its "functional population," 139,035. By 1975, the data base was estimated to have grown by 35 percent to 162,600, the functional population to about 188,000. The overall density is 277 people per square mile, but this increases to over 3,000 in the northern part of the city and county and to less than 100 in tracts that stretch to the inland corners and the southern tier.

One way of gaining an overview of life and ethos in Sarasota County is to visit its "places of assembly"—from the airport to the beaches, the marinas to the outlying ranchlands, from the shuffleboard courts to the public fishing piers, from the stadium where baseball holds its spring training ritual to the 5,000-seat arena at Venice where "children of all ages" view the premier showings of the "Greatest Show on Earth," from Clown College to New College, from luxurious St. Armand's circle to "The Purple Onion," Sarasota's Frank Lloyd Wright-designed Van Wezel Performing Arts Hall at the Civic Center. I visited them all, and more, to catch the flavor of the place. One day, I made the rounds of the sales offices for Sarasota's modest and expensive condominiums to try to identify with the house-hunting fever that grips thousands of newcomers each year. I heard again and again, "This is a start-over community; you'll love it!"

My first discovery here was that the rise and fall of the mercury in the thermometer determines who comes and goes, how long they stay, and whether or not they settle in. It was February 5, 1976. I had escaped near-zero temperatures up north to enter a balmy, tropical 78°F in Sarasota. Short-term vacationers had already extended their stays "indefinitely," with the result that accommodations were overreserved. The December to March migration was in full swing. My "Whisper-Jet," flying at 30,000 feet over half the state, descended for landing at Bradenton-Sarasota Airport. From the air, I had looked down on endless rows of white rooftops, arranged in checkerboard fashion, the habitat of thousands of winter trailer-park vacationers.

Disembarking, I encountered organized mayhem. Claiming my baggage was an exercise in polite bullishness. The area was jammed with natives bidding *au revoir* to reluctant leavers or crying exuberant hellos to expectant arrivers. I elbowed my way, muttering perfunctory "Excuse me's," through grandparents searching for grandchildren, and middle-aged women (females outnumber males two to one) solicitously peering through masses of bodies for dear ones inching their way, as if playing "blindman's buff," on canes and walkers. Traffic was snarled at the curb with arriving and departing Chryslers and Cadillacs, taxis, and hotel-motel jitneys. The walkways were laid out with the handicapped in mind —no curbs or steps—and the supply of wheelchairs and walkers, it seemed, was enough to handle a small planeload of the retired infirm.

Leaving the airport, I got my first sight and feel of the Tamiami Trail, a car-clogged Tampa-to-Miami artery that hugs the Sarasota, Blackburn, Lyons, and Donna bays, just inland from the narrow keys separating the Florida peninsula from the Gulf of Mexico. In Sarasota City, the Trail hawked accommodations for the "snobs" and the "slobs" in a strip of motels (10 percent discount for senior citizens), restaurants, and one each of every nationally advertised, franchised hamburger, fried chicken, taco, and pizza establishment. From the Tamiami Trail, you gained entry to the Ringling Museum, then farther south, to downtown Sarasota and to Longboat, Lido, and Siesta Keys. "No Vacancy" signs were posted in neon lights by five o'clock. A night's accommodation ranged from $14 at places featuring "efficiencies" to $28, $36, and up as one approached the yacht basins and access to public and private beaches. The Holiday Inn had its private marina, catering to owners of expensive yachts and sailboats.

For about half the population, churches too are places of assembly. Johnson, Picard, and Quinn's study records ninety-one congregations in the county.[3] "Sarasota Scene," a real-estate promotional piece, boasts that "the beauty that is Sarasota is enhanced by the uniqueness in design of its 102 houses of worship, representing twenty-one various religious denominations—93 Protestant, seven Catholic, and two Jewish."

The telephone directory reveals that the religious fare is plentiful and varied. At St. Martha's, the Catholic can find two Saturday masses and choose from among seven on Sunday, one a Spanish-language liturgy. At the Community Baptist Church, an "independent, fundamental, missionary congregation," the inquirer is bidden to savor its bus ministry, youth ministry, bookstore ministry, senior citizen ministry, deaf ministry, as well as tape, tract, music, visitation, and missions ministries. The interdenominational, charismatic Tabernacle bills itself as "the church you have been looking for." One congregation offers "a difference that is worth the distance." America's first "drive-in, inside-outside sanctuary," is located at Whitfield Estates, across the Tamiami Trail from the Holiday Inn. The independent Baptists advertise their differences by name—Missionary, Primitive, True Missionary, and so on. There are also the Deliverance Miracle Revival Center, the Shrine of the Master (Metaphysical Science), the First Assembly of God (a "full gospel church—for all people"), and the Bahai Temple. Many are well attended, as I was reminded by an editorial writer in the *Sarasota Herald-Tribune* eight months later when my published reports first reached Florida and mildly scandalized some of the natives.

Standard mainline denominations present themselves in architectural finery at such places as the Church of the Redeemer (Episcopal), Church of the Cross (Reformed), Siesta Island Chapel (Community), St. Paul's Lutheran, and First Presbyterian. In February 1976, they all had large crowds. Six Christian Science practitioners follow the telephone directory yellow pages listing of twenty-one chiropractic physicians. One can dial 959-2323 for a three-minute devotional by Helen Fugazzi. The Friday religious page in the *Herald-Tribune* and the *Sarasota Journal* adds to the list and variety.

There seems to be something for everyone. The *Sarasota Herald-Tribune* writes, "Certainly this area is not without a gracious plenty of religious opportunities; there are churches here representing nearly all

forms of worship practiced in America."⁴ My statistics indicated however that at least half of the year-round population opted for nothing at
all. I got the impression, confirmed in interviews, that the churches were
busier competing with each other for customers among the minority
who might recognize the "difference" each was marketing. I wrote in
my diary on Saturday, February 7, perhaps too cynically:

> Tomorrow I can choose from a rich menu of sermon offerings. Dr. Grosvenor
> at the Church of the Palms will preach on "I Believe in Angels." At Pine Shores,
> I can learn about "Mr. Lincoln, Man of God." Roger McDuff, Praise the Lord
> Club soloist, will be "in person" at the Tabernacle at six. The Unitarians will
> offer "The Who of You." I think I'll go Lutheran; the sermon title isn't listed.

Church news and advertisements are on the newspaper's sports page, sand-
wiched between feature stories on heart, respiratory, bronchial, emphysema
problems, and the comics, daily horoscope, and "By George," the local advice
columnist. A Sagittarian, I was cautioned to "keep all my senses alert today to
a new opportunity or an adventurous experience." Had I been born a few weeks
later, my advice was "to be analytical and sift through all the wordage until you
ring the bell of fact." "By George" wrote, "If I were you, I wouldn't ask my
advice under any circumstances."

Most Sundays people assemble elsewhere. As an academician, I was
attracted to New College. Students congregate on the lawns between
Hamilton Center and the dormitory complex or in rooms within. Young
men and women visit one another frequently (within the rules) and
share meals (against the rules). One Sunday in February you find them
on the bay front across the Tamiami Trail, behind John and Mabel
Ringling's famed palatial mansion, "Ca'd'zan." The strip along the
beach is banner-bedecked and flags fly with blazoned heraldry. It is the
annual "Medieval Fair" jointly sponsored by the college's Renaissance
Studies Committee and the Ringling Museum. The "world premier" of
an original, bawdy medieval play is performed by students and faculty
at a beach-front pavilion. Leslie Telfer gives her sensuous Near Eastern
belly dance, accompanied by Ali Jihad Racy on his coconut-resonating
lute. Clowns and mimes—some of them faculty department heads, I was
told—entertain with medieval tomfoolery and pantomime (capturing a
butterfly, fondling it, and letting it fly its imaginary escape). On week-
days, students and faculty gather in classrooms to share "the hazards as
well as the liberating spirit of self-directed learning." They paid hand-
somely for the privilege before New College, facing bankruptcy, was
merged into the state university system.

You catch a different scene not far away in Census Tract Number Three, where 99.3 percent of the population is black, although only 6.7 percent of Sarasota County is black. There on the concrete pavements surrounding the "Project," the black children play with broken wheeled vehicles—bicycles, wagons, skateboards—or tumble on discarded mattresses. Inside one unit—they don't call them "homes"—an extended family of ten (all female) alternately feed, change diapers and spank the three youngest, ages three months, ten months, and 18 months. The furniture is cast-off, from the Salvation Army, who got it from the middle-class, who got it from the upper class, years before.

On the bridge between Bird and Coon Keys are the ever-present fishermen and women. "Why?" "For food, man," says a twenty-five-year-old black, unemployed construction worker. "To get away from the battle-ax," says a retired eighty-year-old with the gestured concurrence of his younger, seventyish companions. "Everybody fishes here at least once," volunteered a northern transient dressed as he thinks Floridians dress. No one seems to be catching any fish.

St. Armand's Circle, a shopper's paradise on one of the most affluent of the keys, St. Armond's Key, is another world. Here are specialty shops featuring "winter wear for the summer season." Most are branches with second locations on the Jersey coast, Cape Cod, and Martha's Vineyard. They cater to the credit card users, to those addicted to the elegance of Sarasota's wealthy, the over-seventy connoisseurs of the latest in women's fashions. One couturier told me of a regular customer who buys $700–$800 in dresses "at one clip," deliberately choosing the wrong sizes so she will have an excuse to come back and "while away the time" for second and third fittings.

Traveling north on Longboat Key, I passed entrances to private developments of $100,000+ homes on winding "jug handles" named Hornblower or Outrigger Lane, landscaped with palms, hibiscus, and flowering cactus. There are the Longboat Key Club, the Privateer Apartments, and the Country Club Shores. There are fifteen or more tennis courts at the Colony Beach and Tennis Courts. In rapid succession, I passed the Aquarius Club, the Islander Club, the Far Horizon Restaurant, and the twenty-story high-rise Beachcomber. The key gave me the impression of an ersatz bayou country, with engineered lagoons and a horticulturist's heaven, populated by the rich and the near-rich who are spending their final years in the conspicuous comfort they have spent a lifetime earning.

Pelican Cove offers "bayhouses" and "treehouses" in an "environmentally planned, low-density, wooded location." On the last prime Gulf-frontage in the county, Sansovino appeals to the "new nobility of Venice" to purchase "condominiums of uncommon livability." "Your castle on the bay," with "Romeo and Juliet balcony opening on a tropically landscaped courtyard," is offered for $139,000 (1976 prices) with dock for the yachtsman pride and joy ("limit 44 feet, please"). A "penthouse of elegance," an "exercise in extravagant space, everything oversized except the price," sold for a mere $79,950 four years ago. A double-luxury apartment in the Islander Club of Longboat Key is available with atrium entry, Nutone audio system, and marble shower—"the best value anywhere at $240,000." Seasonal apartments could be found at Bahai Vista, Gulf Horizons, Quarterdeck, and the Towers for $1,000 and up a month. Ruth Richmond's syndicated real estate column sums up what such luxury affords—"peace, quiet, sunshine and security." Here, she writes, you will find "privacy and rest from vehicular traffic, overhead airport noise, children, and the creative neighbor building a boat or restoring an antique car in his garage."

Drinking oases abound. In the "Project" area, they call them *saloons.* "Club Mary," just outside the northern city limits, is a tavern featuring topless waitresses and the exotic nude dancing, in February 1976, of Miss Julie Mist. At the Hyatt House on the Boulevard of the Arts, it is a cocktail lounge or supper club with lush elegance, drinks charged to ample expense accounts. At four o'clock, the bars along the Tamiami Trail south of the city begin to be populated by housewives, construction workers, and the retired. At the central marina, the younger set and their elders who dress young sip long, cool drinks after a day's expedition for fishing tuna or marlin expedition. After dusk, the private bars open in the penthouse condominiums and Bird Key gardens.

There are places of assembly for shoppers—at the Sears Plaza or the South Gate Mall; for import car buffs at Roberts Auditorium; for the more reserved sportsmen and women at the night-lighted shuffleboard courts at the Venice Shuffleboard Club and for the more athletic water skiers at the omnipresent marina docks; for riders on the saddle trails to the east; for boaters, bowlers, scuba divers, artists, baseball fans, and all others seeking their favorite leisure pastimes at places from Bradenton to Venice-Nokomis and from the beaches to Fruitville. As the developers say, "Join the million-dollar lifestyle!" Sunshine, the chief source of Vitamin D and Sarasota's booming population, makes this county fiesta time most of the year.

Fiesta time looks different in the churches. On one Sunday in February, at a mainline church on St. Armond's Key, the church bulletin read, "Most of us have our track records behind us—our families raised, educated, and now on their own. We are on the threshold of our Golden Years. What better way to thank God than to give to our endowment fund?" At another church, a thousand or more gathered to consider "humankind disaster needs" and "the involvement of the semiretired and golden-agers" in relief ministries. The bishop of the Roman Catholic diocese was appealing for $1,547,586 to fund "our people-caring agencies"—places for migrants, children with learning handicaps, and the elderly in need of nursing care. But, however worthy the causes, at least half of the Sarasota County population was on the outside looking in. Having left all "that baggage" behind when they came south, their fiestas were being celebrated differently. "The exfaithful," the local paper explained, "who have given a lifetime of faithful attendance and support to churches elsewhere just haven't the energy or personal need to start up again."

Orange County, California
County seat: Santa Ana
Land area: 782 square miles
Density: 2117 per square mile
Population: 1,420,386 (1970), 1,655,100 (1975)
Population Change: 1970–1975: 20.3%
Population Rank: 8 among 3,143 U.S. counties (1975)
Unchurched population, Orange County: 820,191, 57.7%
Unchurched population, California: 57% (Rank 3)

Orange County is at the far, southwestern end of the Sun Belt migratory trail. "More than a state," the tour book says, "California is a state of mind." So also Orange County. There are as many Orange counties as there are Orange County residents. Each has his or her own Orange County. The stadium and Disneyland at Anaheim. The alligator farm and Knott's Berry Farm at Buena Park. The University of California and citrus groves at Irvine. The artist colonies at Laguna Beach or Lido Isle marina. The mission at San Juan Capistrano and the former Nixon estate at San Clemente. The congested, high-density older communities of Fullerton, Garden Grove, and Santa Ana, the county seat. The newer, walled-in tracts in Huntington Beach and Newport Beach. Silverado Canyon and the Santa Ana mountains. Toro U.S. Marine

Corps Air Station and Rossmoor's 10,700 manors at Leisure World, Laguna Hills. Planned, mushrooming communities at Mission Viejo and Laguna Niguel, carved into the mesa hills from the Pacific to the San Diego Freeway. There are beaches, canyons, and mountains; sixteen-lane freeways and offshore oil rigs; lazy, isolated settlements and bustling cities; tourists and those 1,655,100 who call one of the twenty-five cities or towns of Orange's 782 square miles home. It's all part of the 10-million-population Los Angeles consolidated metropolitan area, second largest in the nation.

Is it possible to make sense of this conglomerate mass?[5] Obviously, Orange County defies simplification, and any attempt to do so is misleading. But a certain spirit, a dominating trend, a central theme runs through all the complexity. Some have called California a "microcosm of the United States"; if it is, Orange County is its supreme exemplar. "The Californian," writes journalist Neil Morgan, "is driven, restless, mobile, probing, innovative, and dedicated to the Western mystique. He [*sic*] has created a putty culture—yeasty, swollen, penetrable, unshaped, elastic, impermanent, but with a tendency to adhere at least for a time to anything solid."[6] A variety of "the California syndrome" is found in Orange County. Michael Davie of the *London Observer* found the county "suburban, new, fast-growing, white, intensely orthodox, patriotic, churchgoing, often puritanical, often rootless, often heavily mortgaged, and often fearful that something unpredictable may happen —factory closures, space agency cutbacks, tax increases—to start its citizens sliding toward the poverty from which many of their parents escaped.[7] That is one side of the Orange County stereotype. Of the other side, Sheldon Zalaznick wrote,

> Beneath its eccentric surface . . . Orange County is more interesting for its typicality than for its uniqueness. A great many suburbias across the United States share with Orange County the problems, preoccupations, and tensions associated with growth and change. They're exaggerated in Orange County, partly because growth has been so very rapid. But seen for what it essentially is, a kind of hypersuburbia, Orange County is, as a Southern California businessman put it, a "demonstration city for the world."[8]

Zalaznick's assessment is probably correct. If so, it leads one to conclude, with Karl Lamb, political scientist at the University of California, Santa Cruz, that it is better to think of Orange as prototypical rather than stereotypical. Orange is less a distinctive place than a harbinger of the future in many places. It may well be that "as Orange goes, so goes the nation." In the years since Jean Gottmann wrote his classic, *Megalopolis,* Orange County, rather than the older industrialized northeastern seaboard region, may be on its way to becoming "the cradle of a new form of civilization."⁹

It is hard to know how religion fits into this montage. It appears that for the 820,181 unchurched people (57.7 percent), at least, the sacral element has vanished from religion altogether. The sacred quality of religion as exhibited in the churches is, for most, gone. In its place, to fill the void, comes hedonism or technology or family or civil religion. Each is a form of authentic secularity, perhaps epitomized in Orange County more than elsewhere in the nation. Not that Orange is an isolate; rather that Orange's secularity provides a window through which we see the direction America may be heading.

My four weeks in Orange County, with daily forays from Costa Mesa, hub of the harbor area where I was staying, was inadequate to probe this phenomenon more than superficially. Many of the local clergy and other knowledgeable VIPs understood it better than I. In this book, particularly in the excerpts from a limited number of interviews that follow, I can only report what I have heard and seen and how I subjectively reacted to both. I traveled almost 3,000 miles up and down the freeways and from the Pacific beaches into the mountains and stopped at hundreds of places along the way. I never completed all the interviews I had planned, because the sample and the geography were so vast. It was an intense immersion, and I had the feeling more than once that the baptism was by fire. There was little time to sort things out in the field, for I daily faced the danger of "going native."

Only in retrospect can some of the pieces be put together. I began this with a composite picture I first dictated into my tape recorder one Sunday morning in March 1976. I have added a few reflections that have emerged since. This is, in essence, what I said then and feel now.

There wasn't much sign of life on Harbor Boulevard that morning as I left Costa Mesa and headed toward the entrance ramp to the freeway. As I passed the Bel Congo Motel, a hundred cars were still parked outside. Inside were those who had paid $26 for two to occupy water beds and watch the porno movies. Massage parlors had advertised in the papers last night the availability of girls ready for "house calls." At the entrance to the San Diego Freeway, youths with backpacks were thumbing rides. Among them were two Marines on their way back to Camp

Pendleton after a weekend "on the town." The freeway was as remarkably free of traffic as the city streets. The few cars besides my own were mostly campers on the way west to the beaches or east to the mountains.

To the south, as I sped along oblivious of speed limits, I glanced toward the foothills of the Santa Anas. Saddleback Mountain this morning was covered with a yellow haze. Whether fog, mist, or smog, the eerie sense of it was inviting, as if the mountains were singing plaintively, "Come on over to me, I'm here." To my right before long, there was my first morning glimpse of the Pacific. I remembered what an artist at Lido Village had said to me last night, "There is something astrological, magnetic about the Pacific. The ocean speaks to people. It pulls people toward it, like a siren's song." My destination was an early morning church service at Laguna Hills. It took will to keep my course and resist the gravitational field that surrounded me.

Newport Beach sweeps up from the ocean and envelops both sides of the freeway. Again, those walled subdivisions. I had asked dozens what those walls meant, remembering Frost's line, "Something there is that doesn't love a wall." I had gotten as many answers as people I asked: "The lots are small, you need privacy." "Just Southern California's modern version of Spanish Mission architecture." "Security, I guess, never thought about it much. The wall was here when we came." "To separate homes from highways." "A big playpen for my dog and the kids." At Leisure World, "America's Number One Adult Community" of 17,400 residents, protective walls with barbed wire atop surrounded the residential areas. Lee Hutchison, saleswoman, had perhaps been more candid about it, when she told me, "Courteous security attendants are on duty twenty-four hours a day at all the entrances. And a protective security patrol is always there to protect you, your possessions, your property." But I could not discover what was being walled out or why the people wanted to be walled in. I was sure that my Polk and Waldo and Boone county free spirits would have felt imprisoned.

The Irvine property came next, that massive corporation landholding in the south central and eastern portion of the county. Orange groves, nurseries, and open ranchland abound in the pastoral counterpoint to what I was leaving behind. It woke me up. I felt good. The temperatures had risen to the 70s. I opened the windows to breathe deeply the fresh breezes.

It was only 9:30 A.M. when I left the crowded Lutheran Lenten service at Laguna Hills. I had decided to be ecumenical, because I had attended the five o'clock afternoon Folk Mass at St. Simon and Jude Parish yesterday. After breakfast at Cocos—you wait to be seated even on a Sunday morning—I headed for my first appointment. Sunday morning is an ideal time to find the unchurched at home! From Laguna Beach, I wound up at Temple Hill Drive. A few of the residents were already up and out—retired, older men, on the edge of the street watering their rose bushes; two preteens careening toward me on skateboards; older teens in shorts with surfboards, heading for the waves. My interviewee wasn't home. He'd driven to town to pick up the Sunday papers.

I joined the exodus to the beach. No one swimming yet, but the volleyball courts on the beach were filled. Traffic on the Pacific Highway moved at a snail's pace. All the stores were open and doing midday business as if it were Saturday. Seventy-five cars were parked outside a handsome structure. I mistook it for a church; it was a tennis club and golf course assembly spa. Somebody must be in church somewhere, I thought, but most were either sleeping late or already enjoying their Sunday fun and frolic. I glanced at "A Day in the Life of the Majestic Empire, Orange County" beside me on my car seat as I waited for the traffic to move: "The good life, the outdoor life, Orange County's way of life, made possible by a utopian-like climate. . . . Fertile plains, rolling hills, the ideal marriage of sea to shore, alluring cities rooted in all their splendor against a harmonious background of lofty peaks. . . . This is a wondrous place to live, work, and play." Sunday is a day to play.

I wondered what else was going on this day that I would miss. Fifty-five thousand youth had been standing in line since 8 A.M. to take in the British rock group "The Who" at Anaheim Stadium. In the afternoon, Reverend Ike would be in town coaching his followers to greet one another with "The presence of God that is in me greets the presence of God in you. . . . Together we'll make money!" I went to hear him and to observe his service. The swallows arrived at San Juan Capistrano yesterday. Today, the Chicanos and Indians would be sweeping up the streets from the annual parade. The art galleries were already open. The freeways would be full by now with people racing from place to place —to the mountains, to the sea, to the forests and the desert, to San Diego and Tijuana. Some would still be in bed getting over Saturday night's overindulgence, others still in robes contemplating the day's excursion, a few ready for a morning's jogging to limber up from the week on swivel chairs at corporate headquarters at Fashion Island.

I recalled the interviews of the past several weeks and wrote in my diary:

This is the kind of place I could be comfortable in—perhaps. Would I, too, be driven to make my life so private? Would I have difficulty making the warm, intimate relationships with others that my humanity needs? Would I fall in love with casualness and make my idol—casual clothes, casual conversations, casual relationships, calling everyone by his or her first name without really wanting to know the person behind the name? Fearful of saying hello because I might have to say goodbye? Is life a game, moving my marker on the board from one pleasure today to a better one tomorrow? Can I make it without a God who can give it all some meaning? In this setting, can the church's Jesus mean anything at all? Can I celebrate this life without transforming it? I wonder—for me, and for them.

Like the places I had been or would be, Orange County had its share of churches, only more, because everything in Orange County is exaggerated. Johnson, Picard, and Quinn count 391, but surely—after adjustment for independent groups not included—there are more, perhaps as many as 500.[10] All but two of the national communions with 100,000 members or more are represented here. At least ten of the smaller denominations and sects are also, along with independent bodies and the newer cults and pseudo-religious associations that spring up in southern California each year. Melodyland Christian Center at Anaheim and Calvary Chapel at Santa Ana, both near Disneyland, have perhaps thousands of devotees of their fundamentalist brand of Protestant Christianity. "The atmosphere is wide open," Gerald Kennedy, Methodist bishop of Los Angeles, once observed, "for every choice possible in religious association or for none." Within the proximate neighborhood of Garden Grove Community Church, the Reverend Robert Schuller estimates there are still 500,000 unchurched people. One Wednesday night, I attended a membership class there with 200 "inquirers" from the unchurched community. Most of them would later affiliate here and swell Schuller's 8,000-membership church.

This openness is not a recent phenomenon, the historians and social critics claim. It harks back to the 1850s, days when gold shaped this land, when gambling, drinking, and whoring were the routine weekday diversions, and when the Sabbath was widely observed as the day of rest and cleanup, not churchgoing. Even in the 1950s, when religion was enjoying its "revival" in America and the denominations were building new

churches in the mushrooming communities of Orange County, most of
the incoming nomads were loners, lured by the climate and the hope
of economic advancement, by their desire to be a part of a nonrestrictive
new society. The churches, which stood for roots, even for an historic
Jesus and a traditional faith, seemed out of place for the masses, who
preferred to be social vagrants with few attachments and still fewer
commitments. Today, "anomie"—a condition of normlessness and rootlessness, of drift without focus—the Orange clergy told me, is "the
disease of most countians, a disease most would prefer to nurse than
cure." So the churches become the tribal cemeteries for antiquated
social mores and Puritanical restraints, and the people gladly serve as
pallbearers at the interment of most Christian virtues.[11]

The dominant motif of the montage is authentic secularity and priva-
tism, despite the obvious vitality of many of the churches. One Catholic
leader observes, "Hesitant churchgoers can attend from the privacy of
their cars or even, via television, in their own homes." A Reformed
Jewish rabbi adds, "A person can observe the Sabbath at home with his
family."[12] To see Orange County's present is perhaps to view the
national tomorrow. What happens here may turn out to be the American malaise or a token of its regeneration. The religionist must learn to
ask, as he or she surveys this place, with Wordsworth, "Whither is fled
this visionary gleam? / Where is it now, the glory and the dream?" Little
comfort that he may end up with words like Richard Armour's in the
concluding quatrain of a poem:

> So leap with joy, be blithe and gay
> Or weep my friends with sorrow.
> What Orange County is today,
> The rest will be tomorrow.[13]

NOTES

1. Data sources include 1970 U.S. Census reports for Florida, especially volumes on
"General Characteristics of the Population," "General Social and Economic Characteristics," and "Census Tracts: Sarasota SMSA," and more current data from
"Sarasota County Population Estimates for July 1, 1975" and "Sarasota County Land
Use Plan" (with maps), both mimeographed and prepared by the Long Range Planning Division of the Sarasota County Planning Department, April–May 1975. Population estimates by local authorities and the U.S. Bureau of the Census (see *Estimates*

of the Population of Counties and Metropolitan Areas, Series P–25, no. 709, September 1977) do not agree; federal statistics are quoted in this report. County and city real estate, tourist, and Chamber of Commerce publications are abundant and reflect the "front stage" impressions of certain segments of the community to the citizenry and the visitor. I express special indebtedness to the Rev. Howard W. Miller, Sarasota, who facilitated my entree to the county scene, and to the late Karl Wallenda, then seventy-one, who shared with me for several hours his reminiscences of 50 years as a circus high-wire artist in the United States and of his life in Sarasota.

2. "Functional population" is calculated by multiplying the number of dwelling units by the number of persons per occupied unit for the area from January through March each year.

3. Douglas W. Johnson, Paul R. Picard and Bernard Quinn, *Churches and Church Membership in the United States: 1971* (Washington, D.C.: Glenmary Research Center, 1974), p. 42.

4. *Sarasota Herald-Tribune*, Saturday, 1 October 1977, Section 6–A, editorial page.

5. Mission executive Howell Foster, of the Lutheran Church in America's Division for Mission in North America, a Huntington Beach resident, helped me plow through the mass of available data on Orange County and shared his "oral history" of the last decade. He directed me to the county research and planning offices at Santa Ana where I perused more statistical information than I needed. The best single source I discovered was the Board of Supervisors' annual *Orange County Progress Report* (County Administrative Office, Santa Ana, CA 92701). (Current issue is vol. 13, 1976.) Also helpful are *Orange County General Plan: Land Use Elements*, January 1976 (with bibliographical references to local planning activities); *Housing and Community Development Program*, Environmental Management Agency, January 1976; and H. W. Otto, *If Farmland Goes on California's South Coast* (Santa Ana: Orange County Board of Supervisors, 1974). The Rev. Ellwood Moreland, Laguna Hills, was my contact with the religious community and its leadership.

6. Neil Morgan, *The California Syndrome* (Englewood Cliffs, N.J.: Prentice-Hall, 1969), p. 4.

7. Quoted in Karl A. Lamb, *As Orange Goes* (N.Y.: Norton, 1974), p. 1.

8. Sheldon Zalaznick, "The Double Life of Orange County," *Fortune* 78, no. 5 (October 1968): 140.

9. Jean Gottmann, *Megalopolis: The Urbanized Northeastern Seaboard of the United States* (Cambridge, Massachusetts: Massachusetts Institute of Technology Press, 1964), p. 9.

10. Johnson, Picard, and Quinn, *Churches and Church Membership*, p. 28.

11. Paraphrased from Neil Morgan, *The California Syndrome*, p. 85.

12. Quoted by Jackie Hyman, "Do O.C. Churches Have Deserted Aisles?" news feature in *The Daily Pilot*, Orange County, 16 October 1977. For a political science perspective, see Karl A. Lamb, *As Orange Goes*, chap. 6, "God, Country, and Enterprise: A Search for the Sacred," in which the author makes the point that the "voice of God is at best a whisper" in Orange County.

13. I have taken the poetic license of inserting "Orange County" in the third line of Armour's "I Loved You, California." Quoted by permission of Richard Armour.

Part Three

PICTURES IN THEIR HEADS: CLASSIFICATION

WE KNOW more about who the churched people in America are, what they believe, what they call themselves, what practices they prefer, and how they are organized than we do about the unchurched. At the very least, we know the labels by which the churched identify themselves or are identified by others. For example, there are about 200 religious bodies in the United States, with individual memberships ranging from as little as 260 persons to memberships as large as 49 million persons. There are undoubtedly more bodies if the independent congregations, unreporting groups, and those not formally organized are included. Most have clearly articulated theologies, books or rules of discipline, elaborated forms of governance, and intimations, at least, of preferred lifestyles. They are, by and large, institutionalized into normative patterns of behavior, which are identifiable and sufficiently discrete that one can differentiate among them.

Not so the unchurched. They have been treated as if, as a residual category—those left after the others have been counted—they were one homogeneous whole. Obviously, logic tells us, this is not the case. Deductively, the unchurched might be expected to consist of four groups: (1) atheists, deists, agnostics, and humanists; (2) once active members of religious organizations who no longer practice their religion; (3) people who have never belonged to a religious organization; and (4) members of non-Christian religious sects or cults.[1] This is inadequate both for meaningful conceptualization or for empirical inquiry. Inductively, working from cases to generalizations, a new understanding can be fashioned.

7. Conceptualizing the Types

It is possible to identify ten different categories of unchurchedness, several with subcategories. This taxonomy or classification is not exhaustive, nor are the types mutually exclusive. Every attempt has been made, however, to create a typology that permits classification of the mass of phenomenological data with maximum discreteness.

The names or labels I have given to each category are my own invention. I have deliberately avoided technical terminology, however common such jargon is valued in some academic circles. In most cases, the names given are self-identifying; that is, meaningful in common, person-in-the-street language. This often means a preference for colloquialisms and slang rather than standard English. The type names are often derived from clues given by the informants themselves, language that they repeat again and again as they describe their status as unchurched people. But, as in any taxonomy, the separate classes or types are social fictions. They exist in conceptual rather than in concrete reality. The anecdotal or illustrative material that accompanies each type is intended to describe clusters of common characteristics. The words quoted are real; the conceptualizations, heuristic fictions.

Each category has two foci. The first is a self-identification of the people interviewed. It describes something about how a person outside the churches perceives oneself as a member of that "outside world," the world of the unchurched. The second focus provides the unchurched person's perceptions of the churches themselves, the "inside world" of which he or she is not a part. When they speak of churches, they talk indiscriminately of institutions *and* people.

Before illustrating, it is helpful to conceptualize, to understand abstractly, each of the types. By so doing, the reader can be brought into the researcher's world and method. Each type has been constructed from a clustering of like or related characteristics, derived from what the unchurched say about themselves and the churches. The analogy of what a cashier does at a supermarket at a checkout counter may help. As each item is rung up on the register, the cashier mentally notes the category of the item as well as its price. The item is "produce," or "meat," or "drugs," "canned goods," or "household," and so forth. The cashier has "typed" each item according to a classification system established by the market for its own purposes or as required by law to determine state or local sales taxes. This is a taxonomy of sorts, and an efficient cashier knows intuitively or by training which item belongs in which category. A conceptual scheme lies behind the classification. When the researcher "codes" or otherwise identifies words, phrases, or sentences used by an informant, he or she does essentially what the cashier does—puts each item into a particular niche or type or category. If the research is quantitative, each item is counted; that is, "rung up on the register." If the inquiry is qualitative, the clustering is done simply to focus attention on the differentiation of types of responses and on the common characteristics of each.

The sequential ordering proceeds alphabetically. It does not imply ranking or response frequencies.

Type 1: The Antiinstitutionalists

This category includes responses of persons who are defectors from the church on the basis of what they perceive to be the church's preoccupation with its own self-maintenance. Such persons reject the organizational structures as inessential or inimical to "true religion." They may object to the political nature of the church, its form of governance, or its leadership. They may find the liturgies too raw (warmly emotional) or too elaborated (objective and cold). They may see in the church's history a scandal, a betrayal of the very faith they believe the church was constituted to communicate. They may fault the church both for its irrelevance to the needs of humankind, or, conversely, for its accommodation with the world or its meddling in secular affairs. Frequently, they object to the church's emphasis on finances, buildings, and property. In common, they perceive a sickness that might be diagnosed "morphological malaise."

A frequent complaint of the antiinstitutionalists is the disunity of the churches. They observe a proliferation of "true believers," each of whom claims exclusive possession of the keys to the kingdom. They view the sectarians, for example, as exemplars of exclusivistic doctrines and practices, and therefore as divisive. But they are scandalized, too, by the more inclusive churches who appear to them to be equally imperialistic in their faith demands. They fault the churches from the church's own scriptures, which holds up the hope that "they all may be one." They ask, "If Christianity is one, why are there so many competing branches?" What they observe as competition, they see manifested in "knifing" or "knocking" one another. Until such factionalism is healed, they argue, the churches cannot expect to claim the allegiance of those who feel they are entitled to unequivocal answers spoken by the churches in a common voice.

Antiinstitutionalists think of themselves as solitary Christians or unaffiliated fellow travelers. By avoiding membership in the institution, they can avoid some of the contamination and thus be "purer." They often describe themselves as able to be "better Christians" outside than in.

Type 2: The Boxed In

To be boxed in is to be cornered, to be enclosed in a compartment, to be put in an impasse. Responses of the unchurched that fit this category are those which describe past experiences in a church or churches as overly confining. Such persons are ones who, for the most part, have once been church members and have left. Inside, their lives were restrained and controlled. They complain of not having had room to move or breathe.

There are several varieties, or subtypes.

The *Constrained* are those who have felt themselves forced or cramped in boxes that are too small. Doctrine or ethics have been so narrow as to smother them. Outside the church, they now feel the fresh air of freedom. The sides of the boxes have crumbled or fallen.

The *Thwarted* are those whose boxed-in-ness has prevented their continuing growth toward maturity. They are often grateful for the aid a church has given them to grow at one or more stages of their development. But now they feel stifled, arrested in the stage of growth they have attained. They particularly resent the tendency of the churches to continue to treat them as children or adolescents. They reject what they perceive to be the church's excessive-emphasis on passivity, quietism, and dependence.

The *Independent* constitute a subclass of the boxed in who are fierce individualists. They view the church, at worst, as a prison; at best, as a straitjacket. Their psychological state is expressed in such phrases as "Don't fence me in," or "Unhand me!" or "Let me go!" They want no external restraints. They will be captive to no one. They have taken charge of their own lives. They want to have the freedom to move in and out of the boxes at will, to go in when the box contains something they want or need at the moment, but to leave when they have been satisfied. The Independent views the church as a box that limits freedom for them to "do my own thing" or to "do it my way."

Type 3: The Burned Out

The Burned Out are those whose stories tell of energies that have been utterly consumed by the church. They have known the inside, and it has depleted their resources, talents, and time. The burn-out phenomenon is gaining attention today in studies of the middle years of marriage and in studies of a period of stagnation in vocational career development. By 1900, the standard English phrase "to burn oneself out" meant "to work too hard and die at the task." The term here is meant to describe a category of withdrawal marked by the "dying of the embers." Among the unchurched, this is expressed in two related ways, as follows.

The *Used* feel that they have been exploited or manipulated. Often they were once church leaders or extremely active participants in church programs and activities. They found themselves unintentionally overly involved, without space or time for respite. Or they sought leadership and accepted too much. In either case, abstinence rather than moderation seemed the best course. The church has used up all they had to give but continued to expect more. They are now "worked out" and weary of the continual demands they feel will be made if they maintain affiliation.

Another type of the Burned Out are the *Light Travelers*. This is an exaggerated consequence of having first felt used; although they brought that use on themselves, they will admit. The baggage that was once needful is no longer needed. These describe previous years when their church involvement was for them desirable and essential—to be a part of what they wanted for their children, to provide a proper example, to keep everyone together ("praying together means staying together"), or to share in the formation of their children's values and beliefs. They do not regret the experience so much as they have now reached a stage in life when such baggage can be considered optional or dispensable. With fewer years of life remaining than before, they want to travel more lightly. "An overnight bag will do. You can't fit the church into that," they say.

Type 4: The Floaters

The Floaters are often those who were never really committed to the church in the first place. They bobbed and drifted on the surface. They never put down anchor in a church community. Their involvement was peripheral. It may have been occasional attendance in the Sunday church school, or periodic participation in the recreational aspects of a youth program, or infrequent participation as spectators at festival services, weddings, funerals, or church bingo or suppers. Their first communion, confirmation, conversion, or baptism was a perfunctory activity, accepted because expected by parents, peers, or spouse. The Floater was never more than a fringe member and is now either completely outside or continues to float from marginal association with one group, one day, to marginal association with another group, tomorrow.

Thus there are both the apathetic and the marginals. The *Apathetic* Floaters lack any deep feelings for or sensitivity toward what the churches stand for, say, or do. That for which the churches stand fails to make any impress on their minds or hearts. They are indifferent to the point of saying, "I couldn't care less." It is a listlessness short of overt hostility. They are insensible to claims or loyalties. They simply take it or leave it on an extremely superficial level.

The *Marginal* Floaters are those whose association with churches have been so superficial that drifting from place to place without ever establishing strong ties has become habitual. They may fear the demands of responsibility to others or to programs. They never opt in sufficiently to own for themselves what the church teaches. When inside, they are really on the outside. Lacking attachments, they move at ease from belief to belief and from group to group. Perhaps with the same fears as the Boxed Ins, they play it "loose and thin." Essentially, they cop out, in the sense of withholding commitments, involvements, or meaningful ties.

Type 5: The Hedonists

The Hedonists find their fulfillment of life's purpose in momentary pleasures or a succession of pleasure-satisfying activities. Almost universally, they are "happy hedonists," "happy" because they exude complete satisfaction over what they are enjoying. If there was an unconscious or hidden unhappiness, it was not evident in my interviews with them. Their hedonism was most often manifested in their idolization of leisure pursuits. Obviously, large and increasing numbers of Americans, inside and outside the churches, enjoy unscheduled hours of nonwork or free time. Some bear longer or shorter periods of enforced leisure. But the leisure-lovers in my sample were compulsively hedonistic. Theirs was an explicit or implicit avowal that one's free time is the time when life for them was fulfilling. It constituted life's greatest good and goal. Obligations of church membership were consequently seen as intrusions on the time they can more profitably spend on instant gratification, as participants or spectators of those things that "turn one on."

They seldom wax philosophical about what their preferred mode of existence means. Unlike utilitarian hedonists who might maintain that pleasure is the chief good of the community, they simply claim that good for themselves as individuals or families and utilize nonwork time as fully as possible for sentient pleasure. As the intensity and breadth of hedonistic claims on the person grows, the churches are viewed as poor competitors. Either "the church doesn't want me to have a good time," or "compared to the other excitements I can find or buy, the church can't compete."

Type 6: The Locked Out

The Locked Out are the opposite of the Boxed In. To be locked out is to be prevented from entering, to be barred from getting in, to be thought of as "unauthorized" without benefit of a key. Unchurched people often feel that the churches have closed their doors against them, via formal excommunication, slight, disregard, or discrimination, overt or covert. For various reasons, they believe that the churches do not want them inside. Although some may have locked themselves out, the effect is the same. There are three subtypes, as follows.

The *Rejected* often express deep hurt that their desire for full communion and fellowship has been limited. Because of divorce or disapproved birth control practices, for example, some have had the sacraments withheld from them. Others are locked out because of persistent disobedience of a church's moral codes. Some perceive themselves as "not good enough" as they match their behavior against expectations of holiness or perfection.

A second subtype consists of the *Neglected*. Many of the poor, the ethnic minorities, and the aging feel locked out less because of overt actions by the churches than because of simple neglect of them and their needs. They feel slighted, overlooked, and disregarded by the churches, their members, and their clerical leaders. They feel forgotten and lost.

The *Discriminated* differ from the Neglected and the Rejected in that they can cite specific overt acts of prejudice against them. They tend to be the most hostile of the Locked Out. They have not been simply overlooked, they have been looked at and deliberately excluded. They often perceive the churches as consciously maintaining closed memberships according to status or class. They thus see the churches as participating in and maintaining the class structures of their communities, effectively barring those who are different from the majority. They believe that persons "of their kind" are not wanted, often frozen out, snubbed, or openly excluded.

Type 7: The Nomads

The Nomads are the wanderers in the American society, rovers with no fixed abode. They are incessantly on the move and seldom stay in one place long enough to call it home. Some, as a consequence of upward occupational mobility, are periodically uprooted and transferred from place to place. Others, in order to find employment or a better life, move to the cities or the open places. In either case, ties with community are severed. They have learned to expect this to continue. No community will ever be for them more than temporary. They become casual in their relationships and develop loose, transitory, nonbinding patterns of associations with others. Some of the Nomads resemble the Burned-Outs who "travel lightly" and leave excess baggage behind, or the Floaters who drift, but they differ in that they know from experience that the new territory will be another waystation on the road to someplace else.

Among the Nomads are former churched folks who now feel themselves in virtual exile, a diaspora from the homeland. They can find no church in the new community with any semblance of or continuity with their past church affiliation. They test the waters of the churches in the new community but feel out of place in them all. The nearest church of their old communion may be 50 or more miles away. Thus, at a deep level they feel they are strangers to the religious communities they find along their migratory trail. They often speak of their religious preference as, say, Lutheran, Presbyterian, or Episcopalian, but have long since severed meaningful relationships with such bodies, because they are not there. They are reluctantly unchurched and say they would reestablish relationships if their former denominations had representation in their new communities. Their unchurchedness is a function of their nomadism and their minority religious preferences.

Type 8: The Pilgrims

The Pilgrims are those unchurched who describe their religious beliefs as in the process of formation. Unlike the Nomads, who may be purposeless rovers, they are on an ideological pilgrimage, searching for satisfying meanings and values. They fear premature closure. Like Erik Erikson's adolescents, they have declared moratoria on specific life philosophies. Some, in college years, for example, want to survey "all the options" before commitment. Others, long removed from adolescence, are still on their journeys and consider themselves open to new evidence. They tend to "tolerate" the opinions of others, including those with Christian convictions, with sympathy, understanding, and curiosity. They also expect to be tolerated by others for their own inchoate or imperfectly formed beliefs. They abjure designation as *secularists, humanists,* or *agnostics* as implying closed positions antithetical to the Christian faith. They are locked into no position but are open to all. Their central characteristic is tentativeness—a provisional stance toward final or ultimate truth.

Type 9: The Publicans

The Publicans constitute by far the largest group of the unchurched. They perceive the churches to be primarily populated by Pharisees. They call those within the churches hypocrites, phonies, fakers, and persons living double lives, or to use Ellul's image again, those whose lives and acts are just like the Publicans' own, not corresponding in the least to what the churched are saying. This dissonance becomes, for those outside looking in, a scandal. Their own self-image may be either that expressed by the confession "God be merciful to me, a sinner," or by the judgment "I thank God that I am not like them." They perceive a discrepancy between profession and performance among the members of the churches. Of themselves, they say in effect, "If we cannot live up to expectations, we prefer to stay on the outside. There are already too many half-hearted on the inside." Variations on this theme are almost universal among the unchurched.

Type 10: *The True Unbelievers*

The True Unbelievers may be subdivided into such categories as *Atheists–Agnostics, Deists–Rationalists,* and *Humanists–Secularists.* Except for the latter sub class, there were few authentic unbelievers in my sample. This is consistent with opinion polls that count more than 95 percent of all Americans as holding a belief in God. While many of my informants were quite vague or inarticulate about what that belief implied or its salience for their lives, a small number of them owned up to being True Unbelievers. Yet, for the few, the categories are essential to complete the taxonomy.

The designation *Agnostics–Atheists* is conceptualized according to its common meaning—those who deny the existence of any ultimate reality (as God) or hold that such reality is unknown or unknowable.

The *Deists–Rationalists* comprise those whose theology, whether formally or informally articulated, is based on human reason rather than on revelation.

The *Humanists–Secularists* are those who embrace worldliness, in the sense that the dignity or worth of people lies in their capacity for self-realization through reason, without benefit of supernatural revelation, of clergy, or of church. It is to be expected that frequently this category overlaps with that of the Hedonists. The religious ideas that the churches proclaim are meaningless to them. A composite of them seems to be saying, "I don't think religiously. God-talk is superfluous." However, their commitments to justice and love may parallel that of the Christian church member.

As in any classificatory scheme, there are residuals in this taxonomy. Analysis of the tapes reveals many who either cannot or will not give reasons for their rejection of church membership. When asked why they

are not church members, they respond, "I just don't know." This may
be deliberate or unconscious evasion. But it may represent a type of its
own.

This discussion of classification should not create the impression that
persons are types.[2] People are neither statistical ciphers nor abstract
entities. Type labels comprehend a cluster of pictures that unchurched
people draw. Thus, the clustered *responses* of people form our heuristic
categories. Single autobiographical portrayals, as in the cases of Mary
Lou, Emily, or Carlos (Chapter 2), do not necessarily fit single types.
Several types may be drawn from individual accounts. The pictures they
draw of themselves and the churches they have known may take on
different colors in the oral unfolding of their life experiences. At different stages, the accounts may change and often do. That this should
happen is normal and consistent with the essential ambiguity of human
nature and the changing circumstances of life development.

The excerpts from stories that make up the categories are often
unfinished. One cannot predict what the endings may be. In-depth
probings might uncover hidden stories untold in single interviews that
would "explain" a person's alienation more fully or differently than
appears on the surface and would provide alternative scenarios of the
future. Followup interviews over extended periods of time, not feasible
in this project, would likely uncover more than a person felt free to relate
in a single conversation. Further, remembered experiences from the past
cannot be predictive of the future. Just as external circumstances and
internal response have combined to cause certain kinds of past and
present behavior, so myriad, new or changing circumstances of life and
environment—together with the intervention of others—may shape
new futures neither intended nor expected. We cannot exclude the
possibility that the unchurched I met may move back in from the
outside; some may have already done so. As Carlos has put it, "Maybe
something happen!"

From Conceptualization to Anecdotal Documentation

Understanding the enigma of the unchurched more fully requires
illustrating the types with anecdotal detail. Actually, the typology de-
rives from the stories themselves. The material in the next three chapters has been culled from the 165 actual interviews. No longer do I
invent "social fictions." Rather, I now quote the words and phrases that

comprise the real situation of the unchurched. Here they speak for themselves.

Obviously, not everything everyone said can or should be reported. Some of what I heard was insignificant, redundant, or only peripherally related to this exploratory study. This was to be expected in unstructured interviews. The unchurched often told me more than I needed to know. Not all people use language as colorful or as expressive as others. In selecting illustrative materials for this reporting, I have chosen to include expressions that seem best to unveil the phenomenological field—words, phrases, and sentences that convey both thoughts and emotions. The sentences people speak are not always grammatical. Local colloquialisms and slang, occasionally vulgarities, have been retained. If articulation means an expression via language of how one thinks or feels, all the responses I have chosen are articulate. They communicate to the reader and listener who the unchurched person is and what it is he or she is sharing. The uneducated often express themselves as well as those with years of schooling.

The anecdotal information in a typical interview in an informant's living room flowed freely from an initial question: "Think back, please, as far as you can about your first experience in a church. Tell me about it." Most respondents would then begin to reconstruct and share a "religious autobiography." I listened, asking other questions, such as "Tell me more about that—how did you feel when . . . ?" or "And what sort of thing happened next?" If the flow stopped, I sometimes waited, or interjected casual conversational banter until the respondent was able to continue. In nondirective fashion, I often fed back what I felt the person was saying about himself or herself to test the accuracy of my hearing. Occasionally, I became explicitly directive and probed to help the person focus the conversation. Not infrequently, a person would tell a story of progressive disenchantment with the church that lasted several hours with few interruptions on my part at all. I did not correct contradictions or ambiguities but often tried to help the informant do this for him- or herself. The large majority felt comfortable in the situation, more or less oblivious to the tape recorder, and seemed anxious to share information and feelings that they told me they had not expressed out loud before. I thanked all for their participation. They thanked me for listening. Many of them expressed the desire to read this report.

I have indicated that the ethos of the community of residence may be linked to what was said or the way feelings were expressed. This should become apparent in the conversational excerpts that follow in the next three chapters. The stories have been grouped alphabetically according to types. The sequence implies neither a hierarchy of frequencies nor necessary clusters of logical relationships.

NOTES

1. John Runda, "A Preliminary Research Proposal to Identify and Classify the Unchurched in Six Rural Counties," prepared for the Glenmary Research Center, Washington, D.C., 1971, p. 12.
2. It may be, as some have argued, that sociological literature is strewn with the debris of discarded typologies. Nonetheless, typologies, in the "ideal-typical" tradition of Max Weber and others, are often aids in conceptualizing, an indispensible first step in operationalizing ideas for empirical research. All typologies, this one included, are meant to be disposable; they have no eternal sanctity.

8. The Antiinstitutionalists, Boxed In, and Burned Out

This chapter includes excerpts of stories told by the unchurched, classified in three types: the Antiinstitutionalists, the Boxed In, and the Burned Out.

Antiinstitutionalism is not a new phenomenon in religious history. From the time of the establishment of the imperial state church under Constantine in the fourth century, there have been outbreaks of anticlericalism that, especially in Roman Catholic countries, have challenged the exercise by the clergy of influence extending beyond what was deemed their proper sphere. The opprobrium "churchianity," in contrast to "Christianity," has been standard English in the United States for decades. Even within religious movements in America, revivalism and other brands of fundamentalist religion have appealed for personal conversion, often implicitly or explicitly railing against the established churches' claim to sole possession of the keys to the kingdom. It is not surprising, then, that the stories of the unchurched are punctuated with vivid language describing rejection of the power and authority of the institutional church. This may also have some connection with the widespread reaction against all institutions of "the Establishment" common in the counterculture rhetoric of the 1960s. While the charges may be a latent theme in the American culture and religion, certainly preceding the excessive antiinstitutionalism of the last decade, their persistence and frequency may constitute evidence that the unconventional mores of counterculture youths have infused parts of the society never formally identified with "the Movement." In fact, although six in ten Americans nationally, according to a Gallup poll in 1978, express higher confidence in organized religion than they do in big business, Congress, the schools

and other American political institutions, the churches are widely criti-
cized as having lost "the real spiritual part of religion" and for being "too
concerned with organizational as opposed to theological or spiritual
issues." A phenomenal proportion—86 percent of the unchurched and
76 percent of the churched—agree that "an individual should arrive at
his or her own religious beliefs independent of any churches or synagogues."[1]

The Boxed In give stories that illustrate Gallup's finding that 37
percent of the unchurched identify with the statement, "Teachings
about beliefs were too narrow" and that 28 percent identify with the
statement, "Moral teachings were too narrow." For many, of course, this
is simply an expression of a human reluctance to accept uncritically the
external demands of others. We see here this natural proclivity as it
applies to the faith and ethical demands of the churches. Where the
spirit of individualism is high, as in Central Appalachia, on the West
Coast, and in New England, the rejection of the church on this basis
is especially vocal. The existential force of this argument is revealed in
the autobiographical sketches that follow.

The Burned Out were found everywhere, but particularly in places
like Sarasota, Marion, and Orange counties, which attract the highly
mobile in the American society. The experience of being burned out,
for the most part, appears to occur in the middle and later years of life
after long or intense previous involvement in the church. Some, not
surprisingly, trace the burn-out to enforced "overexposure" to church in
childhood and early adolescence. It may be related to other experiential
burn-outs, like the stagnation that oftentimes occurs in marriages or
jobs, taking the form of withdrawal or marked change in lifestyles.

Type 1: The Antiinstitutionalists

No, I don't think that membership means I'm a better Christian. I feel that
we live perfectly good, Christian lives as it is, and I think that we do good and
I don't think we have to be a member of the church.

This feeling, expressed by an active community leader in a Penobscot
(Maine) river town, is legion among the unchurched everywhere I went.
Almost the same words were used by a retired policeman in Huntington
Beach, California, "I don't feel a person has to go to church to live a
Christian life. I'm not against church. Just that I don't feel that I have

to go to church to be a Christian." A community action worker in Polk County, Oregon, held a similar judgment, "I think churches are pretty much social structures. I think many of them end up being social institutions instead of religious institutions." For him, his religion could better be expressed outside the church. An executive of a southern California United Way organization told of her long, previous leadership and involvement in national church agencies. Now she is disillusioned.

> I think the churches have gotten like a lot of parts of society. They have to worry so much about paying the rent that they have forgotten the good news. They forget the evangelized message. They forget love. I find some of the clergy are very wonderful people, but a lot of them have to seek out the almighty dollar so much . . . that [they] are robbing the people of the great heritage of the church. . . . The leaders are afraid of theology.

Reference to the "almighty dollar" is illustrative of Gallup's finding that 32 percent of the unchurched fault the church for its "too much concern for money."[2]

Parts of the autobiography of Mary Lou, reproduced in full in Chapter 2, describe her rejection of an institution in favor of a privatized, personal faith. For her, the church had ceased to be a "helping, understanding or loving" representation of the God she found "so beautiful."

The institution's leadership often stands in the way, according to a number of the unchurched. In West Virginia, a miner told me about the preacher next door. Mirroring the people's suspicion of outsiders, he said, "for all we know, he come out of a prison some place. They send him in here and say, 'This is your pastor.' "

> They send out there some place and get somebody and they ship him in here for six months or a year. They ship him back out, and we don't even know where he goes or what happens to him. I don't want none of it. . . . Back when I used to go to church, the man that was the pastor of that church, he worked. But the pastors now, they won't even pick up a broom and sweep. Yet they want a big salary. They set around and not do anything. They don't do nothing except preach. They get up and preach and the next thing they start in on—want more money, more money, even though they are getting all the money. That preacher next door, he don't do one thing. All he does is walk around and holler for something. . . . I told him, "Now, preacher, you stay over there, and I'll stay over here. You tend yours, and I'll tend to mine. If anybody gets hurt, it's going to be you, it ain't going to be me."

In a similar vein, an Oregonian said he was still "partial to the Lutheran church," although he didn't go any more. "The thing that disenchants me is the pastor involved," he said.

Throughout most of my life, the pastors have pretty much impressed me by their need for money in order to run their organization. I can understand their need to have some monetary funds to run their organization, but I don't believe that a pastor has to get on us most Sundays and stress the need for money all the time. This is getting away from the spiritual side of things and becoming more and more into the materialistic world. I don't think the church should do that.

Former church members from European state churches and from South America expressed their inability to adjust to the American voluntary system of church support. (State church systems are, of course, supported by taxation.) A Swedish immigrant to southern California was typical, "Back home, there was no pressure on you as far as raising money, money, money. 'Til I came to this country. That is all it is here. Raise money for this, raise money for that, need this, need that." A Lutheran from Germany said, "It really shocked me to go to church here and you have to pay to be told about the Bible. You even have to pay before you get the merchandise."

Some former parishioners have had good, even intimate relationships with a local minister. Then, when the ties with one leader are severed, the church ties are also lost. "I would probably be in the Christian church now had it not been they fired the best man I ever knew," one Orange County resident told me. "We hunted and fished together, and the first thing you know half the faction didn't like him and out he went! Well, that made me so mad, burned me up. I didn't join that church, and that is the only reason I didn't." Or there was the complaint that parishioner-minister ties never developed. "They have a habit of only keeping them [the pastors] until they have built up the church. Then, they move them on and bring someone else in. . . . They haven't kept a minister long enough for you to get acquainted." In a coastal Maine town, the unchurched complained that the parishes were small, had to be "pastored" by seminarians from Bangor who "never quite settled in," and left the local churches bereft of any continuous leadership. "Every time a minister comes, he uses us as a stepping stone for something else."

Part of the problem in attracting and keeping ministerial leadership in the smaller community was the small parish's inadequate financial base to meet ministerial costs, but the people saw the demands of the pastors too high. "The ministers always want too much," an Isleboro, Maine, woman put it. "They want a fully equipped parsonage, a good salary, heat, and utilities. They want car allowances and to be repaid for every time they make a visit to the hospital and pay a ferry fare when they cross over to the mainland." She concluded, "I think that the ministers have lost their religion, and that may be the reason there is not much religion left on the island." Isleboro's former four churches, one dating back to 1835, have shrunk to one, with only 30 members. More than 90 percent of the islanders belong to no church.

It was the same in the smaller communities in Oregon and Alabama. Unlike the West Virginia miner, however, who wanted a pastor willing to "pick up a broom and sweep," many were turned off by the churches whose ministers were only "part-time preachers." "They have no education, get hooked on strange doctrines, and murder the King's English. They simply have nothing to say that makes any sense to the guy who thinks."

A systems analyst for a large corporation in Huntington Beach, California, faulted the institutional church for its preoccupation with the future—heaven and hell. "The more remote a problem is from your immediate locale, your immediate time, your immediate situation, the less percentage of your time you spend thinking about it." The churches he knew were too remote from his needs—"making a living, inflation, keeping the kids healthy, getting them educated." He saw the churches so buried both in the past ("the beginnings and history of Christianity") and in the future ("too much concern for the hereafter") that "the translation of those teachings to day-to-day life is left to the individual to develop by accident. The pressures that we have to deal with right now are not being addressed at all. They [the churches] are giving answers to questions people aren't asking."

The irrelevance of the church as an institution to immediate needs and issues was expressed by a young Alabama plant manager. He recalled his youth in the culture of the "flower children" when the churches simply didn't provide "what I needed at the time." Later as a Navy officer in Vietnam, "I saw my buddies blown up by twelve-, thirteen-, and fourteen-year-old kids. I lost a little bit of my faith. Organized religion just didn't set well with me." Now, he went on,

I see the church as not much different from government—it's overpowering! Local people don't really have a voice in what happens to their money. They tend to perpetuate the system. . . . They just build buildings, take our money away from local needs. The cathedrals and the foreign missionaries are nice, but the church has gotten to be a kind of power broker. That is not religion. That is not what a church organization is for.

In all six counties, I found that the unchurched made a distinction between *joining* a church and *going* to church. In places dominated by conversionist and independent Baptist forms of religion, people would recall numerous conversions, "being born again," with several baptisms to seal the experience, but they never found their way into membership in a local parish. In New England, several told me that it was simply "not fashionable" to belong to a church anymore. Membership was seen as a denial of "Yankee tolerance." In Florida, in the "start-over" city of Sarasota, one retiree said he went to church "once in a while." He said that he was "no longer on the rolls of the church up north—they knowed I was moving and wouldn't be coming back. They took me off." Now, he saw no point in joining, "It doesn't make any difference if you join or if you go. I could never say, 'That church is mine.' If a person asked me to join, I'd say no. Why should I lie about it? It doesn't matter whether I belong or not."

The church as institution is, as one might expect, faulted both for its conservatism and its liberalism.[3] A college youth in California thought that "the hierarchy could be taking stronger stands on current events." It should be helping "to set up a much more human, just and equitable world. The church should be taking the lead." Another former Roman Catholic reiterated the same point: "The church hasn't led the way in breaking down barriers—socioeconomic, racial, national, ethnic. I don't feel they have led the way at all. It's the church in our society that's sick." But, a professional man in the same community, once active and now on the outside, dropped out because his Methodist congregation was affiliated with the National Council of Churches, "supporting causes like Angela Davis and other political philosophies." He wants the church to go back to the "old religion and stick to the Bible." He admitted to a kind of "void in my life," but that was preferable to belonging to a church that was "mixed up with the National Council." A farmer on Lower Salt Creek Road, outside Dallas, Oregon, echoed this: "There is no separation between the church and the world any-more." Holding his arms high above his head, he said, "The church ought to represent something up here." Then, shifting his arms to the ground, he said, "The world ought to be something down here. There ought to be a difference, and there isn't." If the church is the same as the world, "you might just as well stay in the world."

Some of the Antiinstitutionalists focus on the scandal of a divided Christendom. They had heard the claim that "the churches are one in Christ," but they fail to see the unity and are turned off by Christianity's competing denominations and sects.

In the larger, metropolitan counties, the unchurched see an array of churches representing the major Christian denominations. They also are acquainted with local independent tabernacles and chapels that vied with the standard churches for members. In Polk County, Oregon, they were scandalized by the divisions within historic Anabaptism. In the Appalachian counties, the more bizarre of the Pentecostal sects attracted the most attention and further alienated the unchurched. In Waldo County, Maine, denomination made little difference to most. I was told, for example, that few of the members of the rural United Church of Christ parishes knew that their former Congregational affiliation was no longer in force. The problem, from the vantage point of the unchurched, was that each group claimed to be the true believers. They were confused that there could be so many "keys to the kingdom" and that each of the marketers of the keys seemed to be "selling the only key that fit."

"If every church could get together and be one big, happy place instead of always knocking the other one," an elderly, former Freewill Baptist woman in Winfield, Alabama told me, "that would be fine. When I was saved," she recollected,

> I told the preacher that didn't mean I was going to join his church. I did for a while, but then sort of drifted away, what with my husband Jack sick, and having to work two jobs. But then they starts pushin' me. "You got to come here" or "You got to go there." I'm a-thinkin' now about the Catholics. The priest's not pushing. . . . I just wish they weren't so many against the other's church.

Also in Marion County, a nonpracticing Catholic was of the same mind: "This church teaches this way and that church that way. Each says, 'This is the way it should be.' Who is to say this is the only way it should be? All [the Protestants] tell you about the differences in their teachings. I think they all follow the same guidelines. A lot of it is just in interpretation. Which interpretation do you decide to like?"

The scandal is particularly observed by immigrants from Europe. Sarah Erdahl noticed the difference when she emigrated to the United States ten years ago. She was married in the Lutheran Church in Norway, but when she came to Denver, then to Newport, California, she said,

All the different churches turned me off. Which one is right? Which one is wrong? My mother-in-law tells me her church [the Church of Occult Science] is the best. Her sister preaches at me all the time, "If you're not a Catholic, you're going to hell." Either they are all right, or none of them is right, or there's a right one somewhere in between. How do you know? I just don't know. . . . If there were a state church here, I'd probably go. At least I'd know. Right now all I see is a big race, "Mine is bigger or better than yours." I just don't go for that stuff.

On board a small yacht tied up at the Nokomis Marina in Florida, Charles Rebert, a retired Ford Motor Company executive from Detroit, philosophized for several hours about his view of religion. Luther, he said, had "messed up what Constantine had started—one holy Catholic Church. It's all gone wacky."

I'm saying that there's got to be a new direction. The churches have to get together. Everybody around here instead of getting together is building, building, building, a new little church on every corner. They have fractioned themselves off and gotten into little groups. If you love me, I'll love you, and the hell with everybody else. I'm almost inclined to believe that in Sarasota we have more churches than we have Christians.

This theme among metropolitan people was expressed this way: "There are too many different churches." "They do right, the others do wrong—that shouldn't be." "I think all the churches are for one thing —what I can't understand is the discontent." "We all believe in God, why the differences?" In Appalachia, where sectarianism is rampant, the chorus was more strident:

Either believe or you are lost. They all tell you the same. Theirs is the right way.

Even the little churches can't agree among themselves—one hillbilly can't agree with the next and the first thing you know they start a new church.

Where do they get the idea they are right and everybody else is wrong? Does one church have a corner on the truth?

This is spite-church country here, sir. People is always gettin' mad. Uncle 'gainst brother, grandpa 'gainst wife. All 'gainst the preacher. Disgustin.'

The Methodists just fired their preacher, half the Baptists left with theirs. It's all bitterness, that's all.

Always fussing and feuding, backbiting with each other.

For a few, the institutional church's sickness lay in its failure to be an effective institution. "The church," said one Oregon entrepreneur, "has the most wonderful product in the world. It just doesn't know how to present it. If you're reaching only 50 percent of your market, something's wrong with your communication. If I presented my product that poorly, I'd be out of business tomorrow."

Type 2: The Boxed In

The feeling that churches box people in was expressed in three ways —by those who felt constrained, or thwarted, or prevented from full freedom and independence by the churches they had known.

The *Constrained* had their exemplar in a newspaper publisher on the West Coast who had left the Catholic church when he moved to his present community sixteen years before. What he said of himself he claimed was true for many Westerners who shared the area's frontier spirit. He illustrated his situation by drawing boxes on newsprint. He labeled each with the organizational title of what he called the town's "in groups"—the Rotary Club, the Roman Catholic Church, the Fire Department, and so forth. Outside all the boxes, he marked a heavy, black dot. "That's me," he said. "I am on the outside. I go in when I need the ingroup for my personal satisfactions and for the realization of my own independent drives. But," he emphasized, "I remain flexible, mobile, fluid by staying outside. Then I am not responsible for them, nor they for me. I am on the outside. I make my own decisions. Boxes constrain me, even, maybe especially, the churches."

Others among the Constrained, especially some former practicing Catholics, recalled the boxed-in feeling of early parochial education. They often spoke of the fear of the teaching sisters, "frustrated old nuns" who frightened them, slapped the kids when they didn't behave (as in the Mary Lou autobiography), or "made you wear hot corduroy pants with a long-sleeved gray shirt," as another put it. "One nun," a bitter youth in Winfield, Alabama, remembered from parochial school years in Chicago, "comes up behind me, grabs my ears, and says, 'You stupid idiot!' I don't know what for. I'm just staring at the crucifix on the altar and all this stuff. That really turned me off." "You had to go to confirmation every Saturday and memorize questions and answers backward and forward," said an Orange County resident, "I *had* to do it. I dropped out right after confirmation and never went back again."

But it was not only former Catholics who spoke this way.[4] A California woman recalled her upbringing in a Norwegian Lutheran home in Minnesota. "I never did feel comfortable in church," she remembered. "Maybe it was because I had to go to church. If I didn't, I didn't get to go to the show in the afternoon. I resented that. Church was the punishment I had to endure to have a good time." Another described his experience of conversion at age twenty in a Baptist Church:

> It was a Billy Graham type of thing. The call came to come forward, and I got kind of a weird feeling all over. I found myself getting up, then kneeling down, really emotionally involved, I guess. Then, when I got up there, I said to myself, "My God, what am I doing here?" First, I felt pretty good. Then, it was kind of frightening and it bothered me. I continued going to church for two or three months afterward. Then, I stopped. . . . I felt I had really been exploited.

A similar boxed-in feeling was expressed by Leila Palmer, a young mother in West Virginia, who recalled her adolescent experience in the Church of God in Texas:

> We was all dressed up in blue jeans, kind of grubbylike, sitting on the floor. Except the minister. He was dressed very nicely and was standing on the platform. He told us all how wrong we was. I thought, "Who is this guy making judgments up there?" Then he claps his hands and everybody is singing and their hands are waving in the air. They all start praying, "O Jesus, come down on us. We are sinners." Then they start dancing. . . . After it was all over, the man came up to me. He said, "You're new here. You have got a problem. A situation you don't know how to handle. You just keep coming up here, and you're going to find the answer you need." I thought this guy is seeing inside my brain. I didn't want to get up and dance like that to find my problem. I thought this was the craziest church I had ever seen. That turned me off an awful lot. I left the church and the town. And I ain't never been back to either!

Some of the unchurched said that the teachings of the more conservative churches were too narrow. "Just negative in their teachings," said a schoolteacher in Nellis, West Virginia. "You can't get a high school ring, because the church doesn't believe in wearing jewelry. They frown on drinking. It's all 'Don't do this, don't do that.' " Said Clarence Porter, a construction worker in Marion County, Alabama, "You wouldn't believe what some of the people around here believe in. Ain't supposed to touch beer and whiskey, the preachers say. If you touch it, you are sinning and you're going to hell. . . . The people who do, they won't go to church because the preacher set up there and say it is wrong and they are not supposed to do it." Mrs. Porter agreed, "They can't have their cake and eat it too."

A criticism of the Catholic religion had the same focus. The rules were too constraining. "You have to do what I say before the child is baptized," was a non-Catholic spouse's impression of a recent conversation with his wife's priest. "If you don't, she will not be baptized."

"You have to do what I say and come to mass every Sunday. You have to come for the holy days. You have to do this and that. If you don't, I'm going to get mad at you and make you feel bad about it." I didn't like his attitude and I wasn't going to play along. He made me very angry, like I said—when somebody says you have to do it my way and no other, I get mad. Nuts with that!

His wife was angry, too. "Last time Father Riley came here," she said, "I suggested he turn around and leave. He was upset about it, said it was the first time he had ever been thrown out of someone's house. I didn't throw him out. I just didn't let him in." I asked how she felt about it now. "It doesn't bother me in the least," she answered.

I just don't worry about it. If I want to go to mass, I can. If I don't, I won't. I don't feel like I have to. I think all those years of knowing that I had to go for no other reason than the fact that the church said I had to go or I was in a state of sin. I don't buy that. . . . I don't know when the last time was that I went to confession. It makes no difference to me at all.

The anger of those who felt unnecessarily constrained was epitomized by John Staughton, a former Methodist from Tuscaloosa, now in Madison, West Virginia: "I don't want anybody telling me that if I don't believe this and believe that and believe this way and that way I'm going to hell. I think they are fools. I don't think anybody can say that."

The *Thwarted* Boxed Ins are often found where the human potential, personal growth movement has had its influence. An exminister in southern California, for example, recalled "chafing under the fact that I couldn't go to baseball games on Sunday night" in his Scandinavian pietistic home town back in Nebraska. "But I used to sneak away anyway and go." After he was ordained, he sought out a "call" at a church in Reno, Nevada.

I built up the Sunday School, tripled the membership, got the place on a good financial footing. Things were happening there. We were doing things. But, it wasn't enough. My consciousness had changed. I chose not to remain in the church any more, not because I was down on it. My needs and directions were not the same as the church's.

He went on to describe six weeks he spent at the Esalen Institute, at Big Sur, just before his decision to leave the ministry.

I became quite involved. This is a funny thing. I want you to hear this out. I got interested in Eastern mysticism, took some psychedelic drugs, did some inner space kinds of exploring. Lots of things began to happen. I wanted to know me. . . .
I couldn't talk to the bishop or church people. There were other people outside the church who were much more open. People in the church, well I got a lot of judgment . . . in terms of what I was doing. The environment wasn't accepting at all. So I went to outside people, outside of the church. And I found much more acceptance, much more affirmation of me as a human being. . . . When I stepped outside of the church, I learned to resolve [a lot of things]. I found I cannot accept responsibility for anybody in this world except me.
The church perpetuates irresponsibility, dependence, a reliance on the authority of others. And I don't see that as helpful. It wasn't helpful for me in terms of my growth as a person. I feel that I'm a much more spiritual person now. . . . My consciousness has changed. The need for the institutional church, for the church's orthodoxy, has no meaning, no meaning at all.
There was something about the shelter of the organization that I got security out of. They said, "If you fall on your ass, they'll pick me up," the Ma Bell sort of thing. . . . But now I have to become self-sufficient. I don't know what is going to come. But, for me—and I'm not talking about anybody else, they can be OK —I had to get out of the box.

A doctoral candidate at the University of California, Irvine, was moving in a similar direction, a direction that had already left the church behind.

There is a way of redemption that can happen if we get out of our cubicles and get out of our narrow visions . . . in free movements apart from pietism and apart from dogma, in the deep recesses of the spirit, relating to other people as an emotional service—loving, humanizing. That would be a pretty vital church. But I don't see it. . . . And if I can't find it out there, I guess the only other way is just to turn inward to inner space. So I say, "Don't infringe too much on my turf." I can't get locked in to the traditional, historic culture out there any more, where a person is kept within certain traces, or certain guidelines, or certain tracks. We throw out the tracks out here and create our own.

A student in a California community college had just read Sheldon B. Kopp's *If You Meet the Buddha on the Road, Kill Him.*[5] She told me it had legitimated her own lifestyle, "There is nothing outside the person that is important. When we find it, in the church, for example, kill it. The things outside prevent us from realizing the potential that is within." A young sculptor at San Juan Capistrano said that he had to leave the church and enter a commune to "find what is real, caring about the person that isn't so strong, finding brothers." A public school teacher in Anaheim looked back on his churched past,

> It was something I needed along the way. It was a stepping stone for me.
> . . . Relatively speaking, I'm now more of a whole person, a mature person. Now, I don't want to stop growing. I say to the people at church, "You do your thing, let me do mine," because I think I know where I'm going.

He had found freedom beyond the boxed-in-ness of a church in which his growth, he felt, had been arrested, thwarted.

The extent of new religions, growth potential, and spiritual movements is not known, although Gallup has projected a total of 10 million devotees of yoga, Transcendental Meditation, and Eastern religions.[6] One guide[7] lists 800 "spiritual communities" in California, 300 of them in the San Francisco area alone. Some of the community members may, of course, retain more conventional church ties, but the West has consistently shown less commitment to conventional religion than other regions.

The fierce individualism of the *Independent* is sometimes the product of a painful need for survival. The wife of an alcoholic found in Alanon the surrogate for what she couldn't find in her church. "I am now a basically strong person. I can take anything and bounce back. I am very independent, outgoing, say what I think. I don't have time to go to church. I don't feel that is important." In Boone County, in the heart of the coal mining country, a school administrator, a West Virginia native, talked about how,

> Nobody will push me around. You see, I'm kind of rebellious in that I'm not really a follower. I don't march to a different drummer or hear a different beat.

I just am a leader. It's a trait of my family. . . . I had a person from one of the churches here to talk to me. He's welcome in my home, but when he came I told him that the time may come when I will decide to become a member of the church. That may be today or tonight. But I'm going to do it on my own. Nobody is going to pressure me into it. I am a pretty independent guy. I am responsible for my own decisions and nobody else can make them for me.

"No priest, no church is going to possess me," an Oregonian said, in language that was typical of the state's "Don't fence me in" mentality. "The church isn't going to tell me how to vote, how many children I should have. That doesn't cut any ice with me, even if they quote the Pope in Rome. No institution is going to control me, even the church." Another, a Polk County farmer, put his "independentism" this way: "I don't have anything against the church. A certain amount of people need that kind of life. They need to believe, I guess. To each his own. I'm not opposed to any of that. Great, as long as they don't shove it down my throat, they can do whatever they want." A suburban house-wife in West Salem, Oregon, told me, "I would be repelled by anyone who said, 'Bow down' or 'Kneel' or 'Come forward.' That's phony . . . I always like to feel free to do what the spirit moves. . . . I don't want to be boxed in or on a routine or whatever. Not that I can't stand discipline. That's OK. Just give me some space. I'm funny, I don't want to have anybody give me the load and have to carry it. I'm really frightened with that." When asked to describe a church that wouldn't box in her independent spirit, one respondent expressed her preference for "a fairly large church, where I could remain anonymous, if I felt like it. If I care to become very involved, that is all right. If I don't, then that is probably all right too. I would resent the pressure that says, 'Why aren't you involved?' or 'Why aren't you like the rest of us?' I know I am not like the rest of them at all. I am like myself only—period!"

A dock worker in Belfast, Maine, was openly hostile:

Well, I'll tell you. I have been down to the Pentecost. I have been over to the Baptist. I have gone to the Methodist back along. I have been to churches up that way, and the guy came down and dragged me up front. I told him, "When I get ready, I can walk up on my own two feet." Nobody's going to drag me down, coax me up. When I want to go down on my own, I will. I'm going to do it on my own. If they would leave me alone, probably I'd go more often, more often than when they start pushing me. Not me—that's just the way I feel about it.

Such rejections of the churches were based on their alleged restraint of the human spirit. Whether the unchurched spoke of doctrines that were too narrow, restricted lifestyles, or stances that arrested continued development of the individual, they spoke of the need for space and room to grow. The church, they felt, boxed them in. It smothered them. It was too hard to breathe. Being pushed into corners was not for them.

Type 3: The Burned Out

I found many of the Burned Out in Sarasota, Florida, where retirees, especially, rejoiced in their freedom to "start their lives over again." They had been active in previous church affiliations "up north," but they felt they had "done their bit" and didn't want to be "tied down" again. They felt their energies had been "used up" and were not anxious to carry "heavy baggage" again.

The *Used* seemed to be expressing both a previous exploitation of their talents and time and a fear of overinvolvement in their present retirement years. Some simply spoke of a childhood in which they had felt pressured into religious activity that was "too much." "In Brooklyn and then out on Long Island," an Oregon college student recalled, "we went to church every Sunday, religious classes every Saturday. I had to do it. I was pleasing my parents. . . . But we made a deal. If I would stick with it until I was thirteen, then I wouldn't have to do it. When I stopped, the whole family dropped out. You see, we had a boat, and it became increasingly difficult to make church. I haven't been to confession since then, maybe fifteen masses. I always attended at Christmas. Now, it's two years since I've been."

Helen Faix, of Searsmont, Maine, a "marginal Methodist" as she described herself, said that her withdrawal from the church began very early in life:

I would say it was overexposure as a child. My parents were so involved. Their whole life was church activities. Just got so that every time my father turned around he was back at church. I was pulled to church on a sled. There was prayer meeting every Tuesday, Women's Christian Temperance Union on Wednesday, Ladies Sewing Circle at the house. That was my whole life until my father died, that was all we knew. It was just overexposure and developed in me this tremendous negative attitude—I got so I was bored to tears—so I just can't. I go occasionally, but I just hate it.

"I used to be a deacon up in Michigan until we came down here eight years ago," one Florida retiree, a former school administrator from Minnesota, said. "I helped build the new church, was chairman of the finance board and all that stuff. Attended every week. Member of the usher corps, a teller. I counted the money." Now, he was living in an adult community at Sorrento, near Venice, Florida. He wasn't sure he was going to stay. "I might go to church, but I'll keep my membership up north. I'm not going to get involved like that again."

"My wife and I just got tired here in the Episcopal Church," a formerly active church member said.

Up north, if you belong to a small church, the total program is pared down accordingly. If it's large, you have enough members to handle the tasks. But in Sarasota, a 100-member church gets a transient population from November to April ten times that size. To keep things going, the core workers, about thirty-five of us, had to do everything. You get bombarded. We felt guilty saying no. The church wanted all our time—and too much money. They felt we should do everything, and we weren't ready to do that. We're out now.

"At first," a Californian in San Clemente told me, "we just attended council meetings. Then I ended up on the council and became vice-president. We lost our pastor, and there were some internal problems. . . . Now, there's a new pastor. I dropped out. They don't need me anymore. I began to appreciate the worn out guys before me. They're used up, too."

A husband and wife, formerly Presbyterians, recalled with obvious satisfaction their former church involvement.

The minister was just a super guy. We attended regularly, got involved with the youth and adult organization, did some teaching, got elected a trustee. I felt I was needed and could be useful. . . . Over the years, the congregation grew, got too large, I think. Things got too organized, needed money to keep things running. . . . I finally decided I'd done enough. I felt I'd really been exploited. . . . Eventually I drifted away completely.

Another, once a Methodist, said, "They kept saying, 'If you come to church, why not every Sunday?' If you go every week, there's pressure for more involvement. I tried it for a while, but no more." A woman active in community affairs in Santa Ana, California, complained, "When they see a leader, they hook you. They say, 'Here is an executive. She is in our church—let's use her and make her do these things.' Before long it's, 'Will you teach Sunday School, or will you do this, will you do that?' I really can't get that involved. Once in a while, yes, but not just giving, giving, giving."

Perhaps the epitome of the Light Traveler was June Baker, a forty-year-old mother of three, living in an upper-middle-class development south of Sarasota City. She spoke both about her impression of the community and her own childhood rearing as a Catholic. She had had early religious instruction prior to her first communion and had attended a parochial school for a few years. Her parents were marginal Catholics. Neither she nor Mr. Baker, also reared in a Catholic home, had been confirmed. They were married by a Catholic priest in her former home in Indiana.

Since the Bakers' marriage, they have not practiced their religion. "I'm a Christian—period," she said. "That has sustained me. All the other goodies I don't believe in at all." Although she is no longer able to accept the church's teachings on divorce, birth control, and abortion, June Baker recalls the older liturgies with nostalgia. "It may have been Victorian or older," she said, "but I enjoyed the old mass. The Latin was beautiful. There was a mystery—moving, dramatic. That has all disappeared. It's incongruous to me." She compared herself to other Catholics she knew from the "old church": "They will not join another church. The indoctrination worked. They are in limbo like me."

Mr. and Mrs. Baker are not retirees and resent being associated with the elderly. But Mrs. Baker says she shares with them the chance that Florida gives to do something new.

This is a start-over state. Many of the people moving here are looking for a fresh start. Either they are severing the ties from back home. Or they are looking for the Fountain of Youth. Or they are looking for different opportunities or a different way of life. I fall in that category, a fresh start, a completely different way of life. You sever all past relationships in a church or whatever and make a brand new start. Life down here is entirely different, a different feeling, a different structure, extremely casual. I would call it, "So what?" If it doesn't get done today, it will next week.

It is rather funny here. People are friendly, more friendly than up north. Your neighbor helps you here. They don't belong to the church, but they are more Christian. You see, all of us come from some place else. We don't have the traditions. So to ask, "Where are you from?" is an instant communication starter. It is very easy to get to know somebody down here.

She went on to describe the associational differences, as she had experienced them, between the communities "up north" and "down here."

Up north the smaller communities were very structured socially. Clubs and organizations were handed down from parents and stayed the same—segregated according to money and ethnic background. Here it's different. There must be 3,000 clubs in Florida. You can't possibly be lonely. You have so many choices that the church is no longer the important thing [that it was up north]. It is rare to find even a church person who really works within the structure of the church. . . . Your own inventiveness comes through. And it's phenomenal how people will stick together and help each other.

Mrs. Baker is totally happy with her light baggage. She says she will never leave. "I'm a sun person. I thrive in the sun. Dreary days depress me." She has found a place where

. . . you are allowed to do what you want to do as long as it doesn't infringe on the rights of others—freedom, liberty, and tolerance. Universal values—the churches haven't done that, too provincial. That's self-defeating. They talk a lot about love but then they condemn you to hellfire and brimstone for the little things. Even if there is a message buried in the heart of the faith, somehow or other it's not getting across.

What has gotten across, Mrs. Baker rejects.

A Florida college professor summarized from surveys he had conducted in Sarasota:

These people, in their previous associational attachments, including the church, needed them in their earlier years. Belonging to a church helped them in their upward mobility. They needed the church in the same way that they needed the Country Club, the Masonic Order, the neighborhood association, and other groups.

Now, these people have no further need for organizational attachments to reach future goals. Those goals have already been achieved. Now they just pick up and choose. They float with light baggage from one interest to another. This obviously affects the church. They have changed their whole lifestyle. The church, which served them well earlier, is optional. They either never join down here, they become inactive or, overtly, they reject what the church has to offer.

Less eloquently but with an autobiographical authenticity, Martha Stoner of Bradenton, Florida, in her mid-fifties, described her final withdrawal from the church.

I taught Sunday School back in Ohio for eight years—every Sunday. We were involved in all the programs. This is what I wanted for my four sons. It was a strict Missouri Synod Lutheran Church, and I liked that. . . . But, now the boys have grown up and gone away. It's always more fun when you have children. Church connections are most important when the family is a unit. Perhaps when I get older, when I don't have too many years left, then I'll go over to the church to be comforted. Then it will be the only way out. . . . Now, we just get up on a Sunday morning, look through the papers, go golfing, take a drive into the country. That's about it. I don't know. I just don't feel moved to go to church. I don't know why.

NOTES

1. *Survey of the Unchurched American* (Princeton, N.J.: Gallup Organization, 1978), pp. 5–16. See also Tables, pp. 27ff.
2. *Ibid.*, p. 53.
3. In Gallup's 1978 survey (see *ibid.*, p. 53), respondents were asked to identify the problems they had with the church. Twelve percent expressed "a dislike for church or synagogue involvement in social or political issues." Sixteen percent expressed "a feeling that the church or synagogue wasn't willing to work seriously to change the society."
4. Gallup found a comparable phenomenon in his national sample. The chief reason given for nonattendance at church by 22 percent of the churched and by 34 percent of the unchurched was, "When I grew up and started making decisions on my own, I stopped going to church." *Ibid.*, p. 40.
5. Palo Alto, Calif.: Science and Behavior Books, 1972.
6. *Emerging Trends* (a new monthly periodical published by the Princeton Religion Research Center) 1, no. 1 (January 1979): 2.
7. *Spiritual Community Guide for North America* (San Rafael, Calif.: Spiritual Community, 1972–1975). There is no estimate of the number of persons who may use the new group therapies as surrogates for conventional churches. Several of these, founded or headquartered in California, are reputed to have followers in the thousands, such as Thomas A. Harris's popularized version of Transactional Analysis, Werner Hans Erhard's "est," Paul Bindrim's "Nude Marathon Regression Therapy," and the eclectic "encounter" therapies at Esalen, to cite a few. Several of my interviews show the influence of one or more of these groups. For a discussion and critique of psychotherapy as the "key ritual of twentieth-century psychological religion," see Martin L. Gross, *The Psychological Society* (New York: Random House, 1978), pp. 34–35 and 277–317. See also Jackson Carroll, Douglas W. Johnson, and Martin E. Marty, *Religion in America: 1950 to the Present* (San Francisco: Harper & Row, 1979), pp. 25–26, 99, and 107–108, for an assessment of the effect of such groups on organized religion now and in the future.

9. The Floaters, Hedonists, and Locked Out

Three diverse types of unchurchedness are illustrated in this chapter: the Floaters, Hedonists, and the Locked Out. Unlike the Burned Out, whose stories were told in Chapter 8, the Floaters are seldom heavily involved in the life of a church. Theirs is an apathy, born of loose commitment, neither comparable to those who move from activity to inactivity nor an alternative lifestyle characteristic of the Hedonists. They express no hostility toward the churches and do not crave an acceptance by the churches that the Locked Out feel is denied them. The Floaters prefer looseness and marginality and express relative satisfaction with their apathy.

The Hedonists, the compulsive pleasure seekers of the new leisure society, find weekends especially suited for their varied leisure pursuits —camping, hunting, fishing, swimming, skiing, surfing, attending or watching sporting events, pleasure driving, and other comparable forms of recreation. The shift from a work-oriented society to a leisure-oriented society, in which the Hedonists are key actors, is the consequence of number of related changes in the society: more free time for workers, earlier retirements, increasing affluence, accessibility and proliferation of recreational areas, and the broad marketing of leisure products and pursuits by commercial interests, to cite some of the more obvious. If activities reflect new values, these pursuits represent the acting out of a changing American character.

One in three respondents in the Gallup poll of the unchurched gave as a reason for reduced involvement with the church, "I found other interests and activities." When pressed to describe those interests, 38 percent cited "sports, recreational activities, and hobbies."[1] In a supplemental survey probing the "spiritual significance of Sunday," respondents were asked "Which, if any, of these [fifteen activities listed on a card] do you usually do on Sunday?" Sixty-three percent said, "Take rest and recreation." One-third of all Americans take a pleasure trip in a car, one-third watch professional football on television, and one in five goes shopping.[2] Obviously, these activities are neither fully hedonistic nor necessarily substitutes for attending church, but they portend cultural patterns at odds with the traditional "keeping of the Sabbath" once dominant in the culture. The stories told by my respondents indicate that, for many, such pursuits have become substitutes and are intentionally elected in preference to church involvements.

The pictures the Locked Out draw pose a challenge to the church's claim of inclusiveness, a universal tenet of the Christian faith. They also document the findings of numerous research studies that conclude that the churches tend to be stratified according to class and caste.[3] These pictures, then, do not produce stories that are new. They do document the persistence of this pattern in American communities and reveal the deep hurt and hostility that felt rejection by the churches produce. The dissonance between the outsiders' perception of what it means to be "out" and the church's self-understanding in official proclamation that all are invited "in" is marked. The stories also put flesh and blood on the bones of statistical findings.

Type 4: The Floaters

The *Floaters* are of two varieties—the Apathetic and the Marginals. Both were once marginally inside the church, but the commitment was only skin deep.

Michael, a youth living in a Maine commune, grew up in Ohio in a large Catholic family. His father's indifference to the church rubbed off on him. "My father—I never talked to him about this, he never talked to us about anything—never went to church. I didn't know where he was coming from. I'm not sure. He is dead." But his mother "went to church every Sunday, and she expected us to go and sent us to parochial school."

> At quite a young age, I really rebelled. I couldn't believe I'd go to hell for missing mass and eating meat on Friday. I couldn't believe that stuff. So I started disregarding the things I didn't know. I didn't know if I believed or

disbelieved. It just seemed ridiculous to bother with that.

[As a teenager] I went as a hypocrite to save my face. Funerals, weddings, and things like that. I was even married in the church, found a priest I liked, a pretty good man in what he was doing. . . . Then I was divorced. . . . Five years ago when I moved up here, my idea was just to get away from a pretty sour society. I didn't see anything worth taking. . . . Now it's anything goes, just so you don't hurt anybody. It doesn't make any difference. God probably doesn't exist anyhow.

Michael revealed later in our conversation a recent search for meaning in his life, but for most of his childhood and youth he was among the Apathetic, for whom nothing much mattered. For others, asked when they had lost their interest in the church, a typical answer was, "Oh, I don't know that I ever lost my interest. I just don't have the time. I believe in it and everything. There's a church down in Liberty. If I was going to go, guess that's where it would be." Another reiterated Michael's story.

My mother was a Catholic, my dad never really did go to church. As kids, my brother and I, we always went to Sunday School. It was a kind of fun thing. All the other kids went. I never really got involved. I never could grasp it. After I got married, I got busy. Construction work. I'm not home that much. When I'm home, I just as soon be with the family. I feel religion is fine for some people, if you need it. Some people use it as a crutch. They need something to believe in. I believe in myself.

An assembly-line worker in a Belfast, Maine, chicken-packing plant said that she "work[s] all day and I'm just willing to sit right here when I come home from work. I don't care about going too much." Someday, she said, "I'll fool those little grandchildren of mine. I'll get up and go to church with them. There's no reason why. I just can't seem to get started."

Monica is an emigrant from Argentina. She liked the "religious scene" there better than in Laguna Niguel, California, where she now lives. "Nobody went to church back home," she said. Her family was Catholic, but she became interested in the German Lutheran community there. "But it didn't make much difference. You just belonged. You are always a member even if you never go. . . . We're members of a German Lutheran congregation in Los Angeles. But we barely go."

George and Gwen Huber, a couple in Garden Grove, California, spoke of their status as nonmembers of the church. "We went to dinners and meetings and things like that. Probably even to worship a few times." I asked if there had been a decision not to be a part of a church. "I don't think we ever deliberately said, 'We are not going to do it,' " said George. Gwen added, "We just never said, 'Let's do it.' " The kids, they said, go once in a while to the Baptist Church. They make a big fuss about coming and picking them up. "If they want to go, we let them, but don't force them." So, I asked, "You can live without it?" He and she: "We can! We have!" Neighbors on the same street as the Hubers say they had been to a Christmas midnight mass, and once went to a Mormon service, too. "I don't want to sound disrespectful," I was told, "but I found it all rather amusing."

Sigurd Jensen, a former Canadian Lutheran and son of a Lutheran pastor, expressed his present apathy with respect to the churches in Newport Beach, California. "I guess I just don't want to get involved. I just drifted away. I just stay away. I don't know what it would take to get me back." He went on:

> Back in Canada, the community was small. Rural, a one-horse town. The church was the center of the community. Everybody went to church. When your community gets to 30,000 or more, things change. The majority here don't go to church. I have been up there to see the church twice when I've had relatives in town. A lot of them go, so I have taken them there. But me, as far as getting out my horse and off my fanny and going myself, I don't know. . . . I like what they do in South America, preach the Word and let the people do as they please. That's what they ought to do with the heathen in southern California.

Washington Owens, a black farmer in the hills of Marion County, Alabama, needed some prodding. This dialogue expressed his apathy:

> "Tell me a little something about recent years. You don't go to church very often?"
> "No."
> "Can you give me your reasons why you don't go to church?"
> "Just don't go."
> "Nothing there that interests you?"
> "No."
> "What do you think about the church?"
> "It's a nice place to go."
> "But you don't go?"
> "No."

"What might interest you?"
"I'm not in it."

In Belfast, Maine, a factory worker simply said, "It doesn't bother me if somebody else goes or belongs. It just doesn't affect me at all. I don't want to argue religion with anyone. That seems sort of a waste of time. You don't accomplish anything. If they want to believe, well, it's all right with me." Another, "I have nothing against the church. We attend church functions and we get along with them. Some of my best friends are directors of the church here."

A native Oregonian, Charles Felton, a Baptist in his childhood home in Albany, recalled that his last time in church was "when I was a teenager. I went with a Mormon girl from Corvallis. When I went with her, I didn't have anything against the Mormons! When I quit going with her, I didn't go any more. The only reason I went was to satisfy her. Because I frankly never had any interest in the thing. People interest me. Not religion." Felton introduced me to his neighbor, Mark Hoffler, also a native Oregonian. Hoffler had lost interest in the church in his preteen years.

I never got interested to the point of baptism. I was always a visitor. I kind of made sure I was. I really didn't want to get attached, didn't want to feel, "This is it, I'm stuck. I have to make this decision. Now I have to do something with it." . . . It never did occur to me that anything more serious should be happening.

A woman near Brush Creek, West Virginia, had been described to me as a "loose woman" by one of the clergy. I found her rundown trailer on the "holler" lane; her current boyfriend was repairing a Honda motorcycle on the kitchen table. "When you became a teenager, you stopped going to church?" I asked. "Just quit going," she said. "Just quit all at once." "Anything happen in the church that made you feel uncomfortable?" I probed. "No," she said, "just not interested any more. Not even thought about going since then. Most of them church folks just goes for the big argument. That happens around here quite a bit. I'd just as leave stay home if that is what they have to do."

A prisoner in a southern county jail on a grand larceny charge had this conversation with me through his cell bars.

"Were your parents religious?"
"Yeah, my mom is."
"What church does she go to?"

"Baptist."

"What about your daddy?"

"He didn't go."

"Just indifferent or what?"

"No, he didn't have nothing to say against it. Just didn't go."

"Not interested?"

"No."

"What about your childhood?"

"Used to go every Sunday. I didn't like it."

"What turned you off?"

"I just hated to go. My sister, she goes."

"What made the difference?"

"I was just wilder, I guess. I go now once in a while."

"Tell me about it."

"It's a good church. Baptist. Preaching and singing."

"How do you feel while this is going on?"

"I feel nothing. I don't believe half of what's going on. About going to hell, that is about all."

The Marginals are the Floaters whose ties are so loose that they drift from belief to belief and church to church with little sense of belonging anywhere. Some recited a long list of previous loose connections. It was not unusual for the Marginals to have had peripheral associations with a series of churches.

Joyce Edwards has lived in Florida for ten years, on Longboat Key in an upper-middle-class home for three years. "When I was a child," she recalled, "I was very active in a Disciples of Christ congregation in Georgia. Our whole social life [as a family] revolved around the church." At the University of Georgia, she became friendly with Jewish classmates and began to ask, "How can these people be condemned to hell?" She taught Sunday School and attended a rural Christian Church where a friend was a student minister. Her church involvement continued until she was married and "started enjoying sleeping on Sundays. Mr. Edwards and I wanted to find a church together. He was Baptist but didn't want the children raised where they'd be scared of the devil and get a lot of guilt feelings. So we started visiting around." In Tallahassee, they found a Disciples of Christ church. "But it was different from the one I had gone to—very fundamentalistic." Then, she went on, "We started going to the Episcopal Church. I was confirmed there." Two years later, the Edwards moved to Sarasota County. "I started going to the Episcopal Church here, and here I had another big change. It was very high and very big, more like the Roman Catholic Church. My husband didn't like it at all, so we started shopping again." Their search took them to the Longboat Island Chapel, an interfaith church, "very liberal and open, has Christians, Jews, and several of Asian background too."

Mrs. Edwards would prefer an Episcopal church, but her husband, whom she described as an agnostic who "feels hypocritical saying the Apostles' and Nicene Creed"—is uncomfortable there. "We've tried the Unitarians, but I could not get interested. I could never become interested in that church because of their theology." She described herself as one who believes

. . . that I could go to any church, whatever denomination. I visit the Methodist and the Christian Church with my mother and mother-in-law. I feel right at home with them. But in the chapel and the Unitarian Church, I miss the weekly communion. I am looking for a place, though, for my whole family. . . . The lower economic group seem to be more involved in the church [than we] because they feel the need of it. People who are successful think they have found it, but maybe they haven't.

Joyce Edwards apologized for cutting the interview short. She asked the maid to take coffee to her husband, who was sunning himself on a chaise lounge on their private beach on the Gulf.

The Edwards are Marginals, perhaps more Pilgrims than Floaters, but their pattern of movement without long-term commitment will probably continue, given the markedly different religious convictions of husband and wife.

An immigrant German family from Frankfurt fits the type. Gretchen Müller, a widow with three children, lived in California, Louisiana and Indiana before moving to Florida twelve years ago, where she now works as a telephone operator. "I've been to different churches," she told me,

I thought I'd find one similar to the church where I was born and raised in Germany. They have all disappointed me. . . . When I first came here, a babysitter took my children to the Salvation Army. They like it and have been going and going. I go around Christmas time and Easter and on special occasions when I just feel the need to be with the children. But I just haven't found the right church for myself.

I feel funny about the Salvation Army. When I went through a bad time two years ago, they helped me pay my electric bill, gave me toys and a turkey for Christmas. They were wonderful . . . helped me in a good way. . . . But my children haven't been baptized. They have never heard about confirmation. But the children enjoy it so much I don't want to put them out. Maybe later they'll join up. . . .

On Sundays, I watch religious programs on TV. But I am really doing nothing, just resting up for the next week.

A plant manager in Hamilton, Alabama, Malcolm Pusey, described himself as a "paper mill tramp" whose father's work took him to North Carolina, Arkansas, Tennessee. His church connections were loose, "Didn't stay in one place long enough to settle. I never really did more than drift." Jim Walters, twenty-eight, a forester, was born in Michigan and has lived in Wisconsin, Ohio, Florida, Texas, Virginia, North Carolina, and Alabama. Baptized Presbyterian, he has also attended Congregational and Methodist churches. He doesn't see a lot of difference in the churches. He said,

> If I had been brought up Jewish, I would have been taught that there wasn't a Jesus. Or, in India, I would have grown up in that sort of religion. I was brought up over here and taught another thing. What is the real truth? They don't differ that much. . . . I am sure that there is somebody that made this world. They say God created the heaven and the earth. But who created God? It kind of makes you wonder.

Jim and his young wife, Sue, say they may try out one or two churches in Marion County, but they doubt that they'll find anything "that will hold us."

Martha Preston, in West Salem, Oregon, was another Drifter. "As a child, I probably attended the Baptist, Christian, Seventh-Day Adventist, Methodist, and Catholic churches," she recalled.

> I'd be with friends, and they'd say, "Let's go to church," and I would. But I never got into any church very deep. When Charles and I were dating, we did some looking around at the churches. Thought this would be the real American thing to do. We hadn't done it and we probably needed to. We found a nondenominational group, real nice atmosphere, not too much pressure. We asked if we could get married here. The minister said "This isn't a wedding chapel," and he wasn't going to have it used that way. We were turned off.
>
> Then, we found this little Lutheran church. We chose it for looks, the right location, and so forth, nothing else.
>
> About a year ago, we visited an Episcopal church. Our impression was favorable except for the ritual kind of thing. I felt real dingy doing this stuff, because

I don't believe any of it. I really can't participate without feeling like a hypocrite.
. . . Commitment would be too phony for me. I think I can do better on my
own.

Type 5: The Hedonists

The lure and addiction of leisure makes happy hedonists of large
numbers of people in today's society. A retired policeman in Southern
California expressed what I heard again and again from the unchurched,
coast to coast.

Look on every block around here, and you'll find ten or fifteen campers. On
a Sunday like this, you can go out and do anything you want to do: tennis, golf,
fishing. . . . Our weekends are precious. We want to get out of town. . . . There
are so many activities that people don't want to spend a day or half a day in
church.

That same balmy day, a young man was leaving his bachelor's apartment in a neighboring Orange County community. In haste, he said,
"Just finished surfing this morning in the Pacific. Got to get to the
mountains now to ski. . . . The churches can't compete with this!" Some
families choose a homesite "to be near the beach so I can get lost—I
leave my problems behind." Where a couple both work and the weekend arrives, "You catch up on this and that, then get in some recreation.
If free time is Sunday, it's either church or recreation. Recreation wins
out!"

It was the same at the other end of the Sun Belt, in Sarasota, Florida.
A minister complained, "They come down here for leisure. What can
you do?" I checked this out in his community, and he was right. Said
a retiree at Spanish Lakes, formerly from Pontiac, Michigan:

First we vacationed here, up and down the Keys, then settled here. No more
bitter Michigan winters for me. . . . We don't have anything we *have to do*
anymore. We can go shelling or swimming in the Gulf. We can go and play
Bingo tonight. We were slaves to the clock for forty years. I'm so tickled to be
out of it. I'm independent.

"Peace, serenity, security, the good life! The real estate people are
right," a once-active Roman Catholic woman told me.

You've got so many choices here that my church is no longer the most
important thing. . . . When it comes to priorities, I come first. If I can't be happy

myself, there is no possible way I can make my family happy. You find your own thing. I'm in the garden club, a cooking club, belong to the Camellia Society. If you've got money and the time, there's art, painting classes, sculpturing, pottery, folk dancing, belly dancing—you name it. . . . So for the church to survive it has got to have something pretty distinctive to offer. You better believe it!

A New College social scientist in Sarasota called people in his community "a limited liability group,"[4] people who buy into groups only for those things that interest them. He expounded:

> For the retired, this often means floating and flitting, with no deep commitments. Life is too short for them. They *take* from a group—arts, opera, ballet, a cultural smorgasbord at bargain rates, whatever they need for immediate satisfactions. They don't buy into the liabilities, the risks and costs of belonging.

Moving to a company town like Valsetz, Oregon, where the Boise-Cascade Company takes over, in large measure, the government, the schools, and the church, belonging to anything other than job and family is superfluous. A local schoolteacher says, "If the weather's good, the people are gone on Sundays—out to the coast fishing, or back down in the valley to see friends. A couple of families may go to church, but not many." The Plywood Plant Studmill superintendent, in his youth an acolyte in an Episcopal Church, now outside the church, agrees. "A guy doesn't wake up on a Sunday morning and raise the question 'Am I going to church today?' He doesn't even think of it. We work a six-day week here. The seventh day is the only day for recreation."

"We are just too busy on weekends," said a former Kansas woman now living in Monmouth, Oregon. "Sometimes I think it would be nice to go to church, but then you hesitate because they draw you into this and that, and it takes a lot of time. You get too involved. . . . I want to be free. 500 miles, shorter or longer, that's not too far to go if you've got a whole weekend. . . . There is always something to do."

A businessman in Rickreal described his own lifestyle after his move to Oregon from New York thirty years ago:

> You don't plan. You do things as they move you. There is space everywhere. Distances don't matter. I have a cottage on the coast. In the middle of the week, if it's too hot here, my wife and I drive out after work for a swim in the Pacific, stay overnight, come back the next morning. Or, if my wife doesn't feel like cooking tonight, maybe we'll go up to Portland—that's only 60 miles. Once in a while, my wife will go to church in Salem. If I go, I'll put a few dollars in the

plate. . . . But, if you want to be an Oregonian, you do what the rest do in your first two years.

I got the impression that for him that meant not getting involved in a church.

Sometimes a compulsion for play on the part of the husband spills over on the wife as well. "I never went to church while Mac was alive," a widow told me. "When a woman goes to church alone, you feel the stigma. People criticize. That wasn't fair to Mac. He had his right to make his own choice. He was an avid golfer," she recalled, "he spent his Sunday mornings on the golf course, came home and got me, and we'd spend the rest of the day together golfing. In the summer, we golfed every night. I never went to church without Mac." So now she doesn't go at all.

Few felt guilty at all. In fact, more than once I heard the complaint, "The trouble with the church is they don't think you ought to have a good time. That's sinful. I don't buy that." Good times were differently defined. In West Virginia, Maine, and Alabama, particularly among the working class, a good time meant "boozing it up, gettin' drunk." "Why not?" they asked. "Life's too short." For the eighty-year-old millionaire on one of Sarasota's more luxurious keys, the sentiment was the same. "I'm dying, have cancer. . . . But what's life for it you can't enjoy it?" He was enjoying it quite well—a yacht at his backyard dock on the lagoon, a private indoor pool, his own pet blue heron, and a $250,000 home decorated with Renaissance art.

There are certainly thousands of church members who enjoy leisure. There are thousands more outside the church for whom it is life's greatest good.

Type 6: The Locked Out

The Locked Out include three subtypes: the *Rejected,* those whose full participation has been restricted or severed; the *Neglected,* those who have been slighted, overlooked, or disregarded; and the *Discriminated,* those locked out by class- or caste-conscious parishes.

Among the classic examples of the Rejected were Mrs. Darlene Hurlocker of Dallas, Oregon, and her thirteen-year-old daughter, Christine, who participated in the interview. Mr. Hurlocker started his occupational career as a farmer but is now employed at the local planing mill.

The family had formerly lived "on the Coast" but were native Oregonians. Their earlier religious participation had been variously in the Nazarene, Christian, and Four Square Gospel churches. Relatively poor in their early married life, the Hurlockers felt "out of place" in the Dallas churches. "We didn't have good clothes, and some of the ladies in the congregation kept talking," Mrs. Hurlocker said, "I kind of felt put down."

Gee, it's just a feeling you have really. They put people down. If you are not dressed right, like in blue jeans, you are put down. . . . In this town, you are in or you are out. We have lived here for twenty years, and we are not in.

I asked what a person needs to be or do to be "in." Without using the term, she began to talk about social stratification in Dallas. •

You have to join Kiwanis. You should be a business person or a member of the fire department. You have to belong to a lot of these different groups to be "in." They run the whole thing in the churches too. You go in there and listen to the minister and everything. Church ends, and you walk out of there. Not one single person is going to shake your hand, thank you for coming, and ask you to come again.

Christine, the Hurlocker's junior high daughter, was more explicit.

The "in's" are the people with good names, with money or with businesses in town. They are the big-shots in the churches. They seem to think the churches are places for "in people," not "out people." The only way you get in is to look for and try to date and get married to a guy who's in. It helps if you play around with the big-shot guys, like the doctor's son or the son of some lawyer or banker. If you're not so good, that's what those boys are looking for. That'll get you in all right. . . . But I want to be me. I want to be accepted for me.

Christine didn't see that happening in Dallas. She wants to go to Wales to college. "That's where my mother's family comes from. Maybe there I'd be 'in' instead of 'out.' That's the only way I can be 'in' anywhere."

In Black Rock, outside Falls City in central Polk County, Oregon, I found a series of small youth communes, in groups of six to ten persons each. In one, I asked if they had ever visited a local church. "I think they would let us come in if we didn't cause any trouble. But they'd probably laugh. It would be pretty funny [to them]." A shopkeeper in town confirmed what was the local attitude toward such youth. "There are some hippies appearing around here. I don't know if any one of them ever attended church. Where they come from is a mystery. They just seem to come out of the woods. There is some resentment here about them. I don't know if they are really hippies or not, but they look like hippies."

The poor—or "us common, working people" as some preferred to call themselves—were especially conscious of their appearance and lack of money, which they felt locked them out. Said an Alabaman,

> If you just got common clothes on, you see, a lot of them are going to look down on you, and they kind of turn their nose up at you. . . . A friend of mine up there one time wanted me to come up and sit with some of those people who makes fun of the poor people who haven't got clothes like the rest of them have. You think I'm going to come up there and sit with them? He said, "You don't have to look at us." I said, "But they do look down on you."

Another said, in words that I heard repeated in all six counties among the poorer classes,

> I know poor people has a rough time in churches. 'Cause we have been down there. We just ain't got clothes fittin' to wear to church. If anybody goes to church to worship the Lord, they shouldn't care what other people are wearin'.' That is what I feel, but you know there are people who makes fun of you if you don't have. See, I got my feet all sore up, and I'm wearin' some old pieces of shoes. They don't look on me kindly like.

Financial contributions were an obstacle. "I was always raised up Baptist," said an older woman in the hills of Marion County, "my mother and daddy always went to church and paid their tithe. But I would feel it wasn't right if I didn't have the money. You can tell when anybody don't want you real bad." Said another, a West Virginian, in the same vein, "I say a lot of people, they go to church, and they pass this plate around. It takes everything they got. People turn up their nose at them that hasn't got it." A poor dirt farmer said simply, "If you ain't got the money you ain't in. Maybe you don't have enough to just go around. Well, we ain't able. You don't have any kind of money to do like a lot of white folks do."

Many unchurched people feel rejected because their lifestyles differ from what they feel the churches demand. "I don't want a minister who comes here every two weeks to see if I'm having a beer or a party or whatever," a Guin, Alabama, truck driver's wife said.

But I would be interested in somebody dropping in occasionally and saying, "Hi, how are you?" I hope I don't expect anybody to make a fuss. But when they shake your hand, it's like let me touch your hand and get out of here and let's get the show on the road. I just don't feel good about the greeting. There isn't even a sincere smile. There is something lacking in perhaps feeling, or sincerity, or something. I'm not sure what it is.

A black woman in a Sarasota public housing project, when I asked why she didn't go to church, said bluntly, "My man, he's a drunk. They don't want me." "The Freewill Baptist up there," a Marion County coal miner's wife said, "they got a trailer set over there. But if your husband's a drunkard—everything he gets he drinks it up—they look down on that family because of the husband. They keep a'watchin.'" In Waldo County, Maine, a gas station attendant said, "I'm not ready to start going to church. I'd have to change my whole way of life. No more cussin' and drinkin.' No sir!" Molly McCoy, a former tavern owner on the Nellis Road in Boone County, said,

I run this tavern for seventeen years or maybe more. I had a lot of good friends. All my old customers is in the churches. . . . Closest I get to the church down the road (I got my pride) is the big whiskey bottle I fills with pennies. I just pulls up to the church and dumps out the money in a shopping bag, about $28 or $30 worth, and I say, "This is for my son who is in the army." They takes it all right.

The Neglected are especially present among the elderly. In Searsport, Maine, an elderly widow asked me to "stop by for a bit." She said she was just lonely. "Haven't seen the minister since I buried my husband a year ago," she said.

I grieved for four months. I cried day and night constantly. I don't think anybody could have comforted me. Nothing they would have said or done would have taken that grief away, but they could have shown their sympathy for me. . . . I was just abandoned, that was all. Not a soul has come here. I was just abandoned. . . . My sister says to me, "Maybe you expect too much of the churches." I said, "Maybe I do, but you don't expect too much of Christians."

A former vaudeville singer, now elderly and ill, was bitter about the church people in Winterport, Maine.

I'm an old lady now. I have exhausted all my money. I have to do a lot of scheming. I get everything I can from public assistance and food stamps. But you gotta have money to have friends around here, enough money to have a bottle to offer people a drink, enough money to have a nice house, enough to invite people for dinner and feed them. They are the kind of people who go to church. So I just don't associate with that kind of people anymore.

A woman, now ninety-two years old, lives in a small, modest bungalow near Liberty, Maine.

> I came here with a sick husband. He didn't know he was going to die. He passed away back in 1967. . . . So, I was here, and not one person ever came to see me. That is the truth. . . . When I die, I'm not having any funeral. He had a nice funeral. But I'm not having any—no funeral, no visiting, no nothing. Just bury me alongside of my husband. Because when I was alive, nobody would come to see me, dear. I guess I'm vindictive. They ain't going to see me when I'm dead if they wouldn't come to see me when I'm alive.

Another Waldo County resident told me, "I'm sure the church don't help me. They don't do nothing. When I was in bed, I never seen a minister come over and see me and say a prayer or anything like that. . . . When you do see a minister on the street, and he don't say 'Hi,' why should you go to his church? He don't know me. So that's why I stay home." An elderly, handicapped man in San Clemente, California, said, "Maybe they have a full church over there. I don't know. But I've never heard of them calling on folks like me." In a West Virginia "holler," an aged woman of seventy-eight said, with hostility, "Maybe they think I'm too mean, but they never has been a preacher near me. Nobody ever sit down and talk to me. I can't walk, the muscles in my legs skid out, and eventually I just get plumbed out. They ought to spend a little bit of their time over here. They don't do it."

The Discriminated cite specific acts of rejection by the churches or feel locked out because of a deviant lifestyle. A topless waitress working at a tavern outside Sarasota City came to my table after I had arranged with the owner for an interview. She opened her makeshift sarong. "Just look at me, sir, a good look! Now, do I look like a choir girl to you?" A homosexual, who arranged to meet me furtively in a restaurant in Winfield, Alabama, said he "like[s] to spar, intellectually, with the ministers in town. I say atrocious things to them. But nobody really takes me up on it. I can see they don't want people like me." A former Mennonite from Iowa, now in Dallas, Oregon, volunteered for military service in Korea: "That didn't set well with these pacifists." Another Anabaptist, from an Old Order Amish family "back east" said that when he registered as a conscientious objector in Orange County, "These

church people just thought I was a coward or communist or something."
A prisoner in a Boone County jail said, "A church is the kind of place
where you get hit over the head, not loved. . . . I don't think very much
of them. I just don't like them."

The feeling of being discriminated against was expressed by Gordon
Wiley, a construction worker in a lower-class neighborhood off Tuttle
Avenue, in Sarasota, Florida:

> My wife don't go. She don't have the clothes like the rest of the people.
> . . . This church right here—I would not be accepted. I would be looked upon
> as a good bum, because I was dirty. Maybe my clothes aren't dirty, but they are
> ragged looking, and I'd be a bum to look like this. I'd be considered a bum from
> the preacher right on down. . . .
>
> They are not concerned about a man's religion. They are concerned about
> how he acts. From what they say, I don't think if I drink or smoke I can be a
> Christian.

In Anaheim, California, I met a Danish war bride who had met her
husband when he had been stationed with the army in Europe. Their
first home in America had been in Albuquerque, New Mexico, where
they were charter members of a new mission congregation. Mrs. Gon-
zalez is a professional soloist and sings occasionally in churches in Los
Angeles. When they moved to Buena Park ten years ago, they joined
a congregation there. "Manuel had a personal conflict there. He is
Mexican-American. That didn't seem to make any difference in Albuquerque, but it does here. Certain remarks were made by certain
people. He won't go to that church again." In another California
home, a Guatemalan woman married to a Jew left the church because
she knew her husband would "never convert. I didn't want my children growing up in conflict," she said. "Remarks were made, and I
didn't want my children to feel that there was anything wrong with
being Jewish."

Jim Crowfoot, a young sculptor in San Juan Capistrano, recalled one
happy experience from his Marine Corps years at Jehovah Witness
meetings.

> These people were open. There were blacks and whites and reds, all colors.
> . . . It was a warm place. You were automatically filled with life, just like you
> got a squirt of oxygen in your face. There was a flow and people shared, and
> things were always going on. You felt like you knew these people all your life.
> It was a growing process. It was like everyone of them glowed.

But this was not duplicated in his church experiences after he left the Marines. Reared a Catholic, he tried the Catholic Church again. "The religion was dead," he said.

Dead people going in, no life in them, sitting in those pews, coming out. Rich people sit in the front, poor people in the back. Years of that makes you dried up. . . . Being a Christian is the toughest thing in the world. It is easy to be bad, to mouth off, to go out and drink, to chase girls, to do the lazy things. But it's hard to turn to the God that is in you. . . . The churches don't help with the way they separate people. I'm very dried up now.

"I've been in places that I just feel like, boy, they don't want you nowhere around," was the judgment of a black domestic, working in a wealthy home near Hamilton, Alabama. "They got their own little group, their own little people. They don't want nobody else in it at all." The Hendersons, at Isleboro, Maine, said that the churches were class churches. "At the lower end of the island, Dark Harbor," Mrs. Henderson said, "are the fifty or more mansions of the wealthy—Abercrombie, Dreyfus, Dillon, Choate, Strawbridge. They have their own Episcopal Chapel, St. Mary of the Isle. The rich people bring in their own chaplain every summer from Boston or Philadelphia. Everybody knows it's private, for the rich. Used to be, the oldtimers say, they had a sign at the door that said, 'For Members Only.' "

"We have very wealthy people in the Congregational Church here," another Maine resident said. "The church needs money, I know, and a wealthy person can give more, but it doesn't seem fair to cater to them. And that's what they do. That's the reason I left." Some others felt that the wealthy were "not doing their share," as one dock worker put it. "The rich people are the ones who are not paying their taxes. Same in the church. It is the poor man who is out working hard for a living that is doing all the giving. That is so unfair. . . . There are many poor people in Waldo County that don't feel they can afford to belong to a church." A Social Action worker in Liberty, Maine, believed the poor had sized up the situation correctly. "You have the lower-class and middle-class and the upper-class churches here," she said. "It is nice to have the sweet, little old lady with white hair who smells of lavender in one of the middle- or upper-class churches, but if you get some woman from the hills who just smells, they don't want her around."

The poor felt locked out. It appears that, in many places, they are. The discrimination is deeply felt.

NOTES

1. *Survey of the Unchurched American* (Princeton, N.J.: Gallup Organization, 1978), pp. 40, 52.
2. *Emerging Trends*, p. 3.
3. See, for example, N. J. Demerath III, *Social Class in American Protestantism* (Chicago: Rand McNally, 1965).
4. See Morris Janowitz, *The Community Press in an Urban Setting* (Chicago: University of Chicago Press, 1967). According to Janowitz, a "community of limited liability" is a highly mobile community in which people, though involved in local institutions, are prepared to sever these ties and switch involvement when participation fails to satisfy immediate needs or aspirations. People tend to buy into satisfactions but avoid the risks of belonging. Such behavior patterns are heightened for those who are new to their communities or stay for short periods. See also John D. Kasarda and Morris Janowitz, "Community Attachment in Mass Society," in *American Sociological Review* 39, no. 3 (June 1974): 328–339. While aging tends to promote intensification of social attachments, this natural tendency in retirement communities like Sarasota is reduced. Older people are simply not there long enough for such attachments to develop. It may be that some of the new residents intentionally choose such life-styles. My evidence suggests that this is the way Sarasota presents itself to the newcomer (see Chap. 6). Pleasure pursuits offered abundantly in Sarasota do not require deep attachments; they spawn hedonism.

10. Nomads, Pilgrims, Publicans, and True Unbelievers

Four remaining types of responses by the unchurched, when asked about their separation from the institutional church, are illustrated in this chapter. The clustered responses permit the construction of the categories I have labeled *Nomads*, rovers with no fixed abode; *Pilgrims*, wanderers on a journey in search of meaning and purpose; *Publicans*, so-named because they perceive the churched as *Pharisees*—phonies, fakers, and hypocrites; and the *True Unbelievers*, a mix of agnostics, atheists, deists, rationalists, humanists, and secularists.

If quantified, the Publicans would probably constitute the dominant group among the unchurched. Jacque Ellul's observation that those outside the church say of those inside—"Look, their lives and acts are just like our own; they do not correspond in the least to what they are saying"[1]—was explicit or implicit in most of my conversations with the unchurched. These selected excerpts from the interviews are probably the most colorful of all I recorded, many of them taking on the character of vintage "atrocity stories."

The True Unbelievers, by contrast, were more difficult to find. Either because of their reticence to reveal deep-seated disbelief or simply because they may represent a small minority of the unchurched, few of my informants exhibited a wholesale rejection of the fundamental tenets of the Christian religion. The excerpts suggest that in most cases they have, like the Pilgrims, not permanently foreclosed the possibility of faith and belief.[2]

The humanists-secularists that are included in the True Unbeliever

category may be more manifest among the unchurched than this taxonomy suggests. If secularism is understood as the loss of demonstrable
relationship between religious beliefs and values and what people actually do in their everyday lives,[3] large numbers of the stories here (and
included in other types) make plausible the hypothesis that there is a
pervasive functional secularism among all the unchurched. Given also
the probability of comparatively weak commitments among large numbers of church members themselves, particularly in liberal Protestantism, functional secularism may be rampant within the churches as well.

Type 7: The Nomads

Half of all U.S. heads of families live more than 100 miles from their
birthplace. One out of five lives more than 1,000 miles from what was
once home. About 40 million Americans, between 1950 and 1960,
changed their home addresses at least once each year. Probably one in
five, or more, moves from one location to another *today*. Vance Packard
has called the United States "a nation of strangers."[4] The unchurched
among them I have called the Nomads.

The classic type of the Nomad was first revealed to me in an interview
with a successful, upwardly mobile middle-management executive, in
Huntington Beach, California. He described not only his situation but
also its psychological consequences with this comment:

> This is my thirteenth place of residence in fifteen years. The first time we
> moved, we went aggressively into our new community and made friends, joined
> groups, found a church. . . . [Then] 18 months later we had to say goodbye. That
> was hard, real painful. The next time, it was even harder. . . . Now, we've
> discovered that to prevent the pain of saying goodbye we don't say hello any
> more.

The trauma experienced by ethnic minorities in predominantly
WASP towns, like one town in Polk County, Oregon, is expressed
differently by different people, depending on how long they have lived
in the town's Chicano ghetto of 400 people, their age on arrival, education, opportunities to find skilled employment and other factors. Rinaldo
Alvarado, a young man about thirty, has made the adjustment well. He
began his postsecondary education at Collegio Cesar Chavez, at Mt.
Angel, Oregon, north of the state capital. He is now completing his
education, majoring in Spanish, at Oregon State University. He is unde-

cided whether to pursue a career in sales, the business world, or politics. He has been involved in politics, informally, for a number of years and is known by the Anglos in his town as a "Chicano leader." He was the first Chicano in Oregon to be elected to a city council.

Rinaldo's adaptation has been better than most. Although born in Texas, he has lived in Oregon most of his life. He left Collegio Cesar Chavez when he began to feel the focus was too narrow. "It's important to discover your heritage," he said, "but to be a full participant in Anglo society you have to know how to make deals with the Anglo at the same time you remember who you are yourself. . . . In this town, some like myself have been here for a generation or more. Many of them were born here. They have a self-conscious identity, though, and that's good." Their tradition, if they have preserved it and their language," he said, helps to "bind and cement them together." Although Rinaldo was for a time a nonparticipant in the local Catholic church, he has now become active again.

The church is very important for my spiritual development. I like the mass —even the Irish priests who don't speak Spanish but go out of their way to understand us. The priest is doing a good job here. . . . The church has something to offer—spiritual nurture, a kind of escape from the world, and the knowledge of God and Jesus. If the church just talks sense and no nonsense to people, makes its own way, then it is operating properly.

Another Chicano, middle-aged, described his rootlessness and "home-sickness" differently, as we have seen in the story of Carlos in Chapter 2. Carlos remains a spiritual nomad in an alien community of strangers. He wishes he could make Rinaldo's adjustment, but he can't. "Maybe something will happen!"

Nomadism creates a diaspora for many who can find in their new communities no continuity with their earlier religious experiences. This is especially true for people from main line Protestant denominations who are surrounded by the dominant fundamentalist sects in the small towns of Appalachia. Carol Nelson, a housewife married to a profes-sional man, formerly Lutheran, came from the upper Midwest to north-western Alabama. She recalled her first days in Guin.

When I first came here, it was really out of sight. Still, a lot of these ministers never put on a robe. I couldn't believe I was in a church service. It is like a town meeting. And, of course, I had never heard songs like that. I just couldn't believe that. They said, "Why, everybody knows these hymns." But I had never heard any of them. Could only find three hymns in the whole hymnal I had ever heard. "Holy, Holy, Holy" was one of them.

And revivals? I had never seen a revival in my life. I thought revivals were something you read about in *Elmer Gantry* or *Grapes of Wrath*. Here, it's the biggest thing that happens all year. It kind of infuriated me. You don't need this big push. Every week that you walk into the sanctuary you should look for renewal. . . .

It was like coming to a different world. Everything, from the food, to the attitudes, to the politics, to religion, everything was so different.

Carol Nelson has tried to adjust to the local Methodist church but can't. She is now taking instructions from the local Catholic priest but fears that if "I take that step, I'll lose my husband."

In a central Appalachian town in Boone County, West Virginia, an interview with Jim and Mary Livingston, formerly Episcopalians from Virginia, went like this:

Jim: Well, I have spent all my life getting to know people in different communities. This isn't as bad as some. People out in the county, they are real nice, but here [in town] they are shy with newcomers.

Mary: I guess I have moved so many places and gotten to know people real good and then had to leave them and after a while it just kind of hardens you a little bit.

I inquired about their experiences in the local churches.

Jim: It's partly my fault. I don't really try to get to know people or I don't let them get to know me. . . . If you have a church, well, church is people. You have to have people. I like people. But I don't let them know me. . . .

Mary: The churches here, well, they're all so harsh, no softness to them at all. It's not explainable, I don't think. . . . Soft means sort of closeness, feelings of togetherness, I guess, communication between all of the people. Peace and quiet, like the Episcopal Church back home, pretty music, prayers, the whole service.

Jim: It's cold here. No one even approaches us and asks who we are.

Mary: Well, I'm not quite like Jim. I like people very much. I think the church should be bubbling over with people. It's the people that really count. But I don't like harsh services, like, where the church beats on you. . . .

Jim: I just don't receive any fulfillment from it. I have been in so many churches. But out here the ministers are bad, half the people are sleeping. Not a very good atmosphere. I am not going to go any more.

The litany of the Nomads continued wherever I found them. "You anticipate that you're going to be here for three or four years," an

Orange County resident said, "Why start rooting? Why start feeling part of a community?" Said a schoolteacher, a newcomer in Laguna Beach, California, formerly from Minnesota, "They're just raised differently out here. No respect, no discipline. The children are monsters and run loose. . . . Casualness affects everything, casual attitudes about everything." "In the churches?" I asked. "Especially in the churches," she answered. "One of the first times I went to church here, I was really surprised. People in shorts! I was just completely taken aback to see this kind of atmosphere."

Another Orange County resident gave her instant analysis of the "California syndrome": "I think people sort of uproot themselves. A divorcee, for example, she comes out here to try to make some sense out of her life. She doesn't turn to the church. The first thing she does is head for the bar or the beach." Another, obviously homesick for Michigan, from which she had been transplanted, did not find the same casualness: "Rather, [it's] extremely conservative, a little bit standoffish from my experience. We haven't been truly happy here. People tend to be a little bit reserved. They—well, we, get so busy—we don't have time for church."

In the company store in Valsetz, Oregon, the local correspondent for a metropolitan paper, told me she had been here for eighteen years.

I grew up in Australia, an Anglican. Kicked around for many years. Came to Valsetz when my husband came to work in the power plant at the mill. I can't get turned on at all by the community church. Too much fundamentalism. Nothing here attracts me. High-Church Anglicanism might, that would be familiar to me. The local church might be a place for the few people—maybe 1 percent of the town—who want solace once a week. But I just don't have any incentive or motivation to go.

In Sarasota, a young couple from Indiana felt out of place. The wife said, "Very few young people here, we don't have anything in common with most of them." Her husband's work keeps him on the road four days a week, "only home here one weekend a month." When he "once in a while" goes to church, he finds it "nice, but mostly older people. Doesn't turn me on in the least." Another Sarasota County couple, with a home near Nokomis, described their situation as "hanging in mid-air." Both from Detroit, he is Armenian, "more or less Protestant"; she is Roman Catholic. Said he, "Eleanor hasn't gone to the Catholic Church, and I haven't gone to the Protestant. We used to trade off. One Sunday in her church, one Sunday in mine. Since we've been down here, it's neither. We are sort of hanging in the middle. We've talked about it, but no conclusions yet."

At a nearby community, on South Shore Drive, John Belerman told me he had company and didn't feel he could be of any help to me. He said he "moves a lot, twenty-eight years in Miami Beach, ten years over in Fort Lauderdale, seven years here. I'm not sure I'll stay. It might be premature to consider a church."

Other Nomads told stories that paralleled and amplified the excerpts already cited. Variations, of course appear, but rootlessness and difficulties of "settling in" to both communities and churches were shared in common. What I heard confirmed Vance Packard's conclusion: "Transients create fissures in a community. . . . By doing their own thing, they become indifferent to all but a few fellow citizens. . . . [It results] in a decline in satisfying group activities, in mutual trust, in psychological security. . . . Whether for better or worse, it encourages hedonism as a lifestyle."[5] Packard is rather sanguine about the ability of the churches in "a nation of strangers" to supply "instant involvement" for the nomads. My interviews failed to confirm this.

Type 8: The Pilgrims

I found many Pilgrims or searchers among youth—college students and young people in communes—but the type was not confined to them. Mrs. Martha McNamara, forty-eight, a successful Polk County businesswoman, is an example. She grew up in the South in Southern Baptist and Pentecostal churches. "I was a little bit, maybe, frightened as a child about God," she remembered. "We went to church every Sunday and my father was proud to line us five children up and into a pew. I taught Sunday School at an early age but some things scared me, the symbols of black for sin and red for the blood of Jesus."

When Martha was seventeen, she went to a Methodist church for the first time. "My parents were open," she said, "and I think mentally I was forming my own rebellion. I was getting a different idea of what religion was all about. . . . But, when [for reasons she didn't know] my mother dropped out of the church and my older brothers and sisters were gone, I was on my own. I continued to go to church."

Martha McNamara was married in Seattle, Washington, in 1950. They moved to Salem, Oregon, in 1966. Both joined a Methodist church. Martha was especially active. Her second child, then eighteen, developed "severe medical problems." Shortly afterward the couple separated. "He started drinking and did things I didn't approve of. Roy wasn't a good father, and I couldn't raise my children that way." Then, something happened that Martha "could never forget. . . . My church friends turned their backs on me. It really hurt. I don't really care to go back any more."

Meanwhile, Martha McNamara had been exploring other religions— Catholic and Jewish. "I like to go to as many churches as I can," she said. "And I have been exploring deeper feelings about religion. I guess I'm concocting my own religion from many religions now. Even though I don't go to church regularly any more, I think I am much more religions than before."

Today she is reading Ron Hubbard, the founder of Scientology. She visits the Delphian Foundation school, a Scientology institution at Sheridan, frequently. "I try to read through Hubbard's book, but I get lost in it. . . . But what those young folks are doing up at Sheridan fascinates me." She is attracted by the "serenity of the place, the peace and quiet of the people. They have space, too, and people need that— space for human activities and for communicating." For the future, Martha has few plans—just to survive in business. Recalling again her childhood, she ended our conversation where she began, "I don't like the hellfire and damnation way of scaring little children. Let them [the churches] just tell us that God is with us." She is still searching.

A woman student at New College in Florida was raised in Los Angeles, her mother Catholic, her father a nonpracticing Mormon. She went to a parochial elementary school, then to a Catholic high school. "It was kind of stifling—things handed to you to believe, you couldn't move out of bounds." She speaks of her last years before entering college as "a period of questioning. I didn't want anybody saying, 'This is the way you do it.' I had to find out for myself. In the end I had to decide." Since admission to college, she has "not been a good practicing Catholic." She told me, "I don't think there is anyone I know this year that goes to church. It is a kind of agnostic sort of place." But she is searching.

I'm examining a lot of things right now. I'm not sure of what I believe. I'm not certain about anything, and I may have to live with uncertainty for a long time. . . . When I go back and see high school friends, I remember what I experienced then: the communion gatherings, praying together, being together. But, here and now, I can't say. . . . I guess I'm much more of a humanist now, a lot of enthusiasm and idealism. I wish the church would be more concerned about planet Earth, to help change the wrongs, starvation, population, war, things like that, than coming out with doctrines that work against what I'm for. . . . I don't know that I will ever be a part of the church again officially.

Another youth, attending the University of California at Irvine, reflected a similar pilgrimage. He was baptized and confirmed in the Episcopal Church in New York City. He said that he liked going to church a lot as a teenager, but "I was having trouble believing what was being said." After private boarding schools in New Hampshire and Vermont, he began to think he was an atheist. "I thought then, for sure, that there was no God and that I would hold that position forever." Then things changed again.

There were some deaths close to my family. Then my grandmother. Recently, several close friends. It made me think that there must be something or some kind of God controlling things. I have a hard time articulating it. I'm confused. . . . If only the church would be more flexible, more willing to listen to what my questions are. At least they ought to be saying, "Hey, hang in there for another couple of years. It may all come together. . . ." I can't envision myself doing a turnabout and believing in God and Jesus as I did way back then. But it is possible.

An older youth, a recent college graduate of Oregon State University, said directly, "I am in a searching process. I need to acquire more wisdom before I can say what I believe. I refuse to pin myself down yet. I hope I can maintain an objective view as long as possible." He plans to continue searching, he said.

In Costa Mesa, California, I talked to Faith Baker, age thirty-seven, a widow with two small children. She has been "connected with" both Lutheranism and Catholicism, she said, although she can't remember ever being taught anything "religious" at home. She is not satisfied anywhere but keeps looking. "I feel I have a real need for something higher than myself. I recognize that. I feel like I need it. I periodically go search for it, but I can't find it. I can't buy the trip that Christian people tell me about. It just doesn't fit for me. I wish it did. I wish I could just believe blindly. I just can't."

Faith Baker is "into Eastern philosophy" just now. "I like the idea that God is in everything and that we are all part of the whole. The thing

I can't go for is that God is up there—supposedly—watching everybody and keeping notes. I can't buy that. No way!" She went on, "Life is kind of a game. That is the way it is. We might as well make the best of it. . . . If life is a game, why not make it a good game? I figure, why not play a good positive game, because I know when I do I feel good. When I'm playing a negative game, I don't feel so good." Her recent "games" have included yoga, astrology, the Metaphysical Church, Life Spring, Mind Dynamics, and est. "It's all trying to get to a higher consciousness. . . . But an awful lot of it is a ripoff. It costs a lot of money, and I think somebody's pocketing it. When I search for something, I keep running into stuff like this." Faith Baker seems to be searching, but what she seeks eludes her every time.

The Pilgrims tended to treat others tolerantly. "I don't argue with anyone, see," said a Georgia Bible School graduate, now unchurched, "I got my belief, let them have theirs." It sounded much like what I had heard in Maine, "Everyone is entitled to his opinion, and I have every right in the world to mine." In Oregon, the parallel was, "It could be right for you. It could be wrong for me. I can't buy one thing as more right than another." In California, "I accept other people's way of thinking even though I maybe don't agree with them. I expect that for me, too!"

All the Pilgrims seemed to need other people as they continued their searching but did not find in the churches the supporting communities that aided their pilgrimage.

Type 9: The Publicans

Hardly any of my informants fall outside this category. The charge that church people are hypocrites, phonies, fakers was made, at least in passing, by almost all of those with whom I spoke. This was anticipated. Most priests and ministers have heard the complaint whenever they have talked with the unchurched. The churches tend to respond to this accusation in one or more of three ways: (1) it is simply face-saving on the part of the nonmember who is trying to justify himself or herself, (2) the church has never claimed to consist of perfect Christians, or (3) the nonmember is making judgments about a few within who are perhaps marginal in their practice. These responses do little to reduce the force of the charge, however. It is a "picture in the head" that is not easily erased.

Leroy Austin, a chemical plant worker in Belfast, Maine, used words almost identical in thrust to our earlier citation from Ellul: "As far as I am concerned, [the church people] are no different from anybody else. I have met a lot of them, people that didn't go and people that did. I have always thought they was similar. I can never see any difference in them." A similar feeling was expressed by Sara Wadsworth, a Waldo County nurse, who spoke about her husband's disenchantment with the church:

His grandmother took him to the Baptist Church to be baptized. He was only a teenager then, and to hide his true feelings he said something flippant, something about "going swimming this morning." The pastor heard him and bawled him out, embarrassed him in front of the other boys, and told him, "You're not fit to be baptized." He went home and said, "If that is a Christian, I don't want to be one. . . ." Afterward, he would look around at people who were so pious in church and what they did out of church and would say, "If that's Christian, it isn't for me."

Frank Yoder is a caterer to the affluent in Sarasota, Florida. He is an unchurched Amish man. He defined what he meant by hypocrisy with these rambling comments.

I know a lot of wealthy people here who go to church every Sunday morning. We cater barbecues for their parties on Sunday afternoon each month. They really booze it up. I have even seen them start on the bottle when they hit their cars on the church parking lot. By three o'clock they are loaded. Going to church and four or five martinis right afterward don't mix. That's the way I think. That's not religion. That's hypocrisy. . . . Now, if a man can't do something out in the open and he has to sneak around people's back, that's a hypocrite. The good Lord sees you even when you sneak it. . . . I believe in right and wrong and conduct myself according. If I'm going to go to church, then I'm going to act the same out as in.

There were dozens of stories like Mr. Jenkins,' often centering on the outsiders' perception that Christianity demands abstinence or temperance with respect to alcohol, a requirement flagrantly violated by "so-called Christians."

The clerical leaders themselves are often perceived as the worst of the hypocrites. A young man in California recalled his days as an acolyte: "I was on the inside and saw all the bull of those hypocrites. I served mass for one priest and would fill the chalice five times with wine. This guy would be plastered by the time mass was over." An Alabaman, the only member of his family outside the church, recalled an evangelist who "left a bad taste in my mouth." He told how he "used to take my wife and kids out to the tent on Sunday nights. He [the preacher] read the riot act to everybody. But he didn't listen to it himself. He drinks, runs around with young girls when nobody's looking. He's darned worse than me." I met Bob Hogan early one Sunday morning at his house in an older section of Sarasota. He was drunk. "That visiting preacher at the Salvation Army. He had a lot of zip and fire. He shoved it to us all right. But I knowed him. He's a hypocrite himself. He don't practice what he preach. . . . I'm lazy. I'd rather have my own beer on Sunday morning than hear that guy again."

One Polk County farmer called the last Baptist minister he'd known, "Mr. Goody Two-Shoes." "He was one of the biggest crooks I ever run into in my life. In church, he was Goody Two-Shoes, but outside he was a cheat in business dealings. That turned me off right off the bat. . . . Every church I have gone to any length of time at all I have run into the same phony people." I asked if he found "phony people" outside the church. "Oh, indeed. But you expect something different inside, and you don't see it. The people who are real religious, at least the ones I have known, make me feel like they're looking down on me. At church they're so nice, it's disgusting; out here today, they won't give me a second thought. I can't operate on two sets of standards. I'm probably wrong to feel this way, but that is the way I feel."

More sophisticated, liberal persons faulted Christians as hypocrites on other grounds. Nonpracticing Protestant sectarians often charged that the Catholic penitential system encouraged hypocrisy. As one said, "A man can go out and shoot and murder, go to confession, and get absolved. I cannot accept that." A former government official, now living in Venice, Florida, spoke with disdain of "one of my good friends—he is the principal financial supporter of the Methodist church over here —[who] continues to tell nigger stories. He wouldn't have a black man to dinner for all the tea in China. When Dr. King got the Peace Medal, he thought that the folks in Sweden had gone crazy." An Army colonel in the South put it succinctly: "Church services in organized Christianity represent nothing more than a sacred canopy that covers the previous week's debauchery of its members." An Orange County housewife claimed that as early as age thirteen she remembered "the conflict in my own set of values and those of church people who thought they were nice but I didn't think they were very nice at all." In Marion County, the newcomers in particular told me about "an old Huey Long-type politician—crooked as can be, a millionaire on a country-town law practice income—who is the pillar of the church. That's the same church that's so loud about justice and things like that."

An interesting twist on the usual reason for separation from the church because of the members' hypocrisy was repeated several times by blacks in Alabama. One version went: "You are safer outside the church. Because then you don't hear the Word and what God requires of you. Then you're ignorant and God may be easier to you. But if you go to church and keep on acting the way you've always acted, God is going to hold it against you. If you goes to church, then follow the devil instead of God, you're in real trouble! You're going to hell. That's what the Bible says. You better believe it."

An Avon saleswoman in Sarasota, now interested in the Jehovah's Witnesses after leaving the Lutheran Church, told me the tale of her difficulty in getting help from fellow church members when she was having problems with an alcoholic husband. "I would think that any true Christian would want to help. They made Ed worse. They were the ones who picked up the check at the saloons," she said. "I think that is hypocritical. I can't stand being associated with people who are like that. . . . It is more important to live a daily life as a good Christian, like being helpful to others, sensitive to other people's needs. Any preacher who will preach that to me I have to take off my hat to him."

Rufus Saxton, eighty-two, a pensioned coal miner in Boone County, I was told, would have some "tall stories" about church people. His "atrocity story" may or may not be true, but he was convincing. He was converted at a tent-meeting revival, he said, in 1950. "Just got filled up, like. Almost raised above and off I went." He quit going to church shortly afterward. "Then same as now," he said.

> Lots of young girls was baptized t'other night at McCallister's place, right on the concrete. When they went out, they tried to tell me, "Now there ain't no harm to go out and take all you want. It ain't no sin." I said, "You're crazier than the devil wants you to be. If that's the kind of religion you have got, I don't want it." They leave the altar and just take off, they do. . . . Folks who do church work are like that, playing in the devil's workshop.

The Mennonite community in Polk County, Oregon, was the target of abuse by many of the outsiders. There was resentment by some businessmen that the Mennonites allegedly had a "Buy Mennonite

Directory": "They don't want to do business with us. But when they do, watch out!" A well-to-do seed farmer had them in mind when he said: "I have no fear whatsoever in business except the real religious ones. I will watch them closer than anybody else. Invariably, the ones that are supposedly the heathens, I don't have to worry about them. It's the 'good ones' that I get had by. In fact, I'm just expecting it now. I just watch them."

"Churches aren't too good for people," I heard from a young man in a Maine commune. "I think they are leading people astray. The churches are kind of hoky and the people are phony, fakers. . . . I look at churchgoers. It's incongruous the way they are. It doesn't do any good to see Richard Nixon and Gerald Ford go to church. When they come out, it's just like they don't believe anymore. If a person goes to church, he should live up to it."

In short, the Publicans view the church members as Pharisees. The charge is one of moral failure, most often when measured against strict, legalistic ethical norms. The perception is that church members, and sometimes their ministers as well, lead "two lives." "Inside," said one of my informants, "the church member thinks he is Jesus Christ himself, he is so good. Outside, you can't tell him from anybody else." The outsiders believe that there ought to be a difference, and that belief, they claim, has been fostered by the churches themselves. They believe what the churches say, but they find no evidence of the difference.

Type 10: The True Unbelievers

This category of response, as anticipated, proved to be small. Either, as Gallup has concluded consistently in his surveys, there are few true unbelievers in America, or, as I have indicated earlier, many unbelievers do not wish to bear the stigma that a public profession of unbelief would bring. My sojourn with the unchurched failed to discover the "village atheists" that are alleged to populate our towns from coast to coast. Had my sample been selectively drawn from academe, perhaps it would have been different. There are surely many Americans, both within and without the existing churches, with unconventional and less than ortho- dox beliefs. Few, however, call themselves irreligious.

Atheists-Agnostics, therefore, were at most only latently or implicitly so. A self-styled philosopher in Nokomis, Florida, was at the edge of agnosticism. "We are said to be made by God. Nobody else made us. Who gave us our minds or the idea of God? They say, 'God.' But what or who is God? Nobody can tell you that." An artist at Laguna Key, California, was more explicit and expansive:

Nothing is created. Everything is always here. Things just change form. Whatever is, was always here. The odds that gases coagulated to make matter and some of that matter became our earth are against it happening. I know. But it did happen. Creation is just change. . . .

There are some questions that are paradoxical, like "How round is a circle?" We have the intelligence to deal with some such abstractions, but others are just mysteries. I think that is as far as we can go. . . . I don't know if there is really a purpose for me or anybody. We are simply here at this particular place and time. Both these questions are meaningless: "Who am I?" "Why am I?"

God created earth? Well, wait a minute. The idea of being able to ask or say that presupposes that it didn't happen that way. Why do people have to be so definite about their answers to meaningless questions?

Even when I paint, I am only interpreting, not creating. I paint what I see with colors that are just there and scenes or people who happen to strike my fancy. Why do I paint? Because an artist has the gift of interpretation, that's all. . . . Could I paint God? Since I have not seen him, all I could do would be to paint other people's interpretations. It might just be a symbol of energy. My religion is my art. I am an interpreter.

A Boone County engineer put his unbelief in two sentences: "I have never thought that religion could solve my problems. I don't think I'm an atheist, agnostic perhaps, I just find it hard to talk about God."

An innkeeper in one of Maine's coastal towns, when I asked her if she had basic questions she would like to pose to the theologians or ministers, answered, "I would like somebody to convince me sometime that there really is a God. I need some kind of convincing about some things I still believe from my childhood training. The truth is, right now, I truly don't know if I believe or don't believe. I do know one thing—just don't get up there and preach at me or quote the Bible. Convince me somehow that this is really true."

The *Deist-Rationalist* is somewhat more common if the latent, unintellectualized versions of pantheism are included. Rather naively, I thought, some of those I talked to were simply parroting the familiar, "If there is a God, God is in the beauty of the flower, the tree, the hills, the mountains." Others had more rational grounds for their beliefs, without benefit of revelation.

"Belief in a personal God is just not rational," a California chemist said, and went on:

The narrowing gap of knowledge is getting smaller and smaller. If that is the area in which churches operate, they have less and less to talk about. It used to be that people would look up and they would see the hand of God in the clouds, the thunder, and the lightning. No more. . . .

There are, to be sure, some ultimate questions that may never be resolved, like "Where does the universe come from?" and "Where is it going?" and so forth. But when you realize the billions of worlds like this one, inhabited by people, you have left a personal God behind. It's hard to believe that anybody "up there" is really interested in your individual well-being. Man is in control of his own destiny as much as he can be.

A Sarasota woman, forty-five, perhaps reflecting her scientist-husband's orientation, revealed her unbelief, as some others did, in terms of the doctrines she rejected. "I do not believe in the Father, Son, and Holy Ghost. I believe in an overriding intelligence that ordered the planets. . . . I don't take communion because I can't believe 'This is my body.' I have found that when the church sticks to logic, I can get along with it. The Unitarians have it—I was very happy at All Souls Unitarian Church in Washington, D.C."

Reudiger Wolfe, a well-to-do German immigrant retiree, aged seventy-eight, living alone in a canyon cabin at the foothills of the Santa Anas, was effusive about his rational beliefs:

The universe is so fantastic, our brains can't understand it. It is absolutely impossible! Nobody knows, can answer the tough questions about it all. To call whatever is back of it all a "person" makes whatever it was too small.

I love nature. I can stay in the ocean all day. I love nature, the colors, the hills. I was out in the canyon walking all day today. I ride. I watch the birds when they fly on the roof. Sometimes, I think all of this is what some people call God.

But we still need churches. They're the only ones who can keep the discussion going. It's important that points of view come into dialogue, conflict in search of truth.

Humanists-Secularists abound among those who seem predominantly the happy Hedonists or the Pilgrims. A few excerpts, however, suggest the desirability of a discrete subtype. A college student, for example, classified herself as a humanist, "one who works for mankind. . . . I am getting a good education here at Monmouth, and I want to use it to change the wrongs I see out there. I think I can be a leader. I don't know how I'm going to go about it. That's why I'm here. To find out." A young Ivy League dropout, now in a Maine farm commune, expressed a kind of youthful idealism that was common among many. "The thing that is most important to me is having faith and love in people. That, to me, is what God is. That's what I'm developing my whole philosophy around right now. I have a loving feeling for myself, for other people. Compassion. That's it in a nutshell."

"I don't know what people are talking about when they say 'God' or 'religion,'" the prototypical Orange County secularist told me. "I just don't think religious thoughts, don't know when I last did. . . . I have my problems—everybody has them—but neither the churches nor religion can help me. I've got to do my best with my noodle up here."

There are, as in all taxonomies, the unclassified, the residuals who seem not to fall easily into any type. There were those who could give no articulate explanation of their lack of church affiliation. A celebrated circus performer, Karl Wallenda, told me of the history of his triumphs and tragedies. He expressed great respect for churches in the same fashion that he admired the Shriners and the Knights of Columbus. He showed me framed tributes from them all. His "religious" faith was best expressed by "Somebody up there protects me" or, when accidents and death occurred, "just Fate" or "maybe I'd let God down." The circus was essentially his religion, the high wire his liturgy, the applauding crowds his congregation. He was a preacher of sorts.

Others, perplexed, said simply, "I don't know why I don't go to church. I just really don't know."

NOTES

1. Jacques Ellul, *The Ethics of Freedom* (Grand Rapids, Mich.: Eerdmans, 1976), see Chap. 3.
2. This study, like existing survey research reports (such as NORC and Gallup), may not sufficiently tap the hard-core unbeliever within the college and university population. Public opinion omnibus surveys generally exclude interviews with students on college and university campuses in their stated policy of sampling "the *non*institutionalized, civilian population." Microsamples of college students are therefore important correctives to this and other research findings.
3. See, for example, the discussion by Wade Clark Roof, *Community and Commitment* (New York: Elsevier, 1978), pp. 28–31.
4. Vance Packard, *A Nation of Strangers* (New York: McKay, 1972). For official statistics, see U.S. Bureau of the Census, "Geographic Mobility: March 1975 to March 1977," Current Population Report no. 320 (Washington, D.C.: Government Printing Office, 1978).
5. Packard, *A Nation of Strangers*, pp. 5, 156, 270.

Part Four

REFLECTIONS:
AN UNSCIENTIFIC POSTSCRIPT

WHAT IS the significance of these pictures in the heads of the un-churched for sociologists of religion and for the churches in the United States?

Actually, the full dimensions of the pictures people have in their heads—in this case, pictures of the churches from which they are alien-ated—are never fully accessible to other people. "Backstage behavior," as Erving Goffman[1] has called the hiddenness of the ordinary person's presentation of the self, can only be intuited. What *really* is going on in people's heads may never be known by persons themselves or by others who presume to analyze and "know" them. What *appears* to be going on, as the phenomenologists argue, is the best we can explore. Howard Garfinkel would go further: "What goes on in people's heads is of no interest; we cannot read people's minds," he maintains. But we can hear the stories minds create. What shows itself is real, even though in people's oral self-revelation they may be playing games. It is crucial to know what the game is.[2]

I have indicated in Chapter 1 that the theory and method employed in this study are eclectic. It should be apparent, however, that I lean heavily on what Monica B. Morris has called the "creative sociologies," pioneered by such theorists as Husserl, Weber, and Schutz; Mead, Blumer, and Goffman; Berger and Luckmann; and Stein and Garfinkel.[3] They represent a blend of phenomenologists, symbolic interactionists, dramaturgiologists, and ethnomethodologists. Their theories and methodologies have in common a rejection of positivism that restricts itself to the data of experience discovered and verified by the methods of the natural sciences. Implicitly, all share Max Weber's central thesis: *Of foremost importance in understanding social behavior is the discovery of the meaning of an act in terms of the actors themselves.*

How do pictures get into people's heads? What do these pictures mean? To answer these questions, one begins with the assumption that the individual is not born a member of a society.[4] The individual *becomes* such. Personhood is the product of the interaction of the stuff of personality with others—people and groups. The individual becomes a member of society as the individual chooses or permits the successive worlds opened to him or her to be internalized; that is, "taken over" as meaningful and instrumental for the self. The progressively maturing child learns the arts of verbal communication, trust, love, play, and thought through meaningful association with significant others. The child "understands" the world as others communicate that world and as the child accepts the outside world as his or her own world. What is real outside is what has been become real inside. In early socialization, a determination of sorts is inevitable, for no child chooses parents, kin, or the significant others with whom he or she relates. They are given. So is the child's "first world." It is filtered selectively according to the perspectives and positions of others.

The simple picture of early childhood changes to multiple pictures as the individual moves into adulthood. Hundreds of new worlds, different and often at odds with the "first world," open up as the person's significant others multiply and as extrafamilial groups and institutions expand one's ever-changing construction of reality. Schools, neighborhoods, places of residence, work experiences, love, and marriage add to one's "stock of knowledge and experience" and introduce new realities and options for one's construction of a world outside that makes sense inside.[5]

With more or less success, people try to fit their several perceptions of the outside together. They sift through and select those worlds with which they can cope and that offer greatest satisfactions. They establish priorities among the options they internalize. They establish routines to maintain the existence of that which has been made their own. They find other people with similar perspectives to support their choices. They join groups and become members of institutions that provide continuing plausibility (that is, reasonableness, meaningfulness, and trustworthiness) for the picture world they have "taken over." The process never ends. People are always constructing and maintaining their world, tearing down and building up, altering and modifying, adding and subtracting. The process aims at coherence and a minimum of dissonance, neither ever perfectly achieved.

No simple instrument has yet been invented to take x-ray shots of the complex pictures people construct of the world outside. But people *do* things; they act. Their definitions of situations (that is, their "pictures") inform their actions.[6] In acting, their world pictures are unveiled. To do and to act is also to tell. People account for what they do in continual story telling, ordinary conversational activity that represents the defining and redefining of their reality. People go about the task of explaining their world, making sense out of it both to themselves and to others, by telling about it. Such talk gives important clues to the kind of picture world people have in their heads. As Peter Berger theorizes, "The subjective reality of the world hangs on the thin thread of conversation."[7] Conversational stories are reflections of the reality people have created for themselves.

The anecdotal material collected in this study reports the perspectives people have of the world we call "church." All the stories have in common a singular behavioral result; namely, separation from the religious institutions of our society. Whether people inside the churches might tell similar stories has not been the purpose of this inquiry, although it might be surmised that their stories bear some resemblance to the stories of the outsiders. We do not know precisely what triggers the exodus for some and what holds others in. The indications seem to suggest that for most the process of estrangement is gradual. The autobiographical accounts reveal an erosion of attachment presaged in childhood or adolescence and completed in young or later adulthood. Because the evidence from other studies is not uniform, one cannot with certainty count on "return to religion and the church" by parents with the birth of children nor by older people in the closing years of life. Transformations or conversions, of course, do happen, but as Berger observes, this requires strongly affective identifications with significant others and plausibility structures that guide people into new realities and sustain them. The stories I have recounted, however, indicate that those significant others are not there for the unchurched. Nor are the structures any longer plausible. For many who still claim to believe, the problem of living is compounded. They live in two discrepant worlds, believing but not belonging.

The final two chapters explore the implications of our findings for theory and research (Chapter 11) and for the churches (Chapter 12).

NOTES

1. Erving Goffman, *The Presentation of Self in Everyday Life* (New York: Doubleday, 1969).
2. Harold Garfinkel, remarks at the American Sociological Association annual meeting, San Francisco, August 1975. See also Harold Garfinkel, "Common Sense Knowledge of Social Structures: The Documentary Method of Interpretation," in Jordan M. Scher, ed. *Theories of the Mind* (New York: Free Press, 1962); and Harold Garfinkel, *Studies in Ethnomethodology* (Englewood Cliffs, N.J.: Prentice-Hall, 1967).
3. Monica B. Morris, *An Excursion into Creative Sociology* (New York: Columbia University Press, 1977). The bibliography, pp. 191–206, is the most comprehensive available.
4. This discussion is informed by Schutz, Luckmann, and Berger. See Alfred Schutz and Thomas Luckmann, *The Structures of the Life-World* (Evanston, Ill.: Northwestern University Press, 1973), trans. Richard M. Zaner and H. Tristram Engelhardt; Peter L. Berger and Thomas Luckmann, *The Social Construction of Reality* (New York: Doubleday, 1967); and Peter L. Berger, *The Sacred Canopy: Elements of a Sociological Theory of Religion* (Garden City, N.Y.: Anchor/Doubleday, 1969); also, Jack Douglas, ed., *Understanding Everyday Life* (Chicago: Aldine, 1970).
5. "Stock of knowledge" is Alfred Schutz's phrase, by which he refers to the internalized accumulation of experience in the everyday world. For discussion, see Schutz and Luckmann, *The Structures of the Life-World*, pp. 7, 9–15, 66–70, and elsewhere throughout.
6. W. I. Thomas is the inventor of this familiar concept. It is central in the thought of symbolic interactionism and contemporary ethnomethodology. See Herbert Blumer, *Symbolic Interactionism: Perspective and Method* (Englewood Cliffs, N.J.: Prentice-Hall, 1969).
7. Berger, *Sacred Canopy*, pp. 16–17.

11. Implications for the Sociology of Religion

The masses of unchurched people that persist in the American society
—40 percent of the population—are a phenomenon largely neglected
by sociologists of religion. Only in the last decade or so has even a faint
interest begun to express itself.[1] Why this is so remains a mystery.
Certainly, as I have documented here, the evidence does not suggest
that the problem is novel in the American experience. Why then has
it not been attended?

One can only conjecture, but there are plausible reasons for the
neglect. While the classic theorists in the early sociological tradition—
Comte, Durkheim, Simmel, Tönnies, Weber, and others—placed religion near the center of their studies, other emphases have tended to
survive and to inform the subsequent development of theory and research. Part of this, undoubtedly, is the consequence of the discipline's
early efforts to carve out for itself a respectable niche in the world of
scholarship. One option was to separate itself from the philosophical
mold from which it emerged. Today, this separation is almost complete
except for the relatively few in the fraternity who persist in their exploration of epistemological problems. American sociology in particular has
run this course. The close alliance between sociology and the world of
religion that characterized early twentieth-century developments in sociology gradually eroded. Although a revival of interest in the sociology
of religion began in the 1950s, the coterie of scholars and researchers
in this field continues to represent a small minority of the whole. Articles
in scholarly journals, the corpus of books, the agenda at professional
meetings, and funded research suggest that religion is peripheral to most

sociological inquiry. Standard textbooks generally treat religion as an epiphenomenon, that is, a matter of interest only as it appears alongside something else that is its cause or explanation.

When renewed attention began to develop some twenty-five years ago, it coincided with an alleged revival of religion on the American scene and with the "coming of age" of sociology as a scientific discipline. These two parallel trends had important consequences. Those who opted for religious research were attracted to the institutionalized forms of religion—sects and churches—and to the social behavior of those who claimed allegiance to them. There was plenty of data to collect, analyze, and explain. The methods employed were increasingly quantitative, and the scarce resources for research, as every scholar in the field has noted, have dictated both the choice of problems and the methodologies employed. In the process, "irreligion," however conceptualized, and the unchurched phenomenon, however quantified, continue to suffer from inattention. The current, alleged new boom of religious interest again appears to be turning attention elsewhere—to the fractures in the religious establishment, to new forms of religious consciousness, and to the more bizarre and exotic manifestations of religion.

The argument of this book is that unchurchedness is a significant social phenomenon and a legitimate field of inquiry. The research methods appropriate to the task will remain in dispute, as will the theories that generalize the findings. Rather than inhibiting study, one might argue that the ferment and ambiguity about where to begin is fruitful ground for creativity. In this exploratory study, a primitive beginning has been made. Like Goffman, I make no claim that my examples are necessarily typical nor systematically gathered. They are not presented as proofs of facts but as clarifying depictions, in a sense, as "frame fantasies which manage, through the hundred liberties taken by their tellers, to celebrate [their] beliefs about the workings of the world."[2] If they render insights for future research, even rudimentary explorations such as this suggest hypotheses for testing.

In Part Two of this book, "Odyssey in the Land of the Unchurched," I have shown that what people say and the way they say it are shaped by and shape the social worlds of which they are a part. For long-time natives of a place like Marion County, Alabama, the world pictures in people's heads bear an affinity with the ethos of their environment. The dominant motif of the culture is created by those humans who have constructed their culture and, in turn, create the humans who are the products of the culture. People in northwestern Alabama carry with them a social construction of reality formed by the familial patterns of home and village that have been reinforced over generations by the institutions they have built. For those inside the old culture, which still survives as a kind of "first world" of childhood, the churches are prime plausibility structures that sustain and nourish the innocence of the past. Increasingly, however as a new way of life intrudes, some face the dissonance between the rhetoric they celebrate in their churches and the economic realities that constitute their daily work routines. They have trouble putting their two worlds together. For those new to the region, the problem is more serious. They bring different values with them that clash with those of their neighbors. They see the traditional institutions as obsolete, at least for their needs, and they build new structures or attempt to build new values into old structures. In either case, the marginality of the new spawns strain and conflict. Unable to cope, both oldtimers and newcomers, especially the newcomers, opt out altogether or retreat into their own fragile private worlds. The churches suffer the most, holding the continuing allegiance of fewer than half the people.

Similar observations can be made of Boone County residents. The fierce "independentism" of a West Virginia mining community, born of the harshness of the environment and the pride that alone guarantees psychological survival, is ripe soil for independent churches. The warmth of the revival helps compensate for the coldness of the culture. Even Joe Turner's snake-handling liturgy, although not characteristic of the religious fare of most of the churches, becomes symbolic as a communion ritual to celebrate transcendance over the mean, the ugly, and the mundane and the inevitabilities of danger and death. The intrusion of the outside world, epitomized by federal courts, which thwart local miners; by the state, which determines school textbooks; by "outside" ministers who are "sent in" to lead local churches; and by economic interests that rape the hills and rob them of revenues—this fosters a religious world plausible only in its exclusiveness and separation from the rest of the world. To be "saved" again and again is enough. "Power, power, wonder-working power," as a favorite gospel song puts it, certifies release from impotence and promises a heavenly bliss this world cannot give. And, with Jesus, they can do it alone; 75 percent of them, perhaps believing, do not need to belong.

In the Sun Belt counties of Florida and California, the people shape and are shaped by their environments. The retirees of Sarasota leave their baggage up north and start over. The community responds and offers not only sunshine but also an overabundance of ultimate or transient values packaged for the taking. People buy in with limited risks by sampling the smorgasbord of institutional offerings and by withholding enduring loyalties. Orange County, California, provides a climate of casual acceptance, an open society with a minimum of inhibitions, the siren song of alluring, pleasurable delights, and a vast array of competing and surrogate faiths. Even religion, Bryan Wilson suggests, in such a culture may become a leisure activity.

Its intimate connection with work and the rhythms of life diminish as men's work activities come to have less direct concern with nature and more with man's own material and organizational products. The goals of working are now located, both in the minds of men and according to the assumptions on which modern social systems operate, and by which motivation is mobilized firmly in the after-work sphere of men's lives. It is "after work," not "after-life," which looms large in [their] thinking. . . . If religion is no longer significant as a fundamental activity of social life, even in the leisure sphere it faces at once the competition of a variety of others, increasingly powerful, technological and dynamic agencies . . . that seek to command more of men's attention, energies, and material resources. . . . Religious agencies which seek no material reward and which emphasize their moral, educational, socializing mission, become, because of these very items, suspect.[3]

Orange County is such a world, and the stories of the unchurched there confirm Wilson's commentary. Again and again the unchurched fault the churches for their failure to express the needs and concerns of nomadic, hedonistic industrial humans. What religion survives among the unchurched virtually has to be private, because value consensus in this urban place is gone. There is no longer, if there ever was, a widespread consensus of religious allegiance, and as Wilson claims, the "postures of dominance assumed by old established religions serve only to irritate men, and to enhance their incredibility and irrelevance." The successes of mass religion in such places as Melodyland, a huge religious enterprise near Disneyland in Anaheim, California, and Robert Schuller's "Crystal Cathedral," the elaborate new edifice of Garden Grove Community Church, in Orange County, California, may be less the evidence of a new consensus around "old-time religion" than possibility cults, highly institutionalized, that promise success for the believer. The subcultures of belief, burgeoning among the youth and infiltrating conventional religion, find expression in Eastern religions

and the growth potential movement. They function as competing plausibility structures against what their devotees call the ossified main line
churches. Old styles, old idioms, old rituals, old religious structures fail
to satisfy the majority who would seek meaning and purpose in Orange
County. If Orange County is prototypical for the nation, as I have
suggested may be the case, the scenario for the future American religious
experience is radically different from that which we have known in the
past.

Polk County, Oregon, and Waldo County, Maine, provide comparable correspondence between what people say about their churches and
the community ethos out of which their talk comes. The frontier mentality that says, "Don't fence me in" is understandably echoed in the
rejection of churches that "box people in." And Yankee "tolerance"
easily becomes warrant for freedom from religion and its institutions.

In the search for extreme unchurchedness, that is, in selected counties
of the nation with exceptionally high rates of alienation from established
churches stratified in regions with similar high disaffiliation, the sample
counties in this study give disproportionate attention to ratios over
against absolute numbers. The findings would suggest that, contrary to
popular opinion, the unchurched phenomenon in the United States may
be primarily rural rather than urban. Such an hypothesis needs further
testing. Provisionally, however, one is impressed that ten of the fifteen
largest cities in the United States have unchurched rates well *below* the
national average. Only the three largest California cities (Los Angeles,
San Francisco, and San Diego), New York, and Indianapolis provide
exceptions. Even New York City's rate, adjusted for its heavy Jewish
population, is a questionable exception.

Yet the sheer volume of absolute numbers of unchurched people in
large metropolitan areas far exceeds the numbers in other places. Would
a scientific sample from these areas provide a different picture from the
one this exploratory study has drawn? Probably not, if the cities of
Orange and Sarasota are at all typical. Neither the survey research of
Roozen nor the opinion polls of Gallup result in marked differences
between urban and nonurban samples.[4] In a limited research study in
1978 by the *Detroit News* of Wayne, Oakland, and Macomb counties
in Michigan, no ideosyncratic findings were reported.[5] *Catholic Life in
Yorkville*, a 1976 research study of church life and religious practices in
the Archdiocese of New York among practicing and nonpracticing
Catholics, corroborates our observations: "For those who no longer

relate to the church, and in serious ways for those who are still regular attenders at church, the church does not offer a plausibility structure to people. . . . Faith, morality, community: These are the central issues."[6] A major study commissioned by the National Conference of Catholic Bishops in 1979 will examine attitudes and behaviors of active and lapsed Catholics in the Washington, D.C., metropolitan area. The findings of such a micro study in a major eastern metropolitan center will be illuminating.[7]

Readers of the anecdotal material will share with me a degree of dissatisfaction with the discreteness of the categories of the taxonomy. The types offered in this reporting represent a modest revision of my original taxonomy. Parsimony would suggest that further reduction of the number of types might be achieved. William McKinney, staff researcher for the United Church of Christ Board of Homeland Ministries, has suggested four broad groupings: the *committed unchurched* (5 to 10 percent of the total population; for these religious faith is no longer an option); the *disenchanted* (the "reactive dropouts," those who covet church relationships but for whom church experiences have been so unsatisfactory or painful that they stay outside); the *searchers* (the "millions of persons of all ages and backgrounds for whom the religious quest is a serious and ongoing one"); and the *otherwise engaged* (those who take a stance of "benign neglect," indifference or apathy, and opt for "more interesting or compelling activities").[8] Rabbi Solomon Bernards, of the Anti-Defamation League of B'nai B'rith, finds the types possibly reducible to the questions of the "four sons" in the Haggadah, the book containing the liturgy for the Seder in the Jewish festival of Passover: the *intelligent son* (who questions the meaning of the testimonies); the *wicked son* (a prodigal disassociated from the religious community); the *simple son* (who asks, "What is this?"); and the *fourth son* (who does not yet know how to ask).[9]

A general profile of the unchurched has limitations, the most serious being the substitution (in most survey research) of ciphers for persons. This taxonomy tends to focus on categories of responses but does not escape labeling persons. The aim has been to provide typifications, from ordinary conversation with "the man on the street," of the variety of reasons persons cite for their disaffiliation from the churches. Their stories provide a multitude of different "pictures in the head" for us. I have chosen to allow the autobiographical anecdotes to construct their own classifications. The result remains impressionistic. If it is sufficiently exhaustive, however, it may lend itself to operationalization in future empirical studies. Despite its limitations, the collection of stories provide a dramatic frame of reference often subdued in quantitative studies. Perhaps the craft of sociological research needs to exploit those methods that further probe the attitudes of everyday life as it is lived and articulated in simple, vulgarized, deintellectualized rhetoric, which is a major medium for the expression of why people are unchurched. Rigorous content analysis of their unstructured accounts might yield more understanding than the researcher's battery of questions in pencil-and-paper instruments or in prescheduled, focused interviews. It may be less productive of meaning to test our hypotheses than to discover what theories need to be tested.

Some existing theories that presume to explain the religious experience in America may be due for modification as our understanding increases of the reasons given for defection from the religious institutions by large proportions of the population at all stages of the nation's history. "Deprivation," "socialization," "secularization," "generational conflict" and other theories may not yet be sufficient to account for why millions opt in or opt out of our existing religious communities. Until there can be minimal consensus on what we are studying and what kind of data is required to study it, conceptualizations will remain fuzzy, methodology will not fit the problem, and theories will offer at best partial explanations.

A promising line of inquiry suggested by this study is that unchurchedness may be linked to another phenomenon, long a cherished field of inquiry among sociologists, namely, alienation. If this is so, unchurchedness may be the epiphenomenon. Its roots may lie outside the religious domain entirely. To be outside the churches in America may also be to be apart from other community-building enterprises, associations, and institutions in our society. A clue that this may be true emerges from parallel findings in the Roozen and Gallup studies. The Roozen data generally show that the unchurched are not only not involved in the life of the church, but are also less likely than the churched to be involved in any type of organization. In the Gallup study, three-fourths of the unchurched said they belonged to no voluntary organization. Both studies indicate that the unchurched have shallow roots in their communities and move more often than the churched. The marginality of the unchurched with respect to the churches may be a function of marginality of people in the culture generally, or they may be linked in ways we do not yet understand.

The natural life history of movement from participation to nonparticipation in a church also needs more attention. This study suggests several patterns: early childhood attrition, adolescent disaffection, voluntary or involuntary withdrawal in adulthood as a result of problems of faith or morality; or disengagement in the later years of life (as exemplified by the elderly "start-overs" of Sarasota). The rites of passage by which people become members of religious communities are well known. The rite of passage by which people leave, the "tipping phenomenon," remains unexplored.

In short, the research potential is promising if there are those who believe that the unchurched phenomenon is important enough to warrant attention. It would be foolish to suggest what methods might yield maximum results. Joseph Bensman and Robert Lilienfeld emphasize this: "Since the world of experience is infinite, subject to an unlimited number of perspectives, there is little likelihood that one will be able to ascertain a true image or absolute knowledge of any one thing" by any one method. The sociological heresy is to refuse to entertain alternative possibilities.[10] Both quantitative and qualitative research have limitations, but both have potentials as yet minimally exploited. Charles Glock, while inclined to prefer quantitative studies using the sample survey, nonetheless admits the promise of depth interviews, participant observation, and content analysis of autobiographies and contemporary writings.[11] Bryan Wilson prefers historical-cultural studies that analyze patterns of social relationships in institutions and communities. We might look at certain elite strata in the society as well as the mass of the population for clues to discover who bears and transmits religion in our society and how.[12] Comparative ethnographic community studies of two or more relatively small communities are feasible—Hooker County, Nebraska, and Alpine County, California, for example, both with less than 1,000 population, the former 86 percent churched, the latter, 93 percent unchurched. Longitudinal studies of changes in the religious experience of Americans over long periods of times offer promise, although most scholars would agree that much work yet needs to be done to identify the significant causal and predictive indicators of change in the religious domain.

Questions abound. Answers are scarce. They need to be sought. This is the stuff of the sociological imagination.

NOTES

1. Armand L. Mauss, in perhaps the first empirical study of the unchurched, confirms this judgment. He writes: "It is probably indicative of a bias in social science that religious *commitment* is considered a research problem, but religious *defection* is not." See his "Dimensions of Religious Defection," *Review of Religious Research* 10, no. 3 (Spring 1969): pp. 128–135.
2. Erving Goffman, *Frame Analysis* (New York: Harper & Row, 1974), p. 15.
3. Bryan Wilson, in Rocco Caporale and Antonio Grumelli, eds., *The Culture of Unbelief* (Berkeley: University of California Press, 1971), p. 265.
4. Survey of *The Unchurched American* (Princeton, N.J.: Gallup Organization, 1978), and David A. Roozen, *The Churched and Unchurched in America, A Comparative Profile* (Washington, D.C.: Glenmary Research Center, 1978).
5. *Ibid.*
6. Philip J. Murnion and Ruth T. Doyle, *Catholic Life in Yorkville* (New York: Office of Pastoral Research, Archidiocese of New York, 1976), pp. 56–60.
7. The project will be carried out by a research team with Dean R. Hoge as director, at the Catholic University of America, Washington, D.C.
8. William McKinney, "The Unchurched—Believers on the Outside," in *A.D. 1979* (United Presbyterian Journal) 8, no. 2 (February 1979): 26–29.
9. Private correspondence.
10. Joseph Bensman and Robert Lilienfeld, *Craft and Consciousness* (New York: Wiley, 1974), p. 344.
11. Caporale and Grumelli, *The Culture of Unbelief*, p. 66.
12. *Ibid.*, p. 126.

12. The Unchurched and Evangelization

Current interest in evangelization within and among the Christian churches[1] has dual origins—theological and ecclesiastical.

Theologically, both conservative and liberal Protestants and Roman Catholics have rediscovered the *raison d'etre* of the church in evangelization. At the first assembly of the World Council of Churches in 1948, the delegates declared that "evangelism is the supreme task of the churches" and the evident demand is that the "whole church sets itself to winning the whole world for Christ." To evangelize is to "participate in the life of Jesus Christ as Savior and Lord that they may share his eternal life. Here is the heart of the matter."[2] When Pope John XXIII convoked Vatican II on Christmas Day, 1961, he called the council to imbue "with Christian light and to penetrate with fervent spiritual energy not only the intimacy of the soul but the whole collection of human activities."[3] Pope Paul VI chose "Evangelization of the Modern World" as the theme of the fourth Synod of Bishops in 1974. He saw evangelization as "the essential and primary mission of the church,"[4] and in 1975 in *Evangelii Nuntiandi* he spoke of the need of "bringing the Good News into all the strata of humanity and through its influence transforming humanity from within and making it new."[5] The 1974 Lausanne Congress of evangelicals affirmed that "in the church's mission of sacrificial service evangelism is primary. World evangelization requires the whole church to take the whole gospel to the whole world."[6]

While the focus is uniform, debate continues within and among the various branches of the Christian church on the proper content, method, and target of evangelization. Within Catholicism, for example, especially in Latin America, the ideological debate between "liberation theology," spawned at Medellin, Columbia, in 1968, and the more conservative, ambiguous theology, which emerged from Puebla, Mexico, in 1979, indicates the persistent strains. Activities of the World Council of Churches in the 1970s to combat racism in South Africa have raised the specter of potential defections among those member churches who see the potential tarnishing of the gospel in any alliance of churches with violent revolutionary forces. Not all evangelicals are fully convinced that "evangelism and sociopolitical involvement are both part of our Christian duty"[7] without distinguishing priorities. Protestants and Catholics agree that in a pluralistic faith world, the choice of faith ought to be free. The old triumphalism that sought to coerce belief by cultural heritage or social pressure is probably dead. Yet the limits and extent of pluralism remain problematic within those churches that see themselves as the established guardians of truth. Few, even in Catholicism, assert any longer the old theological saying *Extra ecclesiam nulla salus* ("Outside the church there is no salvation"). Yet, as Martin Marty observes, the new evangelizers never work wholly outside the context of the religious communities.[8] The central datum of ecumenical thinking—Catholic, Protestant, and Orthodox—remains: "There is no conversion *without* the church . . . and this mission is central *for* the church."[9]

The means by which the peculiar treasures of the churches are to be shared is the sharpest source of internal contention. Revivals, protracted meetings, and rallies, long the authentic symbols of evangelization in the American Protestant experience of the eighteenth and nineteenth centuries, are perpetuated today in new institutionalized patterns by the conservative evangelicals, but are rejected by most mainline churches. Proclamation largely confined to the captured, gathered community of the faithful is seen by evangelicals and others as lacking genuine witness to the world of unbelievers. Recent Catholic emphasis on the "second moment" of evangelization, namely the lived faith response to the proclaimed Word,[10] raises for some Protestants the problem of "works righteousness" and its failure to recognize that the church has no ultimate stake in the outcome of its proclamation. All the churches seem ready to employ modern modes of communication, but they differ on the propriety of billboard advertising and bumper stickers, on communal versus individual witnessing, on "paid" versus "public service" radio and television broadcasting, on tract distribution versus small group discussion. Preferred styles will range from the soft sell of open dialogue to the hard sell of confrontation.

Ecclesiastically, the current renewed interest in evangelization stems from the recognition of membership attrition by individual denominations. The losses have been serious and have resulted in program and personnel retrenchment by the bureaucracies of most ecclesiastical bodies. Older churches in former bastions of mainline Protestant strength have been closed by the hundreds, and educational facilities newly built in the mushrooming suburbs in the 1950s are often unused today. Growing conservative churches seldom increase in membership in proportion to the growth of their communities and lag behind the records established by Christian churches in the Third World. Fewer of the faithful among Roman Catholics attend mass as frequently as they did a decade ago, and the slippage among youth is internally perceived with alarm. Meanwhile, the churches note the widespread "new religious consciousness" as a movement running counter to establishment religion further detracting from the plausibility of orthodox Christianity. However dismissed publicly by mainline churches, many church leaders privately agree with the Church Growth Institute, which candidly says, "The bottom line is numbers."

Some theological problems cannot be resolved here. They will require continued attention by the interpreters of the Christian message. Two conflicting assumptions, both derived from New Testament scriptures, underlie the church's self-understanding of its mission. One interprets the New Testament mandate as "winning people to acknowledge Christ as Savior so that they give themselves to His service in the fellowship of His Church" (William Temple).[11] This implies that the test of effective evangelization is the degree to which converts become incorporated into the life of the institutional church. Church growth—adding to the rolls—becomes the ultimate objective.

An alternate reading sees the Christian movement as essentially a diaspora, a saving remnant, "buried like seed, like leaven, like salt in the earth of a common humanity" (Hans-Ruedi Weber).[12] This implies that the test of effective evangelization is the degree and depth of Christian commitment, as manifested in the activity of Christians in the world. Preoccupation with numerical growth in membership is seen as self-defeating, productive of half-hearted adherents incapable of effective penetration into the world of secularity.

The data of this exploratory study speaks neither to this issue directly nor to the modes of evangelization most consistent with the church's task. Whether growth or commitment is the test (or both, as many in the churches would argue), tendencies in either direction are vulnerable, from the standpoint of the churches. An emphasis on the gathered community and its desired expansion may unleash exploitative and manipulative styles of witness in the church's effort to succeed, styles perhaps destructive of the very message it seeks to share. Yet the rationalization of shrinking memberships, the consequence of emphasis on "authentic commitment," may lead to a "theology of failure." The one risks the danger of overvaluing the institution, the other of docetizing it, that is, denying its empirical reality. Neither adequately deals with the question of whether some of the unchurched whose stories are told here might already have achieved a more faithful and satisfying expression of their faith apart from the existing institutional churches of our time and place. This question has been seriously posed by ministers, priests, and laypeople who have listened to some of the original taped conversations (the stories of Mary Lou, Emily, and Carlos, in particular, as transcribed in Chapter 2). If this possibility is admitted, a whole range of new theological questions is raised that the church's theology has inadequately addressed.

Theologian Paul Tillich is one of the few theologians of recent times to have addressed the problem of communication. For him, the question was less, "What is the Christian message?" than "How can it be communicated?" Tillich's answer was—"participate in human existence." The plausibility of the Christian faith requires that the communicator help others understand their own predicament, mirror their structures of anxiety, and facilitate a process wherein another's free yes or no to Christian claims is made possible. Martin Luther struggled in his time against a doctrine that insisted that making oneself acceptable to God was prior to God's acceptance of the sinner. Tillich was right, I feel, in claiming that it is always the other way around. Orthodox theology has been consistent that this is the meaning of grace. Thus, it is questionable whether the first task of the evangelist is to preach to them or to tell them that the church possesses all the answers to their questions. The church may be most in communication when least self-conscious about it. "Telling it straight" often has a self-consciousness that gets in the way. Thus, indirection may be the more effective mode of witnessing.[13] The first task may be the "wordless deed," the act of entering into the other's sufferings, hostility, and alienation—even with the confession that the evangelist has been there too.

Acceptance of the other, particularly of the unchurched, seldom occurs when the communicator's preoccupation is in winning a debate, in badgering the other person with the inconsistencies of his or her arguments, or in supplying answers to questions the other may not be asking. Plausibility for the Christian story and promise is not won in monologue preachments, nor are human relationships built that way. A student at Hamburg University, in Germany, where I had outlined the method of my 1976 project just a month before I began my interviews with the unchurched in America,[14] asked me whether I was prepared to hear from them articulations of faith preferable to my own. I answered, "I hope so. That's the risk." That dialogue was fresh in my mind during my first interview in Sarasota, Florida. I recalled Paul Tournier's story of a psychiatrist friend who once remarked, "I used to be able to put my patients into two categories, the congenial and the uncongenial. But now that I have begun to get interested in them as persons, I find them all congenial." Congeniality is the sharing of personhood. Such sharing requires active listening.

An unexpected by-product of this exploratory study is that the research method employed provided a clue for evangelization. That was not the study's intention, and the reporting of it here is clearly an unscientific postscript. The overwhelming experience my conversations with the unchurched conveyed to me—the sort of conversion from which I will never recover—was that those outside the churches wanted and needed to be heard. Surely, some of them told me stories about themselves and about their sad and tragic experiences in the churches of America that were far short of everything they might have said. They also told me as little as they wanted me to know. What they said was presumably what they wanted to say. The vast majority, when they sensed that I was honestly open to hear even the most insignificant (to me) or ridiculous (to them) or poignant (to anyone who listens) of autobiographical episodes, appreciated the cathartic moment. What I recorded on dozens of tapes and that portion of the 2,000 pages of transcriptions selected for inclusion in this book convinces me of the storytellers' essential candidness, openness, and truthfulness. They desperately wanted someone to hear. Presumably my promise and willingness to listen helped them to recollect, to feel the experiences they recalled, and to share them with a complete stranger.

The unstructured interview method I employed is, of course, not completely replicable by evangelists, whether clerical or lay. Most "witnesses" from the churches operate on home turf where they are either known or occupy positions with respect to a particular church. By contrast, I was an alien to their communities, not connected with their institutions, nor perceived as one with answers to their inquiries. I studiously avoided, in my role as objective outsider, responding to their questions about faith. I did not attempt to defend either the church or my own commitments. This often dumbfounded and frustrated some of my informants, as any interviewer who is asked for his or her opinions has experienced. The advantage for the researcher, and indirectly a learning for would-be evangelists, is that this style presents no threat, no judgment, and no censure on anything another feels moved to share. The potential dividends in being able to "hear people out" are enormous. Whether the evangelist can adopt such a stance, without deception, among the unchurched in one's own community is moot.

Learning to engage in active listening is, however, a mode of sharing in communication that can be learned by any reasonably empathic person. The skills are known and can be taught.[15] Clergy and laity have used them for decades in personal and group counseling. They have had little use in the church's work of evangelization. It is significant—whether in the communication of Christian truth or in the teaching of any new thing—that readiness to hear or learn is the absolute precondition for change. Prior to any readiness to hear the "good news" of the Christian tradition is the necessity of the outsiders' letting out those feelings that prevent a hearing of that message. Listening—honest, perceptive, nonjudgmental, relational—which conveys trust and acceptance of the other is the requisite element in the communication process. People can't hear until they have been heard.

Dietrich Bonhoeffer believed that listening was at the center of the Christian's ministry.

> The first service that one owes to others . . . consists in listening to them. Just as love to God begins with listening to his Word, so the beginning of love for the brethren is learning to listen to them. . . .
> Many people are looking for an ear that will listen. They do not find it among Christians, because these Christians are talking when they should be listening. But he who can no longer listen to his brother will soon be no longer listening to God either; he will be doing nothing but prattle in the presence of God too.
> . . .
> Christians have forgotten that the ministry of listening has been committed to them by him who is himself the great listener and whose work they should

share. We should listen with the ears of God that we may speak the Word of God.[16]

I am convinced, on the basis of my association with the unchurched in six counties, that the outsider welcomes the insider who patiently listens. Almost without exception, my informants' last words were, "Thank you," or "I wish we could talk more," or "Please stay for lunch, or coffee, or a glass of wine." Many invited me back. Some gave me mementoes of the visit: records, poems, original art, a book, handcrafted jewelry, and the like. Not a few shared a warm handclasp or a spontaneous embrace. Even the more hostile were anxious to convey appreciation for my accepting their anger. Although I did not respond to inquiries about my own faith, many asked. If listening is preevangelism—that is, hearing the other's story—it may be expected to lead to the opportunity for sharing one's own story of faith.

The Christian church, its best interpreters would say, cannot avoid the New Testament saying that the message of the cross and resurrection will always be folly, an offence, or a stumbling block to the world.[17] This expectation, however, can easily be perverted into license to present the "good news" foolishly, offensively or in ways that create barriers rather than bridges to acceptance.

Even the most cursory survey of the anecdotal material of this report is evidence that hosts of unchurched people have been hearing more "bad news" than "good news" from the churches and pulpits they have known. Sectarian versions of the Christian message have come across to many who are now outsiders as overloaded with law, moralism, judgment, and rejection. Many have simply never heard of a loving God who accepts people while they are yet sinners. One may question whether those communions that hold to doctrines of perfection and holiness have intentionally communicated their message in the negative way in which it has been heard. But that is the way the message has been perceived and understood. Similarly, the outsider is not impressed with the intensity with which many mainline denominations are preoccupied with their separate identities, their distinctiveness. They see the churches as incurably narcissistic communities. The unchurched perceive even the more inclusive faiths as unnecessarily narrow, in terms of doctrine, ethical responsibility, and emphasis on venial sinfulness. Further, the scandal of disunity among the denominations is not excused by the outsider who hears rationalizations in terms of diversity. In a pluralistic religious milieu, one can argue that the need of many may be, not a mongrelized pronouncement, but sharp, differentiated interpretations from which the hearer may choose. Yet, for many outside, the Babel of voices from the churches is incomprehensible.

If the Christian gospel is an offense to the unbeliever, it is legitimate to ask whether the central message has in reality been proclaimed and if so whether the offense may lie in the offensiveness of the proclaimers.

The inclusion of community profiles in this report demonstrates that perceptions of the churches may be linked to dominant themes that are identifiable in the communities in which the unchurched reside. Communities in America have their own peculiar mentalities. Sometimes, they are perpetuated in sagalike collective behaviors. The rhetoric of the 165 persons I interviewed is often the rhetoric of the community. The community's spirit or ethos is discernible in oral accounts. That this spirit be understood and accepted, albeit without embrace, by the churches would appear desirable.

Is there meaning for the churches, for example, in the discovery that Orange County residents are secularly oriented, perhaps pacesetters of trends sweeping America? That Polk County residents preserve elements of a frontier, freedom-seeking mentality? That Sarasota is heavily populated by people "starting lives anew"? That the harsh environment of Boone County produces fierce pride and independentism? That Waldo Count people share with other New Englanders the Yankee virtue of tolerance? Or, that in Marion County, Alabama, an old agrarian way of life is being radically superceded by technological and bureaucratic values? If there is meaning, does this call for greater indigenization of the Christian movement? What does the history of early Christianity's adaptation of its story of a crucified Jewish carpenter to a Gentile world imply for the need for contemporary Christian churches as they missionize in different ways among different communities of people?

In U.S. counties that are heavily unchurched, it appears that the reasons for the aberrations should be studied and understood. Such analysis might reveal an historic pattern of unchurchedness, with discoverable explanation, a datum of special import for the churches. Or the churches' presentation of themselves in the past may be discovered to have provided the excuses for those opting out or never opting in. Strategies for evangelization are irrelevant and ineffective without being informed by serious consideration of these problems.

I have argued that a typology of the unchurched is a beginning stage in scientific exploration. It is significant for parsimonious understanding of a mass of data. It is also instructive for the church's task of evangelization.

The reasons people give for disengagement from the church have been clustered in this book according to types of related characteristics. This reduces, conceptually, the number of categories with which one must deal. For churches engaging in the process of evangelization, such a taxonomy limits the varying styles of response and action that need to be considered. No Christian congregation, of course, will disregard the central affirmations of faith to which it is committed. A chameleon-like adaptation to those who contend against the faith as if the faith "once delivered to the saints" did not matter would be an accommodation that no Christian church could affirm and remain the church. Yet the church's message whether in proclamation, or witness, or service will take into account the types of resistance of those outside its ranks to whom the message is, in part, addressed. The churches need to understand the several worlds of the unchurched.

Helmut Thielicke, German theologian-ethicist and preacher at St. Stephen's Church, one of the largest year-round Protestant congregations in the world, assumed that large numbers of his hearers were "would-be believers." Of them, he wrote:

> If I want to take God seriously, the [indifferent] concern me for *his* sake because. . . . God is not simply the leader of his own earthly followers. . . . God is not kept alive by his followers. He is the God of the atheists too. He remains true, even when men disavow him.[18]

How people "disavow" God and/or the church can best be seen when types of disavowal or resistance are identified. It is as if the unchurched populate separate worlds, each of which can be identified and individually addressed.

The implications for the development of forms of address and styles of communication by the churches is clear. The Pilgrims' search, for example, for a satisfying faith may be comparable to that expressed by King Agrippa to St. Paul, "It will not take much to win me over and make a Christian of me" (Acts 26:28, NEB). A Pilgrim will be dealt with in different fashion from the True Unbeliever, whose rejection of the Christian faith is often deeply entrenched. The Boxed In and the Locked Out represent opposing types and call for markedly different responses. The Nomads and Hedonists are varieties among the unchurched for whom strategies of evangelization must be individualized. When unchurchedness takes the form of the Antiinstitutionalists a strategy that seeks to introduce outsiders into the church by way of small groups would probably be preferable to defensiveness or rationalization about the necessity of the institutionalization of religion, however justified. The Publicans raise questions about the credibility of churches that, according to such outsiders, say one thing and do another. Trust may be reestablished as the church acknowledges its own imperfections before the world. "The basis upon which Christians can speak to [others] is that each knows the other as a sinner," Bonhoeffer has suggested.[19]

Correlations of alternative strategies with types of unchurchedness are only limited by the creativity and ingenuity of the evangelist. It has not been my intention to develop formulas but simply to point to possible directions that may be informed by the clustered characteristics of the outsiders the churches seek to reach. Clearly, the unchurched cannot be stereotyped as a single homogeneous group.

It may seem impertinent to remind the churches of their own need for renewal. A Sister of Charity in Alabama responded to a preliminary report of my findings in Marion County by affirming: "What we need to say to our unchurched brothers and sisters is 'You are right in all your criticisms of the churches. We ask your forgiveness.' " To forego self-conceit and to acknowledge its own sinfulness is the extremity to which the church must probably go, not only to reestablish its credibility but also to be true to its own self-understanding.

The resistance of the churches to the outsider's censure is natural. The stories of the unchurched easily prompt judgment and reproach against the outsider, or self-justification and superiority by the churches. Argumentation, intellectual fencing, and reproof will be a more tempting response than contrition. The evidence from the interviews would indicate that the unchurched are quite familiar with that tactic, and it has tended to deepen their hostility and to drive them farther from the church.

Repentance, according to the biblical record, involves not simply verbal action but a "turning around." The imperfect moral behavior of Christians, for example, is the chief offence the unchurched recognize among the churched. It serves as an excuse for their separation. As Jacques Ellul has argued, the churches have provided the excuse for them. There is abundant evidence, therefore, that behaviors need to undergo radical change if witness is to be believable and effective.

Change will need to occur both in personal and in social relationships.

Moreover, the churches may have intentionally or unwittingly communicated an interpretation of the Christian gospel that has reduced it to legalistic, rulebook morality. Whether this exhibits itself in terms of narrow prohibitions and petty prescriptions of acceptable Christian behavior or undue emphasis on good works, the consequences are the same. Christianity has been perceived primarily as an ethical religion whose end is the production of the "good person." If a vast majority of the unchurched have so interpreted the Christian message, it is plausible to assume that this is the interpretation they have received in the churches. Of course, this may be the explicit intention of some churches. Other churches, however, which view ethical behavior as a response of faith, exercised in responsible freedom, appear not to have gotten their message across.

Other internal reforms are suggested by the complaints of the unchurched. The Locked Out, for example, give evidence of feeling not wanted or of being excluded from the fellowship of churches they have known. The Floaters have found worship services dull, repetitious, and unexciting. The Pilgrims crave dialogue encounter and fault the traditional authoritarian style of Christian proclamation. The Boxed In react negatively to what they perceive to be the church's emphasis on dependence and submission. Such accusations probably have basis in fact, at least in the experiences of the unchurched who at one time have been on the inside. If legitimate, the charges confront the churches with unfinished internal business that needs attention before outreach can be effective.

The models of evangelization currently being employed by the churches in their new efforts to wrest the tide of disaffection cannot be evaluated before the results are in. Some models, however, have been tested against their stated objectives. Mass evangelism of recent times, continuous with the patterns of the crusades of Dwight L. Moody and Billy Sunday of the past, appears to have fallen short of the tangible results of the awakenings of the eighteenth and nineteenth centuries. The older revivalism was a powerful force in the rising antislavery movement and in an attempt to adjust the gospel to the needs of the frontier and urban industrialism. Its modern-day counterpart in the mass rallies of the Billy Graham Evangelistic Association, incorporated in 1950, have lost the mainline constituencies to which Moody and Sunday appealed, have no marked social impact, and have failed to funnel new converts into the life of the churches. At best, Graham crusades can be seen as public reinforcements of doctrines and commitments already indigenous to conservative Protestantism, which may have played a part in conservative Protestant church stability and growth.[20]

"Key 73," a nationwide evangelistic effort of nearly 150 Catholic and Protestant churches and organizations in the United States and Canada promoted by conservative theologian and publicist Carl F. H. Henry, never accomplished its objectives. Henry himself concluded as early as 1974 that Key 73 should be "buried with dignity and respect."[21] Deane A. Kemper, a fellow evangelical, has written that the crusade was in need of a more thorough autopsy than Henry had given it. He saw the original plan of "Calling Our Continent to Christ" and its implementation an "evangelistic last hurrah best viewed in the context of the current wave of nostalgia. . . . It was an evangelistic Edsel, an idea whose time had truly passed."[22] Henry's postmortem concluded that "Christian unity is crucial for effective evangelism." William Newman and William D'Antonio, in a microstudy of Key 73 in two small cities in New England, conclude that this is precisely what never happened. They write,

Social movements developed at the national level that do not resonate with a strongly evidenced desire for change at the local level, do not possess either sanctions or the organizational mechanisms for enforcing them, do not develop a sense of group identity, exhibit inherent ideological contradictions, and lack charismatic leadership are not likely to make a significant impact on the social structure.[23]

In this respect, Key 73 was such a movement. In Kemper's judgment, it was a "paper monolith," and the "gigantic offensive" never materialized.

Drawing on these experiences, several packaged plans for parish self-study and evangelistic outreach have been marketed. Garden Grove Community Church in Orange County, California, believes that its success can be replicated by churches everywhere. The minister, Robert Schuller, has prepared study guides and audio tapes of his lectures for use by local congregations. He periodically draws hundreds of clerical and lay leaders to California for training seminars. He claims to apply Peter Drucker's management principles to the achievement of objectives. He believes in "putting the spiritual needs of the nonreligious people just a slight notch above the spiritual needs of the church's own communicant membership."[24] He admits that this means "compro-mise," and his critics fault his avoidance of controversy—a chief means of attracting the outsider—as a dilution of the Christian faith. Success for Schuller means growth: "I don't have any sympathy for the theologi-cal strain that tries to glamorize or glorify failure."[25]

Another packaged program has been produced by the Institute for Church Growth, Pasadena, California.[26] It incorporates a careful socio-logical survey of the community in which a congregation is located. The aim is to discover the types of potential constituents within reasonable distance. The evangelizing congregation then develops programs to ap-peal to the concerns, interests, and needs of these constituents. The "homogeneous unit principle" is central—a parish should consciously concentrate on a single constituency rather than try to appeal to all. This, it is claimed, helps focus the message and develops congregations with maximum internal cohesiveness. Critics often accept the program as sociologically sound but find it troubling ethically and theologically. It "smacks of exclusiveness, segregation, and captivity to a particular life style."[27] Sectarian Christianity has an affinity with such an outlook, but more churchly Christian denominations view this as incongruent with the essential inclusive mission of the church.

The Roman Catholic churches of America have historically ap-proached evangelization from different perspectives. The chief source of membership growth in Catholic parishes has been "natural increase"; that is, births in Catholic families, and immigration of Catholics from foreign lands who were already baptized members of the faith. The parochial school system and catechetical instruction have been twin instrumentalities of socializing and preserving the young. Missions have periodically been conducted in local parishes by outside religious orders to address special concerns, such as marriage and family life, social action, and other issues. No direct address to the unchurched has ever seriously been exploited. Evangelization has thus tended to be, as educa-tor-priest David Bohr has written, "formalistic, static, objectivistic," and proclamation has been "basically out of touch with real-life situa-tions."[28]

The contemporary stance of key leaders in the Catholic Church represents radical departures from traditional practices. The Glenmary Home Missioners, for example, have dedicated themselves to a Catholic presence in rural, southeastern United States, where Catholicism has been historically weak. Their research center in Washington, D.C., is the most prodigeous and prolific producer of studies on the unchurched in America. The Paulist Office for Evangelization has been influential in developing the current national priority on evangelization in the Catholic community. Models, workshops, exhibits, literature, and mass celebrations are being employed in every diocese, "primarily," as the director, Alvin Illig, says, "as a conscienticizing movement." The emphasis is on parish-based evangelization with "a multiplicity of approaches using an array of tools."[29] It is addressed to the reevangelizing of baptized Catholics as well as the lapsed and the unchurched.

The "Word and Witness" program of the Lutheran Church in America (LCA) might be typical of trends in mainline Protestant churches, although more highly rationalized, articulated, and institutionalized than most. It is a congregationally based program of study and outreach, each conceived to be dependent on the other. Congregational leaders are trained by a specially recruited elite from among the professors of theology, successful pastors, and church-wide staff personnel of the denomination. Training sessions run ten or more days after which local pastors introduce the program into their parishes. Lay groups of nine to twelve persons meet with their pastor for approximately sixty hours of Bible study[30] and another 60 hours learning skills in human relations and sharing the experiences of faith. Some 20,000 laypeople have been engaged in the program since 1976, according to Richard Bartley, and denominational leaders hope to involve 25 percent of the LCA parishes by 1984. Lutherans conceive of their experiment as "relational evangelism." Austin Shell, a professor of pastoral care and writer of one of the texts used by the laity, has developed the rationale for communication. He speaks of the need to bring "three stories" together—the story of the other person, the correlating story of the evangelist, and the "intersecting" story of how God deals with his people in history.[31] Central to the endeavor is changing the parish "climate" such that members better understand their own faith and become intentional about witnessing to it and that outsiders perceive the religious community as attractive and plausible. Evaluation of the results will be difficult to assess, inasmuch as the goals are as global as the whole mission of the church, as Lutherans understand it. It is essentially a new departure in adult education and action. Because the program opts neither for membership growth or personal commitment exclusively, achievement in either arena will likely be internally perceived as success. What long-term changes in persons or institutions might be attributed to "Word and Witness" will require continuing research.

Marjorie Hyer, staff writer for the *Washington Post,* has called attention to the current "Bold Mission Thrust," of the 13 million member Southern Baptist Convention, a gigantic evangelization program authorized by the denomination at its 1978 convention at Atlanta. "Even though they have been No. 1 for years," writes Hyer, "Southern Baptists will continue to try harder."[32] To launch the mission, $750,000 has been initially allocated. The denomination is planning to gear its entire program—every agency, board, and office—to "proclaim the gospel to the world by the year 2000." One thousand career missionaries will be added to the current force of 2,776. Plans call for enlisting an additional 5,000 volunteers for up to three-year terms in a Mission Service Corps, modeled in part after the Peace Corps and the continent-wide missionary activities of the Mormons. If such plans materialize, the Southern Baptists' track record of more than a million new adherents between 1970 and 1976 could be repeated again by 1982. While the traditional strength of the Southern Baptists has been the Old South, recent growth has been in the North, the Upper Midwest, and the West. It may be expected that "Bold Mission Thrust" will concentrate in these newer regions, utilizing strategies consistent with their revivalist past but increasingly adopting more sophisticated tactics to deliver converts. The relative absence of internal stress in local Baptist congregations provides fertile plausibility structures for diaspora Southerners, mostly Baptists, who join the nomads populating every region of the nation today. It is not known, in detail, the degree to which this denomination's growth depends more on its ability to attract the formerly unchurched or to emerge as the winner in the "circulation of the saints."[33] Whatever Southern Baptists may lack in breadth of perspective, their local community bondedness is an asset that they will, no doubt, exploit.[34]

It is not possible here to describe the models of evangelization now in vogue in other denominations.[35] All bear some resemblance to the designs just outlined, with variations according to the value preferences of the particular denomination's theology and the styles congruent with their resources and assessment of need. Few denominations, Roman Catholics being the notable exception, are radically reversing the patterns of their respective histories.

An attempt to join the research enterprise with the practical needs of the churches is typified in the founding in 1977 of the Princeton Religion Research Center, specializing in "creative, actionable research, utilizing the worldwide attitudinal and behavioral facilities of Gallup International."[36] Its monthly newsletter promises to "probe the current dynamics of religion to enable leaders to respond to these trends realistically." It plans to measure changing attitudes, behavior, and expectations of people everywhere "so that the effectiveness of outreach programs can be determined." The center's advice to the churches to date consists of seven "possible steps to help bring about renewal": (1) Reevaluate your program of religious education; (2) strengthen your program of spiritual counseling, (3) reexamine the status of religion in the home, (4) develop an active program of evangelism; (5) reach out to new people in a community, (6) build on—rather than compete with—religious broadcasting, and (7) examine and evaluate the effectiveness of your mission.[37] Sophisticated leaders and laity in the churches may be expected to react without enthusiasm to what they will perceive to be self-evident truths.

Peggy Shriver, Assistant General Secretary of the Office of Research Evaluation and Planning of the National Council of Churches of Christ, is more realistic:

> The task of church renewal appears formidable. Beliefs without strong convictions, a faith that seems to require no corporate expression, some persons seeking more vital spiritual depth, many others insisting on more latitude in moral teachings and beliefs—these are familiar stones in the American mosaic. In prayerful response, the church must continue to be the church of Jesus Christ.[38]

How this renewal—prelude to all evangelization efforts—will be achieved remains the unfinished agenda of the churches. Prognosis of the religious situation in the United States in the 1980s is therefore hazardous. Neither a "religious boom" or a "religious bust" can be predicted from the data presently available, and prognostications in either direction need to be viewed with extreme caution. What internal changes in the churches will occur and what new external, countervailing forces may develop are imponderables. The future has not yet been lived. One thing is sure—80 million Americans remain outside the churches now. Their alienation is extensive and deep. They will not easily be won from the streets into the pews. Whether their numbers grow or decline, the unchurched will persist as a sturdy band for whom the churches are optional or dispensable institutions. If "plausibility structures" are required to perpetuate the traditional truth claims of Christianity in the United States, they are not yet evident for 40 percent of the population.

NOTES

1. Evangelization is treated in this book as a distinctive activity of Christian churches. Other world religions have not historically been marked by aggressive missionary or proselytizing work. See, for example, Marshall Sklare and Joseph Greenblum, *Jewish Identity on the Suburban Frontier* (New York: Basic Books, 1967). The term *evangelization* is used here in preference to *evangelism*, which has more narrow connotations and tends to be associated with particular modes of outreach. Etymologically, *evangelization* is simply to bring in or to announce the *evangel*, "the good news." For a series of perspectives, see Gerald H. Anderson and Thomas F. Stransky, eds., *Mission trends No. 2: Evangelization* (New York: Paulist Press and Eerdmans, 1975). No adequate study is available on the black unchurched. A cursory report is Michael R. Welch, "The Unchurched: Black Religious Non-Affiliates," *Journal for the Scientific Study of Religion* 17, 3 (September 1978), 289–93.

2. See "That the World May Believe," in *International Review of Mission* (Geneva: Commission on World Mission and Evangelism, World Council of Churches, July 1975).

3. John XXII, "Humanae Salutis" (25 December 1961), in Walter M. Abbott, ed., *The Documents of Vatican II* (New York: Herder and Herder, 1966), p. 707.

4. Paul VI, "Evangelization of the World: Essential Mission of the Church." Address during the general audience of 30 October 1974, quoted in *L'Osservatore Romano*, English ed., 45 (7 November 1974).

5. Paul VI, "Evangeli Nuntiandi," *L'Osservatore Romano* (19 December 1975), par. 18. English translation, Vatican Polyglot Press, 1975.

6. From the paper, "Theological Implications of Radical Discipleship," in J. D. Douglas, *Let the Earth Hear His Voice* (Minneapolis: World Wide Publications, 1975).

7. *Ibid.*

8. Martin Marty, "What's Ahead for Evangelism?" in *The Lutheran*, December 1974.

9. Paul Löffler, and others, "The Biblical Concept of Conversion," in *Workbook for the Uppsala Convention* (Geneva: World Council of Churches, 1968).

10. The best source of recent attention to the reintegration of Catholic dogmatic theology and moral theology, with a significant historical chapter on Catholic evangelization in the United States, is David Bohr, *Evangelization in America* (New York: Paulist Press, 1977).

11. William Temple, source unknown.

12. Hans-Ruedi Weber, "God's Arithmetic," in the journal *Frontier* 6 (Winter 1963): 298–303, published by the Anglican Society for Promoting Christian Knowledge (England).

13. John Tinsley, "Communication, or 'Tell it Slant,' " in *Theology Today* 35, no. 4 (January 1979): 398–404.

14. J. Russell Hale, "Krisenheit für die Kirche: Lassen Sich Amerikas Unkirchliche Evangelisieren?" *Lutherische Monatshefte* (Hanover, Germany) 15, no. 9 (September 1976): 498–501.

15. The literature is extensive, beginning with the work of Carl R. Rogers; for example, *Client-Centered Therapy* (Boston: Houghton Mifflin, 1951). One book, substantially reflecting this author's point of view, is Earl Koile, *Listening as a Way of Becoming* (Waco, Texas: Regency, 1977).

16. Dietrich Bonhoeffer, *Life Together*, trans. John W. Doberstein (New York: Harper & Row, 1954), pp. 97, 98, 99.

17. I Corinthians 1:23–24.

18. Helmut Thielicke, *How to Believe Again*, trans. H. George Anderson (Philadelphia: Fortress, 1974), p. 8.

19. Dietrich Bonhoeffer, *Life Together*, pp. 105–6.

20. The literature on Billy Graham is extensive. See, for example, William D. Apel, "The Lost World of Billy Graham," in *Review of Religious Research* 20, no. 2 (Spring 1979): 138–49; Joe E. Barnhart, *The Billy Graham Religion* (Philadelphia: Pilgrim Press, 1972); William G. McLoughlin, *Modern Revivalism* (New York: Scribner's, 1959); and Lowell D. Streiker and Gerald S. Strober, *Religion and the New Majority* (New York: Association Press, 1972). Most recent histories of American religion give attention to Graham; for example, Sydney E. Ahlstrom, *A Religious History of the American People* (New Haven, Conn.: Yale University Press, 1977), pp. 956–958.

21. Carl F. H. Henry, in *The Reformed Journal*, November 1974. The progress of Key 73 was covered extensively in the religious press in 1973 and 1974. See especially *Christianity Today* and *Christian Century* for articles and news reports.

22. Deane A. Kemper, "Another Look at Key 73," in *The Reformed Journal* (a response to Henry), January 1975.

23. William M. Newman and William V. D'Antonio, "For Christ's Sake: A Study of Key 73 in New England," in *Review of Religious Research* 19, no. 2, (Winter 1978): 139–153. See also Eugene Meyer, "The Selling of the Lord," in *Ramparts* 11, no. 11 (May 1973): 25–56.

24. From an interview with Robert Schuller by Phyllis Mather Rice, "Robert Schuller: Man With a Mission," in *Your Church* 24, no. 5 (September–October, 1978): 5–9, 15–17.

25. *Ibid.*

26. The definitive volume from an apologist is C. Peter Wagner, *Your Church Can Grow* (Glendale, Calif.: Regal Books, 1976). For a critical discussion, see Jackson W. Carroll, "Understanding Church Growth and Decline," in *Theology Today* 35, no. 1 (April 1978): 70–80. Portions of this article and others on the general theme may be found in Dean R. Hoge and David A. Roozen, eds., *Understanding Church Growth and Decline* (New York: Pilgrim Press, 1979).

27. Carroll, "Understanding."

28. Bohr, *Evangelization*, p. 234.

29. From an unpublished paper, n.d., by Alvin A. Illig, "Evangelizing the Unchurched," and from private conversations.

30. The text, representing modern biblical scholarship, is Foster McCurley and John

Reumann, *Understanding the Bible* (Philadelphia: Division for Parish Services, Lutheran Church in America, 1977, 1978). 2 vols.

31. Austin Shell and John Kerr, *Telling the Good News* (Philadelphia: Division for Parish Services, LCA, 1977, 1978). 2 vols. For a succinct description of the "Word and Witness" program, see the promotional brochure, "The Lutheran Style of Witness," Division for Parish Services, Lutheran Church in America, 1979.

32. Marjorie Hyer, "Southern Baptists Still Trying Harder: Commentary," *Washington Post*, 23 June 1978, p. A30.

33. See Reginald W. Bibby and Merlin B. Brinkerhoff, "The Circulation of the Saints: A Study of People Who Join Conservative Churches," in *Journal for the Scientific Study of Religion* 12, no. 3 (September 1973): 273–283.

34. See Wade Clark Roof, "The Local-Cosmopolitan Orientation and Traditional Religious Commitment," *Sociological Analysis* 33 (Spring 1972): 1–15.

35. See the current survey and assessment by Albert Krass, "What the Main-Line Denominations Are Doing in Evangelism," *Christian Century* 96, no. 16 (2 May 1979): 490–496.

36. *Survey of the Unchurched American* (Princeton, N.J.: Gallup Organization, 1978), inside cover.

37. *Ibid.*, pp. 20–26.

38. Peggy L. Shriver, "Do Americans Believe in the Church?" in Constant H. Jacquet, Jr., *Yearbook of American and Canadian Churches 1979* (Nashville, Tenn.: Abingdon, 1979), pp. 255–258.

Appendix
Unchurched Population
of the United States: 1971

	Total Population	Estimated Unchurched	Percent Unchurched
United States	203,211,926	78,425,146	38.6
Northeast	49,040,703	17,549,092	35.8
New England	11,841,663	3,829,617	32.3
Connecticut	3,031,709	966,930	31.9
Maine	992,048	492,496	49.6
Massachusetts	5,689,170	1,687,146	29.7
New Hampshire	737,681	326,008	44.2
Rhode Island	946,725	168,126	17.8
Vermont	444,330	188,911	42.5
Middle Atlantic	37,199,040	13,719,475	36.9
New Jersey	7,168,164	2,682,871	37.4
New York	18,236,967	7,441,634	40.8
Pennsylvania	11,793,909	3,594,970	30.5
North Central	56,571,663	20,449,325	35.5
East North Central	40,252,476	15,094,751	37.5
Illinois	11,113,976	3,558,790	32.0
Indiana	5,193,669	2,368,043	45.6
Michigan	8,875,083	3,756,050	42.3
Ohio	10,652,017	4,479,751	42.1
Wisconsin	4,417,731	1,132,117	25.6
West North Central	16,319,187	5,354,574	32.8
Iowa	2,824,376	892,933	31.6
Kansas	2,246,578	880,753	39.2
Minnesota	3,804,971	1,057,628	27.8
Missouri	4,676,501	1,759,957	37.6

Nebraska	1,483,493	484,888	32.7
North Dakota	617,761	109,662	17.8
South Dakota	665,507	168,754	25.4
South	62,795,367	21,507,740	34.3
South Atlantic	30,671,337	11,616,124	37.9
Delaware	548,104	236,788	43.2
District of Columbia	756,510	165,657	21.9
Florida	6,789,443	3,023,296	44.5
Georgia	4,589,575	1,540,571	32.8
Maryland	3,992,399	1,631,803	41.6
North Carolina	5,082,059	1,583,007	31.1
South Carolina	2,590,516	639,530	24.7
Virginia	4,648,494	1,888,989	40.6
West Virginia	1,744,237	906,483	52.0
East South Central	12,803,470	4,127,130	32.2
Alabama	3,444,165	1,090,493	31.7
Kentucky	3,218,706	1,152,575	35.8
Mississippi	2,216,912	494,651	22.3
Tennessee	3,923,687	1,389,411	35.4
West South Central	19,320,560	5,764,486	29.8
Arkansas	1,923,295	737,905	38.4
Louisiana	3,641,306	611,597	16.8
Oklahoma	2,559,229	912,847	35.7
Texas	11,196,730	3,502,155	31.3
West	34,804,193	18,718,970	53.8
Mountain	8,281,562	3,400,466	41.1
Arizona	1,770,900	805,097	45.5
Colorado	2,207,259	1,133,716	51.4
Idaho	712,567	291,711	40.9
Montana	694,409	332,492	47.9
Nevada	488,738	261,968	53.6
New Mexico	1,016,000	307,083	30.2
Utah	1,059,273	113,130	10.7
Wyoming	332,416	155,269	46.7
Pacific	26,522,631	15,318,504	57.8
Alaska	300,382	168,597	56.1
California	19,953,134	11,368,601	57.0
Hawaii	768,561	431,591	56.2
Oregon	2,091,385	1,274,318	60.9
Washington	3,409,169	2,075,397	60.9

Note: The term *unchurched* refers to all those persons who are not on the church rolls of any Christian denomination. The source of data on church membership rolls is *Churches and Church Membership in the United States: 1971,* by Douglas W. Johnson, Paul R. Picard, and Bernard Quinn (Washington, D.C.: Glenmary Research Center, 1974). Statistics for the unchurched have been adjusted to compensate for gaps in that study's reporting of Protestant church members.

For Further Reading*

Ahlstrom, Sydney E.
    1977 *A Religious History of the American People.* New Haven, Conn.:
           Yale University Press.
Anderson, Gerald H., and Stransky, Thomas F., eds.
    1975 *Mission Trends No. 2: Evangelization.* New York: Paulist Press and
           Eerdmans.
Bensman, Joseph, and Lilienfeld, Robert.
    1974 *Craft and Consciousness.* New York: Wiley.
Berger, Peter L.
    1970 *A Rumor of Angels: Modern Society and the Rediscovery of the
           Supernatural.* Garden City, N.Y.: Doubleday.
Berger, Peter L.
    1969 *The Sacred Canopy: Elements of a Sociological Theory of Religion.*
           Garden City, N.Y.: Doubleday.
Berger, Peter L., and Luckmann, Thomas.
    1966 *Social Construction of Reality.* New York: Doubleday.
Bohr, David.
    1977 *Evangelization in America.* New York: Paulist Press.
Bonhoeffer, Dietrich.
    1954 *Life Together.* Translated by John W. Doberstein. New York:
           Harper & Row.
Campbell, Colin.
    1971 *Toward a Sociology of Irreligion.* London: Macmillan.
Caplovitz, David, and Sherrow, Fred.
    1977 *The Religious Drop-Outs: Apostacy Among College Graduates.*
           London: Sage.

*This is a selected list of fifty bibliographical resources for readers who wish to explore further some of the issues raised in this volume. Other references are noted at the close of each chapter.

Caporale, Rocco, and Grumelli, Antonio, eds.
   1971   *The Culture of Unbelief.* Berkeley: University of California Press.
Carroll, Jackson; Johnson, Douglas W.; and Marty, Martin E.
   1979   *Religion in America:1950 to the Present. San Francisco: Harper &*
          Row.
Demerath, N.J. III.
   1965   *Social Class in American Protestantism.* Chicago: Rand McNally.
Dickinson, Eleanor.
   1974   *Revival.* New York: Harper & Row.
Gallup Opinion Index.
   1978   *Survey of the Unchurched American.* Princeton, N.J.: American
          Institute Of Public Opinion.
Garfinkel, Harold.
   1967   *Studies in Ethnomethodology.* Englewood Cliffs, N.J.: Prentice-
          Hall.
Gaustad, Edwin Scott.
   1976   *Historical Atlas of Religion in America.* Rev. ed. New York: Harper
          & Row.
Glenmary.
   1974   *Religious Population of the United States: 1971.* Washington D.C.:
          Glenmary Research Center.
Glock, Charles Y., and Bellah, Robert, eds.
   1976   *The New Religious Consciousness.* Berkeley: University of Califor-
          nia Press.
Goffman, Erving
   1969   *The Presentation of Self in Everyday Life.* New York: Doubleday.
Hoge, Dean R.
   1974   *Commitment on Campus: Changes in Religion and Values over*
          Five Decades. Philadelphia: Westminster Press.
Hoge, Dean R. and David A. Roosen, eds.
   1979   *Understanding Church Growth and Decline.* New York: Pilgrim
          Press.
Janowitz, Morris.
   1967   *The Community Press in an Urban Setting.* Chicago: University of
          Chicago Press. ·
Johnson, Douglas W.; Picard, Paul R.; and Quinn, Bernard.
   1974   *Churches and Church Membership in the United States: An Enu-*
          meration by Region, State and County, 1971. Washington, D.C.:
          Glenmary Research Center.
Kelley, Dean M.
   1977   *Why Conservative Churches are Growing: A Study in Sociology of*
          Religion. New edition. San Francisco: Harper & Row.

Koile, Earl.
    1977   *Listening as a Way of Becoming.* Waco, Tex.: Regency.
Krass, Albert.
    1979   "What the Main-Line Denominations are Doing in Evangelism."
            Christian Century 96, no. 16: 490–96.
Lamb, Karl A.
    1974   *As Orange Goes.* New York: Norton.
Lippmann, Walter.
    1922   *Public Opinion.* New York: Macmillan.
Marty, Martin E.
    1977   "A Map of Religious America." *Journal of Current Social Issues* 14,
            no. 2: 4–9.
Mauss, Armand L.
    1969   "Dimensions of Religious Defection." *Review of Religious Re-
            search* 10, no. 3: 128–35.
Morris, Monica B.
    1977   *An Excursion into Creative Sociology.* New York: Columbia Uni-
            versity Press.
Murnion, Philip, and Doyle, Ruth T.
    1976   *Catholic Life in Yorkville.* New York: Office of Pastoral Research,
            Archdiocese of New York.
Packard, Vance.
    1972   *A Nation of Strangers.* New York: McKay.
Pruyser, Paul W.
    1974   *Between Belief and Unbelief.* New York: Harper & Row.
Quinn, Bernard, and Feister, John.
    1978   *Apostolic Regions of the United States: 1971.* Washington, D.C.:
            Glenmary Research Center.
Rauff, Edward A.
    1979   *Why People Join the Church: An Exploratory Study.* Washington,
            D.C.: Glenmary Research Center.
Roof, Wade Clark.
    1978   *Community and Commitment: Religious Plausibility in a Liberal
            Protestant Church.* New York: Elsevier.
Roof, Wade Clark; Newman, William M.; and Halvorson, Peter L.
    1978   *Religion in New England: A Social Profile.* Hartford, Conn.: Hart-
            ford Seminary Foundation.
Roozen, David A.
    1978   *The Church and the Unchurched in America: A Comparative Pro-
            file.* Washington, D.C.: Glenmary Research Center.
Savage, John S.
    1976   *The Apathetic and Bored Church Member.* Pittsford, N.Y.: LEAD
            Consultants.

Scott, Marvin B., and Lyman, Stanford M.

    1968   "Accounts." *American Sociological Review* 33, no. 1: 46–62.

Shutz, Alfred, and Luckmann, Thomas.

    1973   *The Structures of the Life-World.* Translated by Richard M. Zaner and H. Tristram Englehardt. Evanston, Ill.: Northwestern University Press.

Stark, Rodney, and Glock, Charles Y.

    1968   *American Piety: The Nature of Religious Commitment.* Berkeley: University of California Press.

Streiker, Lowell D., and Strober, Gerald S.

    1972   *Religion and the New Majority.* New York: Association Press.

Szezesny, Gerhard.

    1961   *The Future of Unbelief.* Translated by Edward B. Garside. New York: Brasiller.

Wagner, C. Peter.

    1976   *Your Church Can Grow.* Glendale, Cal.: Regal Books.

Weller, Jack.

    1965   *Yesterday's People: Life in Contemporary Appalachia.* Lexington: University Press of Kentucky.

Wills, Gary.

    1978   "What Religious Revival?" *Psychology Today,* April 1978: 74–81.

Wuthnow, Robert.

    1978   *Experimentation in American Religion: The New Mysticisms and Their Implications for the Churches.* Berkeley: University of California Press.

Index